To the one I love

This Is Everything I Didn't Say

My name is Victoria.

And this is my story.

I began to write this when I was twenty six years old. I was living in an 8x10 living space at the time in Petawawa, Ontario. There were a lot of events that took place that led me to that bedroom that I was renting. One October afternoon, I opened up my lap top, and decided that it was time to start saying all the things that I have yet to talk about in hopes that some of my more difficult paths could help someone else. I am now thirty two years old, and I hope to finish writing this story by Christmas.

Over the years I have experienced great losses, as well I have made profound gains. There have been moments in my life that were so black, but upon getting through those times, by coming out on the other side of those moments, there has been the most incredible blessings waiting for me that I have experienced thus far.

If there is one thing I know to be true about life, it is that *it goes on.* It doesn't stop for anyone. It doesn't wait for you to fix your mistakes. It simply goes on. And it is up to you, and solely you, to figure out whatever road it is that you need to be on in order to make your own dreams come true. Nobody will ever be able to do that for you, except you. And once you discover the power you hold deep within you as a woman, nothing will be out of your reach. I know this to be true because I dreamed my dreams, then worked them true. I worked a few dreams true, to be perfectly honest. However I can very easily say that where I am right at this moment isn't my "pure bliss dream come true", but I'm happy with who I am. And above anything else, I can very confidently tell you that being happy with who you are is the ultimate gold medal.

I haven't so much loved all I've endured in my life, and like most hard things, you're often left with some form of scar. Weather on the inside, the outside, or both sides. The only purpose these scars serve nowadays is as a reminder. A reminder of what was once real, and more importantly a reminder of things, places and thinking patterns that I will never need to re-visit again. My mistakes in life have no doubt hurt me. They hurt me in ways I would never want any young girl to feel who is starting out in life. But my mistakes have also made me. Some of my biggest mistakes ended up being the most solid parts of the foundation I have now built within myself.

I have two sisters. Two sisters who are both smart, beautiful, and who are living great lives. My older sister, Melissa, married her wonderful husband in September of 2015 in Muskoka, Ontario, which is a beautiful cottage community right on the water. My baby sister, Lana, is in her early days of being a university student. Lana was from my dad's third marriage. She was born when I was fifteen years old. She is half my age, but wise beyond her years.

I love my sisters with everything I have. I would easily kill for them. Zero hesitation there. However, there was a time when my older sister and I had no relationship. We grew apart years ago, and it seemed as if one thing led to another. Until fight after fight; we finally broke. We no longer saw much of anything the same way, and unfortunately, a few years ago one particular argument we had got so heated that it took us a few years to get to the place where we are now. I can very easily admit that her words came from a place of not just hurt, but more than likely a place of concern. My hot temper didn't make the situation any better either.

Melissa always worried about me. Despite the path I chose in life, or the ventures I endured. To Melissa, I was always her baby sister. And I know better than anyone that with my temper and ability to speak very hurtful words, I have no doubt that every hurtful word she said back to me during our fights, I'm sure one way or another I either pushed her to her limits, or I deserved the verbal lashing.

As my older sister, she is the only person on this earth who remembers what our childhood was like. She is the only person in this world who can look back with me and understand why we both have certain pains in our hearts. I'm not quite sure why we grew up and became so different as individuals that it actually *hurt* us rather than keep us close, but a big part of why I still to this day feel a certain sense of loneliness in my life is because for a period of time I lost the respect of my sister. And I've always hated myself for that.

My baby sister and I will share some talks here and there, but it is tough. She lives in Ontario and leads a busy and very full life, and I am here in New Brunswick. Lana is also an amazing athlete. She rides horses, just like Melissa and I both did. She runs track and field and plays on all the school sport teams. I am so proud of the little woman she has become.

Anytime I am back in Ontario and I get the chance to sit down and talk to her, her words, her wisdom, her beautiful heart, she is a true gem of a girl. And although I never quite shared the sisterly relationship with her due to our age difference, I still look at her as my baby sister, and I look at her with so much pride and love. I never worry about her. Her mum is a great woman. Her and my dad did eventually fall apart which led to their split in 2012. But despite a failed marriage (haven't we all had one?) as a mother, she has done an incredible job raising Lana. The proof is in the pudding.

No matter what, above everything and all things, regardless if the hardships of life have kept us apart at times, I will forever know those two amazing women as my sisters. And I pray that one day we will all be together again. For now, I simply hope they both know how much I love them every night they go to sleep.

The Beginning

As a little girl, I grew up in a very beautiful town just north of the city of Toronto.
Unionville. The sweet town of Unionville, Ontario.

My sister Melissa and I attended a public school close to our home where we ran and won most of the track and field events.
We took part in every school drama production. I think I've been Ariel in the Little Mermaid, the Dodger in Oliver Twist, and some kind of ballerina in the Nutcracker. The list goes on.
We were pretty happy and loveable little girls. As sweet as pie we were.

My sister was always very popular. I always hated Math, or anything else that required you to find "x" inside a triangle.

Unionville is literally your white picket fence kind of town. Well-kept gardens, wealthy families where the father was usually the bread winner. Lawyers, Doctors, Investment Bankers. Picture "Leave it to Beaver" but with a Starbucks and BMW's.

That's Unionville.

My main *home base* was in this town from the time I was born until the age of 22, when I left for the Canadian Army.

But life wasn't always as pretty on the inside as it was on the outside.

When I was young my parents fought a lot, which eventually lead to them separating.

Now, 1994 in a small town where the majority of mothers were stay at home moms and Starbucks regulars, a divorce was gossip worthy news. As well that year, my mum's parents both died of cancer. That year hit us all very hard. She had two little girls to raise and a mortgage to pay. I remember I could feel the nervousness in my bones because of how scared my mum was. And rightfully so. I couldn't even imagine the amount of overwhelming feelings she had to work her way through.

Of course like any small town, there will always be the rumors as to why or how the marriage of my parents ended. There was a lot of talk. And my mum was very much the talk of the town for quite some time. Mum is 5'8, blonde, legs to the sky. She's stunningly beautiful.

My older sister and I were only little girls when it all happened. I was 8, and Melissa was 10.
Melissa very much had a grip on what was going on, she got it. Dad was leaving because Dad didn't love our mum anymore.

Me, on the other hand, I was a little more confused. I couldn't really piece the puzzle together. I remember watching my dad take his clothes out of the dryer the morning he left and put them into moving boxes.
I remember standing on the concrete floor of my garage and staring at the back of a U-Haul truck that was packed with furniture.

For the years to come, I watched my mum struggle to make ends meet. And looking back now, it wasn't anything out of the ordinary for when a single mum has to raise two little girls while keeping a roof over their heads.

She would work double shifts at the hospital for most of her work week. I watched her come home night after night exhausted. Between the monthly child support payments and her nursing salary, we were just getting by it seemed. She has a strong soul, one that will do what it takes to provide for her family. But she is a woman too. A woman with a soft heart and dreams of her own. I think I experienced my first heart break when I was only a little girl. My heart was breaking for my momma.

There were a few valuable lessons I grew up learning: living costs money, (more than you would think), you cannot rely on *anyone* to make life what you want or need it to be, and nothing is promised to you.

Nothing.

All you can do is promise yourself that you are going to do it differently.

At 8 years old I learned this.

I was beginning to become a young teenager, 12, maybe 13, and there was no strong father figure in my life. Sure, I would have visits with my dad on weekends or sometimes during the week. But as I grew into my teenage years, our visits grew further and further apart.
I'm not quite sure if I had a strong connection with my dad to begin with or if I actually lost it when he moved out.

When I look back to my memories of when I was young, it hurts me. Of course there were beautiful moments, happy moments, but there were also a lot of times that were not happy, not beautiful. The fighting between my mum and dad would be so bad some nights, it felt as if our entire house was on fire. I never got an opportunity to grow up and learn what a good love is supposed to look like. My two teachers, my *only* two teachers who were supposed to set that example, never could. I didn't just *fail* that class. But I never had the chance to attend it.

Fifteen years later, this would prove to be vital in my ability to seek out a man who would be good to me. A man who would love me in the ways any father would hope his little girl would be loved. I failed at that. I failed at that because I couldn't recognize what good love was supposed to feel like.

I questioned everything about love.

I knew during that time that I had lost the faith. Those years feel cold to me when I look back to them.

Now, my dad is not only one of the most important people in my life, but more so, one of the most vital people I have in my life. He became my best friend as I became an adult. I can go to him for *anything*, and he's there for me. But it was different when Melissa and I were little girls. He still had a lot of growing up to do.

Today he is a successful Doctor who has saved many lives and has been an incredibly supportive man to many families with suffering loved ones. He is amazingly compassionate with all those he helps. All you have to do is Google him, and the patient reviews speak for themselves. But I believe even he will admit, it took him a lot of years to become who is he is today.
As a young father, he made some mistakes. Mistakes that filtered down into the insecurities that would eventually build within his daughters.

Melissa and I are like night and day, literally.
We couldn't be more different as women.
She is two years older than I am, her skin is like porcelain. Her hair has always been as beautiful as blonde hair could be. Its Pantene-Pro V commercial worthy hair. If you think you have pretty hair, it's got nothing on Melissa's. Everything about my older sister is stunningly beautiful.

She was delicate on the outside, and although she can be strong when she needs to be, the reality is, at times she's even more delicate on the inside. But ever since she became a mum of her own two babies, I've seen this change a lot in her.
She's someone I wouldn't mess with nowadays, I can surely tell you that. She won't tolerate anyone's shit.

And I love that she found her groove with that.

Being a mum was what I believe my sister was born to be. She can do and *has done* a multitude of different jobs in her life, and all of them very well, but what suits her most?

Being a mum. Hands down. She's incredible at it.

I'll never forget the first time I saw her with her first born. I couldn't believe how relaxed and non-overwhelmed she seemed. She could have been on day three with basically zero sleep, but you would never know it.

Growing up, she would always try to protect me.
There were many nights she would come into my room, or sit on the stairs with me while my mom and dad were fighting in their bedroom.
We used to just sit and listen to my parents yell things at each other. Their vocabulary wasn't one we could understand.

But what we felt in our bones many nights a week was the chilling feeling of hate, anger, and resentment.
We always felt that. We grew up feeling that. Those feelings were more recognizable to me then the feeling of love.

My mom did the very best she could after my dad had moved out. I always watched how my mum struggled to make ends meet.
If there was one thing I knew for sure, it was that I was going to do whatever it would take to never be in her situation. I was scared shitless for my future merely because I saw how fast it could flip, even if you had a great career and beautiful home.

Things in life can turn on a dime.

And the faster you stop dwelling on how shit has just hit the fan, the sooner you can be on your road to navigating the mess of it.

It took me almost my entire twenties to learn that neat little fact.

When you want to feel sorry for yourself, sure, do it. But don't stay there very long, doing that totally useless thought process of "poor me". You're only pro-longing your suffering. And people will become pretty sick and tired of repeating their helpful advice to you.

My experiences as a child have 100% carved me into the woman that I am today. I know the ins and outs of my bank accounts better than I do the inside of my own shoe closet. Being a woman who had to struggle was not going to be in the cards for me.

Although I've had my good years and bad years when I *absolutely struggled*, (it happens to all of us) I knew in my mind back then, even as an 18 year old that my life would be more *successful* versus not. I knew I would own a beautiful country home, in a beautiful small town, with a long stone driveway, gardens, and big trees. At the time I was a far cry away from achieving anything like that, but that image of heaven stayed sharp in my mind.

Had I known then that by the age of 32 I would have owned not one, but *four* beautiful country homes, I probably wouldn't have been so nervous throughout the early years of my life. These homes were mine and nobody else's. There was never a "wonderful relationship" or "successful marriage", "divorce pay out" or anything of that nature that helped me when it came to owning real estate. I did a lot of things wrong while venturing through my twenties. Mostly men. But what I always did right, was real estate. And if I had to do it all over again, I'd still take the same trade off.

It has been the money from successful house sales that have purchased *all the blankets* that keep me warm at night these days. If anything I *lost* blankets thanks to failed relationships.

For me, my twenties clearly outlined what would end up serving me and what would end up hindering me.

The relationships I had during those years, although I grew from them, they were experiences in my life that ultimately hindered me.

But the houses? They provided solid and pretty beautiful hardwood floors to sit on when crying through heartbreaks. And anytime I sold the homes, they also all ended up giving me a big *"Thank you for owning me, here's your cheque full of money"* send off.

So am I ok with losing those past loves who kept a lot of my blankets?

Absolutely.

Being a teenage girl with a single parent who works a lot, you get a lot of freedom. There were only so many hours in a day, so my momma had to pick her battles.
Coming home after a 12 hour shift at the hospital, the priorities?

1) Pour a glass of wine (I can definetly relate to this nowadays)
2) Put the chicken breast in the oven for dinner
3) Give a yell upstairs to see what her daughters were up to
4) Make sure the cats were inside before night fall
5) Feed the dogs

As years went by, the differences in Melissa and I started to become much more obvious. She was very much enjoying her life as a popular and beautiful teenager, dating one of the most popular guys in town.

Thanks to my sister and her very popular group of friends, house parties at our home were a normal thing. Liquor, and *lots of it,* dancing on the kitchen counters, pool parties, the obscene amount of beer cans and cigarette butts that my very tolerant neighbours would kindly toss *back over* the fence line in the morning… this became a monthly thing. We partied. And pretty hard at that.

Melissa and I had an incredible amount of freedom. We were always good girls, we never hurt people. Nor were we ever bullies or mean girls. We just simply had a lot of freedom to run wild and crash and burn as many times as we were willing to. We never had a lot of money to get ourselves into too much trouble, but we absolutely achieved living our teenage years to the fullest.

Although for a period of time we were insecure. I know for myself that being insecure or unsure of who you are, it's easy to take on the persona of *aiming to please.* I remember when I was little I would try to be whatever the person in front of me expected me to be. The entire world could fall to shit, but as long as I was behaving better than the rest, then everything would be ok.

I remember I always had this overwhelming feeling of desperately needing to be *approved of* by whoever it was I'd be in front of at the time.

When one parent is absent more times than not, I think it can hurt the kids. I know many single parents raise their babies and all is rainbows and butterflies. But for Melissa and I, there was a certain kind of love that disappeared for us. There was a certain kind of safety, security and reassurance that wasn't around us.

We didn't have that.

Providing a sense of security for myself, *by myself* has been something I still work on every day I wake up.

When my mum started dating my current step dad, Ron, things at our home started to become more and more beautiful. I was about 14 or 15 when he came into our life. One day at a time, our world began to become full again. An abundance of love began to fill the walls of our home when Ron came into our world.

Ron had a beautiful cottage in Collingwood, Ontario; a gorgeous ski resort town. My mum was finally finding her happily ever after. After dating a few duds, she was being swept off her feet by a man who was willing, well, *brave* enough, to take on a single mum in her forties with two very hard headed teenage daughters. Ron has a bigger heart then most men I know. He is incredibly generous and loving. There have been more times than I can count that I have come to him seeking advice, whether financial advice (he is a very successful business man) life advice, or relationship advice. He always looked out for the best interests of Melissa and I. He was always there for us.

Always.

You would have thought we were his own daughters. He came into our lives, rolled his sleeves up, and took on the challenge at showing Melissa and I how we deserved to be loved.

That was a gift so priceless, and something I have forever been so grateful for. He showed Melissa and I just exactly what unconditional love is supposed to look like. And because of that, I have learned what a powerful thing it truly is to love someone unconditionally. To accept them no matter what. Through the good and the bad.

In the beginning, Melissa and I tested Ron, and quite a few times. But through it all he never quit on us. He stood proud beside my momma and took her hand in marriage. He gave her a diamond ring bigger then my head and made her the happiest woman on this planet. And regardless of how out of line or wild Melissa and I got, he just kept on loving us. And looking back, that was the only thing we needed. Was to know someone loved us, *no matter what.*

Although Ron had come into our home and into our lives with all the love and joy that he brought, Melissa and I still had our cracks deep down. If there is one word I could use to sum up the general emotion that surrounded my sister and I as young women, it would be this: *Uncertainty.*

Uncertainty would become a constant theme that would always be on our shoulders, no matter where we went, what we accomplished, or who we dated.

Being little girls, we got a very big taste of real life at a young age.

Nothing lasts forever.

Love can crumble.

And people will fail you.

So be careful if you choose to trust someone, because you may be accepting a dance with the devil.

Every single day carried with it a sometimes overwhelming feeling of uncertainty.

Would we have to sell the house?
Will this new husband of hers actually stick around?
Can we drive him away?
Should we drive him away?
Are things going to be ok now?

This feeling of uncertainty very quickly turned into *insecurity.* Talk to anyone who ever knew or were ever friends with my sister and I, and there will be a common trend; *we are sweethearts.*

Well, maybe more so Melissa. I can be a dick a lot of the time, but honestly, only if a person really deserves it. Other than that, I'm a pretty nice person.

Anyone who ever knew us, or became close to us always knew how big our hearts were. My sister has a heart of gold and has always been a pillar of strength for all of her girlfriends over the years. I can easily say she's as beautiful on the inside as she is on the outside. And getting that combo nowadays isn't very common I find.

I on the other hand started dying my hair a different colour every month during my teenage years. I really destroyed what use to be long, thick gorgeous blonde hair. I as well started getting tattooed twice a year, *every year*. I always saw my older sister as the beautiful one. I ended up becoming a walking, talking, breathing example of *"self-discovery - she's a bit of a mess"*.

Although we come from the same childhood, everything that took place, everything that we witnessed, we eternalized slightly differently. Which naturally gave a different end result in the women we grew up to be.

Now, both my parents have been married more than once. So come early December of 2011 when my dad announced he was leaving his third marriage of 15 years to my baby sister's mum, as disappointed as I was, this wasn't really that news worthy for me. This was simply *life as I knew it.*

Melissa and I were insecure, insecure to a fault, but in much different ways. I think throughout most of her twenties Melissa would find herself on many occasions fighting feelings of nervousness or anxiousness. It always upset me to see her struggle to fight through the feelings of anxiety that can plague a person.

I have done everything and anything to change my appearance. Long hair, short hair, light hair, dark hair. I would wear coloured contacts, ridiculous amounts of eye shadow… anything to help me try to put together this woman of who *I thought I was supposed to be.*

I never really had a sense of myself growing up. The lack of structure, and the non-existent self-esteem, I would make myself up to look like whoever I thought people *wanted* me to look like. This would eventually become an extremely valuable ability during my twenties. But during my early years, I was just lost.

What I wish I could have known back then, was this:

No matter what we went through as young girls, no matter what we witnessed. Who we lost. Or no matter how many suppers we ate at the neighbours because mum was working late, regardless of any of that--Lana, Melissa and I were not only going to grow up and be successful, but that through it all, we always have been, and always will be more than good enough. More than just average. That we would all become young women who achieved, succeeded, loved, laughed, and experienced greatness.

Those are the wishes I have for my baby sister.

Even though she is fifteen years younger than me, that doesn't seem to stop her from growing up into the amazing little young woman that she's becoming right before my eyes.

She has long, thick, natural deep brown hair. A smile that makes the teeth of celebrities look mediocre. And this amazing sense of who she is. She has more followers on her Instagram account than the population of a small city.

I know she knows these words. And I pray she never for a second forgets them. No matter what*

Lana—You were beyond a blessing the moment you were born. I will forever remember the moment I first held you in my arms that day at the hospital. I was just fifteen years old. Like Melissa and I, you as well experienced a loss when our dad left your mum. You as well felt anger and confusion. And at eight years old, you as well didn't know what to do with it.

You are so loved beyond a level you could ever imagine.

Our dad loves his daughters like crazy. Our dad is so incredibly aware of how special you are, how smart you are, how amazing you are in each and every little thing you put your mind to. And I know, as I have known our dad for thirty two years, when he wasn't able to see you, he was a man with a broken piece to his heart.

I want you to take my words and believe every single one of them. Because each word is the full truth.

You lack nothing.

From the top of your head to the inside of your heart, to the bottoms of your toes. You are more than good enough.

And loved by our entire family plus many more.

Never let any person treat you as if you are anything less.

I wear enough scars for all three of us.

So let my mistakes be your road map.

Nobody in my life, nobody that I hold dear to me is a bad person. I have experienced and loved some of the most wonderful people that this world has. But some of those people have made very bad decisions which affected me directly.

When I was eighteen years old I had graduated high school and decided to work at one of our local coffee shops on Main Street. I worked at that coffee shop for almost a year. I really loved that type of work. I handled the baking, ordered the coffee beans, I made the fancy cappuccinos for our town regulars each morning. It was fast paced work, but it was really enjoyable for me. I loved setting up the muffins, the pastries, and the amazing home baked goods. Of course I was only making around $7.25 an hour. If it wasn't for the absolutely shitty rate of pay, I could have done that for years. It wasn't a job that was very hard on the head, but it was good old fashion service work. And to this very day, I love the service industry.

Providing a service for payment.

I'm good at it.

It's easy for me.

A naturally ingrained "talent" some might say.

During our slow times I used to bring my journal and keep it under the counter. This was my dream book. My "big plans" book. I used to write out lists, so many lists every day of everything and all things. My future goals, my current favourite things, a song I really loved. You name it, I wrote it in my journal.

By the time I turned nineteen I decided I would need to go to college in order to one day earn a decent living. I decided to enroll at Seneca College downtown Toronto for their Beauty and Esthetics program. After completing this two year diploma program, I would be a certified Esthetician and I would be able to work in any Spa in Canada.

I enjoyed people for the most part, and taking care of myself is something I have always taken pride in. Even though I was more of a tom boy growing up, more of the *sporty-girl* type, I thought beauty school could be fun. I was sure to meet some great girls. And I did. I lived on campus in residence during the program, and I met and worked beside some really cool women.

Lindsey, Jen and Marr – you girls made my college experience completely worth it. Our friendship during those years alone was worth all the nasty arms or legs we waxed.

One of the things I discovered about myself while being in college was that I didn't enjoy wasting time. On nights when I would be done my classes, there were only so many hours I could spend in the campus gym.

Thanks to my early years of reckless behaviour and party girl antics, for me, college was not a place where I would be at the pub every night drinking with the rest of them. I got my party years out of my system by the time I turned eighteen.

I wanted to be productive. I had goals. I had wants. And partying on my Friday nights was never very appealing to me. I also wasn't dating anyone. I spent two years in college. Two years living on the biggest college campus in Toronto and *not once* did I bring a boy home to my dorm room.

Not once.

College boys really didn't interest me. They were all sort of preppy. Nice guys, but young, immature, didn't have much to offer me. And for all I know I probably had very little to offer them.

Anytime I'd meet any of the sporty guys, athletes I guess, they'd all talk about the same thing. Their hockey game the night before, or the random girl their buddy went home with. I got told this a lot:

"Last night, I scored the winning goal, it was unreal, 3 seconds left on the clock. Just me and the boys straight husslin' the puck".

In my head I'd be thinking *"wow. Super cool. Does that line get you laid a lot".*

I was happier working on my homework, or dreaming up ways of how I was going to create the life that I could see in my head when my eyes were closed.

After completing the two year program, I was no longer feeling very passionate about the type of work I was doing. Somewhere along the lines of fulfilling my class time and studying for my tests, I lost the love for spreading knowledge about healthy skin care practice. My heart wanted something bigger. I knew the rate of pay I would make as an Esthetician in Toronto wouldn't allow me to own a home of my own and purchase that big black truck of my dreams. The cost of living started to sink in really fast for me.

I knew I had to make a new plan.

So, as true to who I am today, I *did* make a plan. I made *big plans*. And due to my ultra-controlling and obsessive compulsive nature, I followed through on those plans.

Not once during this time did I ever think *"I'm going to meet someone, fall in love, get married, and share the bills"*. That reality wasn't one I viewed as an option. What *was an option*, was building my life on my own. My own time, my own blood, my own tears, and on my own dollar.

It's how both my fathers raised themselves, and it's how both of them built their lives. Following suit was what I was hardwired to do.

"Next on the stage, Miss Molly Aitken"

Now, growing up with seeing how hard my momma worked to keep a roof over her daughter's heads, I always knew that the cost of living for the type of lifestyle I dreamed of for myself would very simply require a specific amount of dollars. I managed to fail every single math class I attended in high school, but if you put a dollar sign in front of a number, I somehow understand it.

Money made sense to me.

Money makes the world go round.

Money put dinner on the table for Melissa and I when momma was working 60+ hours a week.

Men may have been able to fuck with my self-confidence, or my sense of self-worth, but those silly buggers never conquered messing with my ability to make money or secure accounts they had no knowledge about. Regardless of how much of my time or attention they had, like a hamster on a wheel, my brain was always working in the background.

My college campus was conveniently located a 12 minute subway ride away from Toronto's top strip clubs.

One evening during the winter of 2006… possibly 2007... it's hard to piece some of the timelines together, I decided to get on the subway and take a walk into this one certain strip club. Or in better words, "gentlemen's club". I remember when I walked in nothing about the situation made me feel uncomfortable. In a very odd and unsuspecting way I felt almost at home in this club. Now, to feel at home in a strip club at the age of 19 or 20 considering the *Leave it to Beaver* town I grew up in, it's a pretty alarming feeling to be aware of, but I brushed it off and simply chalked it up as being just another Toronto bar, but with dimmer lights and less clothes.

I didn't have a resume with me, as I wasn't quite sure if resumes were a common practice when applying to work at a strip club. But what I did bring with me was my sweet charm. That inner attribute has helped me slide out of multiple speeding tickets over the years. And I'm pretty sure it's a skill I gained as a little girl while being in the back seat of my momma's car watching her sweet talk her way out of a traffic ticket. She had skills. And still does. As for most things we acquire at a young age, it was a *learned* behaviour. And a behaviour that would prove to serve me well in the months to come.

I walked up to the bar and ordered a Jack Daniels and Diet Coke. The bartender was a beautiful brunette woman. Eyes as green as clovers. Dark hair, almost black and longer than my arms. She whipped up my Jack and Diet within seconds and slid it across the bar to where I was sitting. She barely made eye contact with me, but was quick to let *"that will be $12.50"* slide out of her mouth real fast. There was an exterior toughness about her that I was immediately drawn to. It was in that very brief moment when it became clear to me what I lacked within myself.

What I lacked as a young woman.

Strength.

And a *fuck you* type of back bone.

I didn't even know her, but I already admired her. She was a hard working woman with a certain edge to her.

It was in that moment that I knew I was looking at exactly what I wanted to emulate.

If you had told me back then that I would have been successful in achieving that goal, I would never have believed you.

I was so insecure at this time in my life.

Before I knew it, a very sharp dressed man had walked in from a set of doors behind the bar. He was clearly someone who was in charge of the place. He was mixing himself a small drink, a double gin on ice to be exact *(I'll never forget watching him do that)*. He glanced over at me and flashed me a quick wink as he said *"Good evening cutie pie, enjoy the show"*.

Now looking back, I have zero idea what came over me, but before he could even make it out from behind the bar, I found myself standing in front of him telling him *"this club needs me"*. True to his character (as I became quite close with this man with the months to come) he smiled, and said *"Is that so sugar pie"* with a deep kindness in his voice. *"Now, you see all my girls, you see all my beautiful girls working my floor? Why do you believe my club needs you?"* I remember I thought to myself *"well shit, good point, what do I say next?!"* And it was in that moment where I proved to myself that my ability to think on my feet and to "play the part" so to speak, was why this man was going to hire me. And was the reason why I was going to make this man, and myself good money.

I looked up at him, with sweetness in my eyes, and simply said *"because I can be anything anyone wants me to be"*. I said it with enough desperation so that the man standing in front of me would be able to feel as if he could have his way with *working me the way he wanted to*, but also with enough conviction to let him know I wasn't scared. I needed him to know that I was ready and willing to bring my all.

I wasn't aiming to be the next *Stage Star*. But what I was sure of, was that I was aiming to work my way into multiple men's hearts in order to retain high paying regulars and to be on the receiving end of the VIP tipping pots. My kind customer service skills and fast serving abilities would run circles around every other woman working in that club.

My appearance that night wasn't overly impressive. I was a small 110 lbs. Short bleach blonde hair. Yes, a cute little body, but I was lacking confidence in so many ways. I was wearing a small black skirt, leather boots that came up to my knees, and a soft pink halter top. Typical 2005 Suzy Sheer clearance rack outfit.

I was far from impressive.

However, either this man was lying and in fact *was* in desperate need of more girls, or maybe, *just maybe*, he saw something in me. As I stood there in front of him sipping my Jack Daniels, he looked me up and down and said *"you really want to work here cutie pie?"* to which I answered *"Yes. Yes I do. I have goals. And serving coffee won't cut it"*

He then called over one of the girls working on the floor. As she walked towards us, I remember this overwhelming feeling of fear came over me. A feeling that she still at times gives me to this very day. This woman who was walking towards me would eventually become one of my biggest money making partners who is currently still an active part of my life. However that night, she made the Russian president look like Mary fucking Poppins.

Tattooed from her chest up onto her throat, to the tip of her chin. The inner and outer parts of her hands. And her entire torso and back. Everywhere. She was covered in the most beautiful tattoos on almost every inch of her body. This was Trisha. My soon to be hot tempered Russian-Puerto Rican counterpart. My ultimate lifelong wing woman. If we ever crossed your path, I'll take a moment now and apologize. Because I know it wouldn't have ended up a good experience for you. We either stole your watch, left you with zero cash in your pockets, took your fancy sports car for a joy ride, with or without permission, or all the above. We didn't leave a man any other way.

And if you were on the receiving end of her temper, you'd be left with a bleeding nose.

She was bat shit crazy when she got mad.

Sorry about that by way the way, *men we fucked over*.

He told her to take me out back, have me fixed up in an outfit, and to put me on stage as "girl number 4" as apparently they had a seven minute slot to fill due to one of the house girls not showing up for shift.

I stood there beside this extremely angry, viscously beautiful looking woman as I watched her look me up and down as if I was nothing but a waste of time and resources. She led me into the back portion of the club where there was about five other girls getting ready for the night. She asked me *"what can you dance to?"* At that specific moment, I had no fucking clue what I could dance to. Was she asking me what I could *slow dance* to? What could I perform a *ballet performance* to? I quit ballet class when I was 3 years old. I took those pink little slippers off and probably said to myself *"fuck this ballerina crap, I'm out"*. In a somewhat state of panic, I simply said *"whatever you think is best. I'll just work it out on the stage"*. And true to my on the spot nature, I fulfilled that promise.

Two of the girls immediately came over and were very excited to dress me up and wish me luck on my "big debut". With my innocent looking face and tiny body, they both shouted out at the same time *"naughty school girl!"* Before I knew it my Suzy Sheer clearance rack outfit was down around my ankles and being slid up onto my waist were light blue panties with gemstones dangling from them, an overly-small white blouse that conveniently had no buttons, a plaid tie, and knee socks.

I'll admit it, I looked cute. But I knew I was only a half hour away from getting on that stage and in some sexy way, I was expected to rip this tiny outfit off and collect money while doing it.

At this point, I had never in my life been on a stripper pole. I hadn't even slid down a fireman's pole during those elementary school trips to the local fire station. Yet here I was, talking a big game, telling this some-what successful club owner that he *needed me*.

As I stood in the wing of the stage, I still didn't know what song I would be dancing to. But I remember I looked at the pole, then mapped out the distance from each part of the stage to the pole. I was pre-planning my working space. Still had no idea how the hell I was going to swing around this pole and look hot while doing it, but I still knew in the back of my head if all else fails, just take my clothes off and touch my body.

That's always a guaranteed hit.

(Never a guaranteed hit when trying to get out of a speeding ticket though, FYI)

As I stood there watching the current dancer end her song, I looked up and saw Trisha (*angry dark haired Russian from Puerto-Rico*) waving at me. I knew my song was about to start playing. Still – no fucking clue what type of song was going to play. But come hell or high water, I was ready. And I was going to show this club owner that I was here for one thing *and one thing only*, money. And then it starts… that undeniable guitar rift that unless you had been living under a rock for the last 30 years, it's impossible *to not know* what song this was.

Kickstart My Heart – Motley Crue.

Yep.

This was it.

My big debut.

To none other than Motley fucking Crue.

To this very day anytime that song comes on the radio, I still laugh. This was the song I made my first ever stripper dollar to. And don't be mistaken, any dancer's first stripper dollar is a big deal. Because after you earn that first dollar, you'll never be able to take back all the nakedness you just threw out to a bunch of total strangers to earn it.

Some girls get honour roll.

Others, a stripper dollar.

I was the girl who got a lot of stripper dollars.

Some girls get honour roll *and* stripper dollars.

I wasn't that talented.

You can laugh all you want. But your first stripper dollar is an exciting land mark. I still have the same string of gemstones that were attached to those light blue panties hanging around the rear view mirror of any vehicle I own. How could I not.

They bring me good luck.

They bring me money.

This was the beginning of a very fun, extremely educational two year portion of my life. I learned more working in this industry than I ever learned from any classroom. Certain old-fashion values I acquired while working among these girls, for the men who ran the place, as well, accompanying their various "business partners" to fancy events. Those learned values have stuck with me until this very day.

Be good on your word.

Take direction, but no bullshit.

Watch – watch as much as you can.

And soak up as much beneficial information as you can before you leave a room.

The education system is expensive. So learn what you can when you have powerful people around you.

Being the quiet girl in the corner holding the drink tray observing how smart business dealings versus sloppy business dealings take place – being that quiet girl holding the drink tray always pays off.

Watch.

And then learn.

But be sure you're taking notes from only the best.

And most importantly, *take care of those who take care of you.*

For the remainder of my college program, I would work here as much as I was able to. The money was good. The environment was safe, and one filled with a multitude of memories I can still feel whenever I think back to them. I met some truly incredible women here. Some were enrolled in University. Aiming to become lawyers, Doctors, psychologists, physicians of various kinds.

We all had one common ground on which we related to day in and day out. What we want will cost us something. So figure out what it is you want for yourself, and do whatever it takes to ensure it happens. With that common ground, most of the shifts with the girls were good ones. We weren't there to blow drugs up our noses (some were, but very few to be honest) we weren't there because of *"daddy issues"* or *"in search of men who will love us"*. We were there because we had a vision bigger than what had been laid out in front of us. And we all had the same amount of guts to use what we could to secure steps on that tall staircase to success. Whether that meant buying a car, paying rent on an apartment, tuition for school, or for no other reason than to put your earnings away to help set yourself up for what you wanted to accomplish next.

This portion of my life at that time wasn't something I shared with my family or friends. I knew all too well it would not be well received. *"Hey mum, I know you've been slaving away at the hospital for 12 hours a day,, but I've been rubbing my bare ass against the chest of a 44 year old balding man who manages a Credit Union on the West Side and I just made double your daily pay in a matter of 47 minutes".*

Call me crazy… but I knew enough to know that my mum who has worked harder over the past 40 years than any other woman out there, I knew that was the last thing she'd ever want or need to know. Therefore, I kept these nights to myself. And realistically, anything I did or *do* is really nobody's business anyways.

And that's simply a fact.

Something I'd become more inclined to get comfortable with the older I became.

What I do on my time for my security – is not a soul's damn business.

Period.

So I Joined the Army and Got Married

I was once married. For about 2 and a half years, maybe 3. It's hard to tell because the end of my marriage was pretty messy and confusing. But what I do know for sure is that on June 8th, 2008, I got on a plane and flew to Quebec to endure three months of boot camp. Meeting a man and have it become romantic was the furthest thing from my mind when I joined the Army. The entire idea of marriage was so far off the charts for me.

But once my college program was nearing its end and my late nights at the club were starting to wear on me, I knew I needed a big change. Ever since I was sixteen years old after watching the movie G.I. Jane with Demi Moore (true story) I had an inner need to at some point in my life join our military and serve the country. For at least one contract.

While going through the first three months of training, the official boot camp part of it, I would meet my *soon to be* husband, and once we were both done our training, by year's end of 2008, I would walk down the aisle to a man who I thought would be the father of my future children.

But I was wrong in the hopes that I had for him and our marriage. The end of my first real relationship would prove to be one of the biggest heart breaks I was going to ever experience. And to this very day, I still hold the memories he and I shared close to my heart. I have this very odd protectiveness over our memoires. Over our marriage. God help the soul who speaks of our marriage in any negative light. I loved that man. And all these years later, we are both more than aware of the mistakes we made with each other.

We learned from them.

And we became better individuals because of them.

Our marriage was a relationship – a moment in time – that I keep treasured in a much protected memory. It sits on my mind and in my heart. And I have a feeling it will remain there until the day I pass.

For many years after our marriage ended parts of me wish I could have turned back the hands of time just to feel the good days of our love happen again. As I sit here and tell you all about this, I still tear up.

My husband would walk in the door of our house and have my coffee order and my favourite muffin. I wouldn't have to get off the couch, or even lift a finger. He did special little things like this for me all the time, and it's those simple things that I haven't had in my life since losing him.

I continue to miss those moments to this very day. Those simple moments of happiness that he brought into my life.

My husband knew how the little things would make me smile. He knew the little things that could make his wife happy. I think it's safe to say, that was something he would forever love about me.

When I met my husband it wasn't anything like I had experienced before. I never had boyfriends growing up, I never had a "high school sweetheart", so when I fell into the arms of a man who seemed to really love me for who I was, and who I *wanted to be*, I let myself completely go in it. I let myself crumble.

Now, anyone who has experienced heartbreak, or a few heavy relationships, they will all probably tell you this*: don't lose your sense of self in the relationship. Remain who you are, and let your partner support you and drive you to become a better version of you.*

Well, when you have no sense of self to begin with, and you fall in love?
Tricky waters.
Tricky, tricky waters.

Very early in my career I suffered an injury that would soon lead me to losing that career I tried so hard to make work for me. I broke my hip right in half while going through some of my military training. During that moment when my hip was splitting, my femur fractured. I can't even tell you what that feels like. Well, maybe I can. It feels something like this: If the devil himself could enter your body with a chainsaw and destroy what he wanted within the general hip area with no warning – that's what breaking your hip in half and fracturing your femur at the same time feels like.

It's hell.

I was devastated. I had been an athlete my entire life. I used to run, run races, compete in Ontario-wide competitions, and win medals, *gold medals at that.* I was also a horse back rider, and like my baby sister, I was successful and often won first place at all the local horse shows in the area surrounding my home town.

After waking up from corrective hip surgery at the ripe age of 23, with having multiple plates and metal implants now keeping my hip together, it was a bit much for me to take in. I was told by the Doctor that I would never run quite the same again, nor would I be able to have a natural birth when or if I got pregnant, it would no doubt have to be a C-section. I was... scared. I was sad. I was angry.

I was now broken.

Not just physically, but I started to become broken within my marriage. The first of three scars to come was about nine inches in length down the outside of my left thigh. It was very big and very sad to look at. Everything I would do from that point on would need to be altered. The pain I would experience in my daily routines due to this injury was immense. This was a major break, and I had no other choice but to learn to live with the pain, and accept the fact that simple things, like getting in and out of a car, or carrying a load of laundry up the stairs would for the rest of my life be a little difficult.

The pain took a hit on my personality as a whole. I knew it was hard for my husband to any longer really connect with me. I wasn't in a good place mentally after my first surgery. But, like any injury a human sustains, you begin to learn to work with your injury. You learn to make those day to day common movements a little different. And I did. I began to stop focusing on the injury, and switched my perspective to focus on the recovery.

My husband and I lived on an army base. I was a full day's drive away from my family. My dad, my step dad, my Uncle, my cousins - everyone. My girlfriends, my closest friends from childhood. The people who knew me best, who knew my story and my struggles.

My husband was loving and gentle with me for the most part. He had a huge heart when it came to his animals, and he was always very kind to strangers on the street. He would be the man who held the door open for a group of old ladies. My husband was always so incredibly honest with me, whether it was the hurtful truth or not, there was never any wondering with him. I always knew where I stood with this man, and for the majority of our marriage, I was his wife, and he was proud to let everyone know it.

He was a man of his word. He would never butter up what he was going to say nor would he bullshit you. If you wanted a straight answer or direct explanation, you would definitely get one from him. Ever since leaving our marriage I was soon going to realize that this quality is very hard to come by in a man. He and I kept no secrets from one another. There were no pass codes on our cell phones. For the most part, he would have me checking his emails to see if there were any new emails from his side of the family.

I trusted him, and he trusted me. And that is such a key element to having peace of mind in a relationship.

Having that with him was heaven.

Being where I am now, and having experienced two pretty awful traditional-type relationships during my twenties after my marriage ended, I can tell you, honesty is a rare thing. If you have that with someone, if you have that trust with someone - that respect with someone; cherish it. Fight for it. Don't ever let it go if you can help it.

I have learned that some men have a funny way of dancing around the truth when you are trying to get an honest answer out of them. This is something I have learned to no longer have patience for.
I never had to go through the dramatics of that with my husband. We were simple, just he and I. And it was wonderful.

He was a good man deep down, and I knew this because I could never imagine that I would have the ability to fall in love with a monster. He simply suffered one slip up, one major slip up involving a very large amount of alcohol which brought parts out of him that I have never seen before. This was the one incident that put our marriage into a tail spin.

It put him in jail for a couple nights, and changed my life, *and me*, forever.

He and I had our two dogs. That was our little family while we lived together and went to work every day on an army base.

We tried all the time to make babies. But for some odd reason I would never get pregnant. Every time that *time of the month* would come, I could see the disappointment in his eyes. And I couldn't help but feel responsible, feel at fault for not giving this man the one thing he always dreamed of, which was a family.

During our first year of marriage, we experienced all the normal things a young couple goes through; learning how to live together, learning the living habits of one another, after all, we got married after knowing each other for 5 months.

Here's a piece of advice ladies… don't do that. *Ever.*

The cracks in our marriage began to show themselves pretty early on.

My self-esteem began to disappear. It was a combination of getting used to my new hip movements, or *lack-there-of*, and probably the knowing that I was going to be medically released from the military. I was becoming insecure with almost everything about myself. And before I knew it, I wasn't the woman he fell in love with anymore.

I lost myself. I was losing our marriage. And my career was most likely falling onto that slow road of a medical-discharge from our country's Military due to the degree of my injury and the future surgeries I had yet to endure.

But before it got this sad, before it got this lonely and cold within our household, something very pivotal took place that would forever change the dynamic between him and I. It would put our relationship into a place beyond repair. And it would take away any last ounce of trust I would ever feel for a very long time.

Now like I said earlier, I have loved many wonderful people in my life, and some of the closest people to me have absolutely let me down, or hurt me. But we are all human, and we all make human mistakes.
Lord knows I've made a lot of my own.

But what was to take place early in our marriage on a summer's night, this was not a mistake that I saw as *ok*.
This was a mistake that would eventually lead me into a depression and force me to evaluate everything that I had become at that point in my life.

In my eyes, I graduated high school thanks to an incredible guidance counsellor who didn't quit on me, no matter how much I hated attending class or applying myself. I left the adult entertainment industry. I joined the army, found love, got a house, built the fence, got the dogs, trying for babies; the domestic dream. I was doing that. Despite never thinking it would ever happen, I was somehow living it.

But at a certain point, the rose coloured glasses that I had worked so hard to finally see through had become dark.

Our little army town was having a fair down by the river. My husband and I had all our closest friends over at our house that night. We had a BBQ on the go, drinks, music, laughs, everyone was in good spirits with lots of alcohol flowing. We were all going to head down to the fair later on and have a good night. A good - simple - small town kind of night.

For the first time in my life, I thought I had reached a place where I was now safe. I was loved and protected. What I didn't see then was that in a matter of hours I was going to be right back where I started. Eight years old sitting on a cold concrete step, alone and with cold shoulders. Questioning the truth of the people who apparently loved me.

There's that funny word again; love.

A four letter word that comes with one hundred different identities.

My husband was very drunk before we left the house to attend the fair. But I wasn't too concerned, because he was in a really good mood. Now, with my past experiences having drinks with my husband, 99% of the time the night ended with us having some sort of dispute. It was never anything serious, but like most people when they drink, some kind of argument would come up, and we would go to sleep with our backs to each other.

We were dancing to the live band down at the fair; he and I both had cups filled with some kind of drink in them. I remember dancing with him. We were laughing. We were happy. In that moment for the first time in a long time, he and I were having a really fun night and I was feeling hopeful for our marriage. I was feeling hopeful in maybe coming out on the other side of the depression I was in.

But unfortunately that sense of hope disappeared very quickly. I threw my hand in the air while we were dancing, and as I did, some of my drink splashed out of my cup and onto him. I didn't really even notice until he stopped dancing. He took his hand out of mine and starred at me. I was giggling because in my eyes it was an accident, and it really wasn't that big of a deal. But he was drunk, very drunk, and he felt *very different* about the situation.

He accused me of throwing my drink at him, *on purpose.*

My heart sank. It felt like I had been hit by a brick. I didn't understand what the hell he was talking about.

I remember one of my very good friends at the time that was standing right beside me, said "*It's ok, he didn't mean it, and he's drunk*".
I remember thinking very clearly, probably the most clarity I have had in years, and I thought to myself, *"No… no this is not ok".*

I may have had very little guidance growing up in terms of love. I may have not ever experienced a healthy relationship with a man, or even a slightly normal one at that. But what I did know for sure, that what was happening right at that moment *was not ok*.

Before I knew it my eyes changed focus from being on my husband to the ten foot chain link fence that was about 100 yards away. I b-lined it to that fence. My hip was still not even a full year out of the first surgery. I still walked with a limp, but I had to get out of there. I had to get away from him. So I threw myself over the fence. When I started climbing it, the two security guards came over and said *"Ma'am are you ok?"* I couldn't really put two sentences together, but I remember telling the one security guard to help me over this "motherfucking fence".

I was about a 20 minute walk from home. I started walking as fast as I could in the pouring rain. All I wanted to do was get home, wash off my makeup, crawl into my pyjamas, and make this night disappear.

As I approached the house, to my surprise my husband was already there. He must have taken a taxi.
He was sitting on the front step waiting for me. I marched right past him and couldn't even make eye contact with him. As I was in the bathroom washing my face, he put himself in the doorway of the washroom.

Now, my husband was a fair size man. He's always been a very fit and strong man. He could easily have his way with me and there wouldn't be a thing I could do to escape it. My only hope was that he wouldn't have the heart to hurt his wife. I couldn't wrap my head around the simple fact that my husband, the one who protected me, wrapped his arms around me, the one who I trusted, the *only one I trusted…* could ever do anything to jeopardize that.

As soon as I was done washing my face, I asked him over and over again to move himself out of the bathroom door way so I could go upstairs and go to sleep. But he was drunk, and in such a faraway place from the man I knew and loved. He wouldn't budge. His eyes were empty as he stared at me and tried over and over again to make me admit that I threw my drink at him. This was so ridiculous… this was so unbelievably un-true. But the more he stood there and scolded me, the more I began to see that this was all probably going to end very badly.

I started losing it.

I started screaming, trying to push through him, but I couldn't. He wouldn't budge. I was trapped in that bathroom.

I remember what it felt like to actually have my brain start realizing that this man might hurt me, in some way, he might hurt me. And that I'm stuck here in this bathroom and that there was nothing I could do to stop it. I became frozen stiff, in fear I think. And before I knew it he was moving right towards me. I took a couple staggered steps back towards the bathtub as I didn't know what was going to happen.

But when I woke up, maybe a few minutes later, maybe an hour later, I'll never be sure how much time passed while I was laying there, but I was laying on my back in the bath tub with a couple shampoo bottles on me and a splitting headache. I will never really know how I ended up in that bathtub, but I do know that I blacked out right before I landed in the tub. And looking back, I'm almost positive my mind shut down in fear. My balance was still on shaky grounds from my injury, so there was a good chance I could have fallen into it myself.

When I woke up, I was looking at the ceiling. Immediately I looked towards the doorway, but he was gone. But I could hear him somewhere in the house. The kitchen? The basement? I stood up, and ran as fast as I could up the stairs into our bedroom. He heard me, and he wasn't far behind.
Looking back, you would think I would have ran out the back door, because it was right beside the bathroom, but in a moment like that, thinking clearly is the last thing you seem to be capable of.

As I got into our bedroom, I immediately tried to shut the door, and I don't even really know why, there was no lock on it anyways. But before the door even closed, he pushed himself through it, leaving me to be flung about four feet backwards onto the hardwood floors. I remember I curled myself up into a ball in the corner of our bedroom pleading with him to stop, but all I could hear was his yelling. I don't even know what he was saying, he wasn't making any sense.

As I sat there starring up at him standing over me, I remember thinking there is nobody around me or close enough who can help me. It's me and this man. And for me, that's a losing battle.
My heart started breaking. I was beginning to feel a little less scared, and a little more devastated that this was actually happening.

My husband used to call me his Peach, his Sweet Peach.
He used to walk along the outside of the sidewalk, closest to the traffic, and always kept me safely by his side.

This was a good man, this was the man I married, and fell in love with. What was happening?

Among the yelling and angry words, I started to feel the sadness that came along with it deep in his voice. He was beginning to re-live some of his own bad memories as a child, and he was doing it right in front of me. From everything he had told me, his childhood was not one that seemed easy. I could never explain it. He's truly a hardened man because of it. Among being scared and feeling trapped by him, my heart was breaking for him.

My heart was breaking for my husband.

This night went on for hours until I was finally able to dial 911.

After I awoke on the hardwood floors, there was broken glass all around me from a picture frame that had been knocked off the wall. There was white plaster dust on my house coat from the giant hole he had put through our bedroom wall with his fist. He had put his fist through a couple walls. My eyes were blurry. My entire body was in pain. But I could see my cell phone. It was for some reason laying on the ground in the living room. I flipped it open and dialed 911.

By four in the morning I was sitting in my housecoat, dried blood on my hands from broken glass, sitting at my kitchen table giving my statement to the RCMP Officer.

My husband was being hand cuffed and put into the back seat of a cop car.

Here we were, newlyweds, and I was signing my name to papers laying charges on my husband.

Two weeks later, after emptying out most of my savings to pay for a lawyer, I helped in getting the charges dropped on him. I remember telling the judge that it was nothing more than a domestic dispute. That I was ok and wanted to have my husband home to fix our marriage and recover from this.

I wanted to make it better. I wanted to fix it. At this point it was obvious that during this time in my life *self-love*, or *self-worth* were qualities I had yet to develop. These were qualities and traits that I was going to learn the only way I learn things, which was the hard way.

Eventually, with each passing day, it became more and more clear that there was no fixing this.

The first time I attempted at leaving this marriage, it happened all rather quickly. It was a Thursday night in September of 2010. I came home from work. I didn't have a particularly good day at work that day, so I already wasn't feeling too great. I walked into my house and my husband was sitting on the couch with our dogs enjoying what looked like a really beautiful meal. And it was, he was an amazing cook. As I went into the kitchen to fix myself a plate, I couldn't. There was no food. He had prepared a beautiful meal, plated it himself, yet didn't even think for a second to make a plate for his wife.

I stood there… looking at my stove, covered in sauce, noodles, dirty frying pans, and that man didn't even save me a lettuce leaf. I still had my uniform on, boots and all, and I walked right into the doorway of the living room and said *"You know, if you're going to cook yourself a delicious supper, at least clean up your fucking mess".*

Now ladies, this might be a common thing with having a husband, you know… picking up after them. But at this point in our marriage he was walking a very thin line. Our marriage was on a thin line. And I had had enough.

Well to my surprise, he had had enough as well. He very calmly put his plate aside, stood up, and squared off with me, and out it came, in the deep voice that he has, he began yelling back.

And that was the last straw for me.

I remember having one of those light bulb moments. Like how Oprah says, that "voila" moment, and I thought to myself, *"that will be the last fucking time any man, husband or not, will ever raise their voice at me. Ever. This is done".*

And within 20 minutes, I managed to make my way through the entire house, grabbing picture frames off the walls as I made my way up the stairs so that I could literally *one-arm sweep clean* my dresser of all my special trinkets into an empty toilet paper box.

I was out of there.

After throwing as many of my things as I could into about 3 cardboard boxes, I called my Warrant Officer. I needed to leave my home.

That winter, after the dust settled down, I went home for Christmas alone and my husband stayed at the house and looked after our dogs. I didn't want to tell my family about all the things that were happening. I didn't want them to know that I was failing at this new life I tried to build, or living in the spare bedroom of a co-worker's house. I didn't want them to think my husband was a bad man. Even though my marriage was over, I still felt that it was my duty as his wife to protect his character. To "do right" by him.

Ultimately, although our marriage was far from perfect, we were young. Early twenties. I knew then and *still know* to this very day that the man I married is in no way a violent man to the ones he loves. I truly believe alcohol can do horrific things with people. And we all have our demons or unresolved issues from our past that alcohol can set fire to.

Sometimes people send regrettable text messages expressing their upset with a person when they are absolutely wasted. Or, if a person is in front of you, you say those words in person.

Either way, I hate, and will always hate what took place that night. What ultimately made separating from him so difficult was because I knew his heart. And despite our past with each other, he was and *still is* a very good man.

Throughout that winter, while living at my co-worker's house, I had time to heal some wounds, have quiet nights with myself and my dog, and be away from the dark memories that plagued the air in the house I once called my home.

After two months of living apart, my husband and I decided to give our union one last try. We still cared about one another, and although deep down we may have very well known that we were broken, we still wanted to try. What made the entire situation as hard as it was, was due to how much alcohol my husband had consumed the night he was arrested. He had almost no memory of what took place that night that led up to the handcuffs being put on him. I'm sure he believed that in no way he would ever hurt me, therefore reading through the police reports more than likely made him angry because in his mind, none of that could have possibly happened.

But that's the biggest heart break in the whole thing, he lacked memory of it all. Which had him show almost no remorse for months to come.

My husband wasn't the man who was hand cuffed that night. That night in no way represents who he is, or who he was.

I loved him. With everything I had in me, I loved him.

And I hate that we fell apart.

But the proof was in the pudding.

I was a mess.

And we had holes in our walls.

And almost ten years later, I can re-tell you just about every minute of that night.

It's a memory that never goes away. And it changed me. It changed a very big part of me.

One early January morning, after packing up my truck with all my bedroom belongings from where I was staying, I slipped my wedding band back on my finger, and I was ready to come home. We decided that if by the spring things hadn't improved enough to continue our marriage, we would part ways, and we would do it with knowing that we did all that we could to save whatever may have been left.

Although at first it was good to be home, it felt right to be putting our photos back on the walls. The dogs were happily re-united, and weekend movie nights cuddled up on the couch with the two greatest dogs - our family was back together. Although, this bliss of ours did not last long. As many would have suspected, the roots to our broken parts still existed. If not in the hollow walls of that house, they existed deep within my bones.
I just knew, what once was whole, would no longer ever be.
I think he knew it as well.

Knowing this fact, knowing this very simple truth is a heartbreak all on its own. I would look into his eyes at night and I knew it was only a matter of time until I would no longer be saying goodnight to him. This love of ours indeed had a "forever ending" that was soon upon us both, it was just a matter of when.

Very soon after realizing that I would no longer call that place my home, and I had already begun house hunting, I received very unexpected news that could have changed everything.

He and I never got pregnant. He and I never used protection because for three years we could never make a baby. Well, I'm not sure why or how, or what message the universe was telling me, but I was pregnant. Six weeks or so with his child. I remember exactly the feeling that went through my body that morning I tested positive. Here it was, our blessing. Our dream, a child for him and I.

But it was too late… we were much too broken. So what do I do? I was 24 years old and I was a few short months away from being released from the military.
I knew in my heart that at the end of the day, no matter what would happen, or where I would end up, I knew I could be a good mother. I would know exactly what my baby would need to feel from me, and hear from me.
I never had any worry about him being a father either. Co-parenting with him would have been a breeze. Despite the downfalls we had with each other, he's an incredibly reasonable man.

My birthday was just around the corner, February 28th, I was to be twenty five. The big "25".
A few days before my birthday I was still living with my husband, as I had not yet decided on a home to buy. But even though he knew I was leaving, he still took me out that night for a pre-birthday dinner. He still treated me like his Peach. Even though we knew it was over, he still gave me a beautiful birthday.

We went to this little diner just down the road. He never liked it very much, but he knew I always loved it.

To top it off, the day before he cooked me this amazing dinner and had brought home a strawberry shortcake birthday cake from the grocery store. Candles and all. I still have the photos I took of that dinner and cake in my photo album. He really did make turning 25 special for me.

That's probably one of the most difficult things about leaving a relationship. Is knowing there are aspects about it that you will never find in any other relationship. But due to some of the bad aspects, the relationship as a whole just can't work itself out. So with that, you lose those beautiful parts.

During the days leading up to my birthday, I still didn't know how, or when I was going to tell him about our baby who was almost 9 weeks old. But I knew if I told him before I bought a home, he might have encouraged me to stay in an attempt to keep our family together.

Being a child of divorce, I knew all too well that staying together because of children is not the answer.

I wanted him to be happy. I wanted him to move on with his life and find someone wonderful so he would never sleep another lonely night. I knew in my heart we were much too broken to function as a family.
Having him visit on weekends, and take part in raising our baby was in my eyes the best possible situation for the both of us.

But waking up on my 25th birthday, that morning, the decision of when, or how I was going to tell him we were having a baby, was a conversation that would never need to take place .

I was having a miss-carriage.

As I lay on the air mattress in the spare bedroom of our house, with pain so immense, I knew right away our baby was no longer going to have a little beating heart.

After a few hours at the hospital in town, I came home to an empty house. He was still at work, and the dogs were curled up on the couch in their usual spot having their afternoon nap. I had birthday cards in the mailbox at the front door from some of my family, but they would have to wait to be opened another day.

I sat on my couch and put a blanket over my lap. I sat there, just sat there. I didn't know what to do with myself. I didn't know how to feel. I just sat there for almost an hour I think. I was trying to process the reality of losing our baby.
My entire body was frozen solid. I can't put into words what that day felt like. All I kept telling myself was that I had to *"keep moving forward, keep moving forward"*.

I remember as I sat there, I closed my eyes one last time and took the little energy I had left and pictured in my mind what it felt like the night before while I sat on that couch in the very same spot,
sipping a Tim Horton's French Vanilla, resting one hand over my belly because I could feel her in me.

I now sat there, and it was empty. I was empty.

I stood up, looked over at my sleeping puppy dogs, and went into the kitchen.

I baked 57 cupcakes that afternoon, and decorated each one with a different design.
I didn't know what else to do. I was more alone that afternoon than I had ever been in my entire life. I couldn't process what had just disappeared from me. My husband, my baby, they were gone now.

Whether you are pregnant for five minutes, or five months, the moment you realize you have a little angel in you, you never forget what it feels like.

Losing my baby that day broke my heart.

The Little Yellow House

By the spring of 2011, with my heart as dead as it has ever been, I bought my own house, took my sweet pupp with me, and decided it was time to move on with my life. I was getting out of the army within a couple of weeks and I had enrolled in school in one of the community colleges in Fredericton to try and get a little more education under my belt so I could start over. Education is key. Take it when you can get it. Even if you hate sitting at a crappy little desk, surrounded by a bunch of catty young women or teacher's pets.

Get your education.

Just suck it up and do it. Because I can sure as hell tell you now, had I known just exactly *all the living* I was going to do while being on my own, having a PhD worthy bi-weekly pay cheque would have been a hell of a lot easier.

That spring of 2011 I had found the perfect house. It was yellow. It had a garage big enough for my big black Chevy truck, and a yard with more than enough room for my dog to run and play in. I was buying this house all on my own. As a single woman, 25 years old, starting a new chapter with nobody but myself and my dog.

My pupp was about to turn 2 years old when I bought my house. His birthday was June 1st. So naturally, after moving in and getting settled, he and I celebrated his birthday. Just my pupp and I. We sat on my kitchen floor together.

With a bottle of Jack Daniels and some homemade cupcakes, he and I celebrated his birthday.

And it was perfect.

There was nobody telling me how to do things. There was nobody telling me that my baking wasn't very good, or that my supper was missing a certain ingredient. That summer all you could find in my house was a constant supply of Jack Daniels, fresh pineapple, baking supplies, and enough ingredients to make ceaser salads for supper.

That summer I made a point to spend a lot of time alone.

My new house needed a lot of work on the inside. So although I may have been very lonely at times, one thing was for sure, my pupp would never leave my side. I always had to drag myself out of bed every morning to give my baby his breakfast and put the coffee on.

Each day got a little easier. Almost every evening I would get in my truck, usually around dusk, tell my pupp he and mummy were going for a truck ride, and off we would go. We would cruise around everywhere. Mostly up and down quiet country roads, and every so often I would bash through some un-discovered territory in the woods. We'd see how long we could drive for before I would have to call my very dear friend Jeremy to come guide me out of the mud.

Jeremy had a great big Dodge, with even bigger tires. He was my saving grace anytime I had truck problems, or needed to know where the good mudding trails were. Jeremy became a very close friend, a best friend at that. He worked beside me every day in the army while my marriage was crumbling. He saw me as his little sister, and he was always there to talk me through those days at work when I could barely hold it together. He's one of those people you meet and you never forget them. No matter how long you go without talking or seeing one another, you always remember them. Because when almost all things in your world were at odds, they were a steady source of support in your life, and your happiness actually mattered to them.

That summer I ended up re-finishing all the wood in my house. I even built some of my own furniture. I was kind enough to leave my husband with all the appliances… yes…. all the appliances I bought and paid off, I let him keep them.

Only to watch his new wife post photos onto Instagram of her various perfect baking creations all thanks to her fully paid for (by me) stove top.

(Don't do that, take all your shit when you leave. Let the new wife pay for something)

But I was starting over in so many ways, so I figured I might as well re-build everything, including the living room coffee table.

I firmly believe that when you go through something, and it changes you, it's important to face your darkest thoughts head on. Face them, don't try to fight them, but understand them, and move past them. If there is self-blame, lift it. If there are thoughts of *"if I did this, or had I tried that"* –let those go. Those cold gates of hell will only remain locked tight around your mind for as long as you let them stay there.

Self-imprisonment.

I think all of us at some point in our lives do it to ourselves.

One of the most beautiful things in life is how we change when things happen to us. I am a big believer in the universe, and I know, I *absolutely believe* that things happen when they are supposed to. People come, and people leave your life at the time they are meant to. I trust that process. And let me tell you, trusting that process isn't always an easy day, but when you've got nothing else to stand on, you don't have a choice. You have to hang on to something.

Summer was turning into fall, and I was ready to put myself out there again. Not date anyone, but have some company.

In come the roommates.

I had two girlfriends move in with me; Angele, and Krista.

We had a very fun-filled fall that year. We spent many nights sitting in the kitchen having drinks, talking about everything and anything. Angele is a lot like me in many ways. She and I met in the army. We are both very independent. Being alone isn't something her or I ever feared or felt uncomfortable doing. We both have a love for all things out of the ordinary, and when the two of us are together, our sense of humor just flows. We can bring each other to tears in laughter. She's a force field. She isn't like any other female that I know.

She knew me while I was married, so she saw my ups and downs, heard through the grapevine at work that "Victoria and her husband were splitting up".

When the girls moved in, the house became more of a home. We had more weird candles and vases to decorate with. More homemade art to hang around the house that would probably scare off any normal guy we attempted to date. But we didn't care; this union of ours worked for us.

Early in the mornings you would usually find me, Krista and my pupp snuggled up together on the big couch I had in my living room, and Angele would be curled up on the oversized chair by the window. We would have our coffees, talk about what we had planned for our day, and update each other on any current love interest. Although Krista usually had the most stories to tell, she was very active in the dating scene. I was still much too scared, well, not scared, let's say skeptical. Yes, skeptical. The very small amount of faith that I had tried to acquire with men had unfortunately been handcuffed and put into the back seat of a cop car. So I just lived through Krista and Angele.

My Piece of New Brunswick Heaven

During the months of August and September of 2011, I would meet someone who would unknowingly become very important to me for a reason I'll never fully understand.

You know that scene in a movie where that broken hearted girl sees her real life super hero? For the first time? Just leaning against his Chevy truck, a smile that makes you melt. This man was a man you wanted to bake muffins for, for the rest of your life. He stands 6'3, 6'4 with his work boots on, eyes as blue as ever, with a little bit of grey in them sometimes I'd say. Hands that once they hold you -- your home. Although he looked perfect on the outside, his heart was one that knew loss. It knew grief. It knew what it was like to have your trust ripped into a million tiny pieces.

He was a little younger than me, but that never mattered because he was wise beyond his years.
We met by chance, sort of. Well, not really.

We actually completely intentionally met. But for the sake of the fairy tale let's go with "we met by total chance, it was magic".

I joined a dating website (not magical) for about three and a half days before I deleted it because as usual, I got nervous. Anxiety attacks to outer space and back. But what I found hidden in the bushes of a small town an hour south of me was the finest gem I could have ever found. We talked for a few weeks before we met. Late night conversations at bedtime, followed by sweet morning text messages that *always* gave me the butterflies.

Being the first man I was meeting after leaving my marriage, I was new and unexperienced in the whole dating thing. I didn't know then the importance of *playing hard to get* or being a little unavailable from time to time. I failed in that area, big time.

I was always available. Never made him chase anything. Why would I? Running from anything was exhausting, let alone running from Mr. Dream Man. Who the hell in their right mind would run from a six foot man with a body comparable to the Empire State building and a smile that silently says *"I'm going to kiss you in your naughty places and you're going to like it"*. Call me crazy... but those factors somehow made me sit and stay.

Looking back, my idea of winning a guy over would have been something more along the lines of *"Here I am, not running. Just sitting. All ears and totally up for commitment"*. My game plan to hook this dream guy was a shit plan. Completely wasn't going to work. But I didn't have a fucking clue back then. All I knew was that I met this man and he somehow in some very sweet way made me believe in love all over again.

Aweee

Now, at this time, I wasn't in love with him, we barely knew each other. But years later? Eight years later at that, I know I love him. Unconditionally. I know it's a love built on trust and friendship.

Having someone who will wrap their arms around your broken pieces and not let you slip from their grip. That was him.
For years to come, whether I was having work trouble, truck trouble, general life trouble, or just a bad day, he was my go-to man.

Anytime I've come calling in tears to him over the telephone, it's as if he moves all the clouds in the sky and he brings out the brightest star of hope and speaks directly to my heart. He tells me what I need to hear, which is usually what I *don't want to hear*. But he always reminds me of the things that I deserve.

"Chin up beautiful". Those words slide off his tongue like butter on a hot bun. Those are his words. His and my words. Because anytime I see those words across the screen of my phone, he may not know this, but it changes my entire day.

He's my greatest reminder to take care of myself. To take care of my heart. And to never lose sight of the things I deserve.

I wouldn't change my friendship with him for all the money in the world. I'd walk to Texas and back, bare foot and naked for him.

We dated for a month or so, a couple sleep overs and lots of phone conversations. Some afternoons I'd be sitting in class at the college I started attending in Fredericton, and I'd get a mid-day call from him. He would tell me how his day was going, how busy he was, but he would always say *"anyways beautiful, I just wanted to call and tell you to have a great day, and that I'll talk to ya later"*. Whether it was a mid-day phone call just to tell me I was beautiful, or a six a.m. morning text, *"Good morning gorgeous"*, he made me feel important to him. He helped me feel beautiful again.

That should have been my first sign.

When you're standing in front of a man and you feel beautiful exactly as you are in that moment – whether your internal world is a mess, or your anxiety and self-love issues are at an all-time rate of daily failure – when everything *in you* and *around you* feels ok when he's near, you know he was brought to you by something much bigger than you.

This person was brought to you to show you that you will soon feel that sense of peace and happiness all on your own. But for the mean time, he was there to give me those moments of relief. He was there to give me those moments of love that I probably needed more than I lead on.

He doesn't need to read these words. Because he knows he's done all this for me. Throughout all these years he's been my silver lining of love. And for that I'll always love him.

Hunting season was soon to begin for him, and with our one hour drive that separated our houses, our moment in time didn't make it past the two month mark. There were no hard feelings between us, it was just the wrong time. He was quite happy being single, and I was probably much too emotional of a girl for him. But his foot prints inside my yellow house left their mark on my hard wood floors and in my heart.

After a few months of not talking, (the normal breaking-it-off routine) our relationship would soon become one where we'd share short phone conversations with each other from time to time, or send pictures back and forth of funny things from the internet. He would eventually move on to date other girls. Some who worked out short term, and some long term. As I was soon going to meet someone quite unexpected as well. But one thing remained a sure thing, he walked into my life during a very fragile time. I was re-building who I was, what I wanted out of life, and I was looking towards my future with hope and a huge hunger to make something of myself.

In a time when there were no warm bedtime stories in my life, those few nights we spent together, he would hold me in his arms until I'd learn to fall asleep again.

He understood me. He could appreciate me for who I was. The good, the bad, the unpredictable. The at times... unreasonable. Or much too over emotional. My love for my dog was something he identified with because he had his beautiful dog, his boxer, his boy - Chevy, who was his entire world.

Little did I know then, thinking he was just a guy who I completely failed at attempting to date, that he would in fact become the first person that comes to mind anytime I think of being home. Not because of lovey dovey stuff, but because he gave me this giant umbrella of happiness that I eventually learned how to hold up over myself, *by myself.*

Jack

In a few short weeks, little did I know, being "single" was all going to change. And let me tell you how un-ready I was for it. Because what happened at the end of it, led me to where I began writing this story, in an 8x10 living space.

But he's not all that bad.

There I was, standing at a bar in downtown, with Angele beside me. It was about 1:30 in the morning, I was pretty sober. We were out that night for Krista's birthday. I remember the events that took place before we went out that night. I remember Krista was going to wear one of my red dresses. She was so excited for this night, as she had been waiting weeks to celebrate. For all of us to go out together, dance in our party dresses, and have a total girl's night.

I remember as I was getting ready in my bedroom, I was in the worst mood. I think I was just having a bad day, an emotional day. You know, one of those days where you're fighting the memories of the past that put you in such a dark place to begin with?

I didn't feel beautiful. I kept applying more and more makeup, trying to achieve some kind of "happy, pretty girl" look. But nothing was working. Nothing could cheer me up, and I felt terrible, because I didn't want to ruin Krista's birthday night. One of my girlfriends who was part of our pre-party get together came upstairs and sat with me while I tried to shake this awful mood I was in. She kept telling me that I didn't need more make-up, that I was beautiful just as I was, and that tonight was going to be *fun,* and that I'm going to get through these haunting feelings of mine.

I took a hard look at myself in the mirror, and said to myself *"Come on Vic, get it together, snap out of it"* Although it is reasonable to have low days when you're fighting memories from the past, tonight wasn't going to be one of the nights that I was going to give myself permission to be sad.

Put on your hot little outfit, throw on some sparkly bracelets, and toughen up buttercup. *Act* happy, until you *are* happy.

Feeling low that night had nothing to do with missing my husband, he and I were very much over. I think I was feeling low because I was still in transition with re-building myself, and that whole process is a tough one. It's not one you can just stop working at, because if you quit the process, you're quitting on your life, and that's just not an option.

After a few good hours of dancing and drinking, Angele and I were standing near the bar waiting for Krista to get her last drinks finished so we could call it a night.

And then it happened, I saw *him*.

Nope. Not my husband, and it wasn't my safe haven, my New Brunswick gem either. This was a man who I had never seen before.

As I was waiting with Angele, someone grabbed my butt. I spun around real fast because it pissed me off. Nobody can just *grab my ass*, I mean, *not for free at least*. To my surprise there were about six very good looking, very physically fit army guys behind me. I immediately locked my eyes on the guy who was closest to me. *"Did you grab my ass?"* And I didn't say it in a sweet, little girl voice. Like hell these boys we're going to grab my ass like it was up for free.

I did the army guy thing.
I married one.
It ended, didn't even get a T-shirt.
Lost my fridge and stove.

I was over it.

Definitely in no mood for some stranger to hit on me as if I was up for round two.

After telling this one guy that he better not touch me again, I immediately distracted him with the cute birthday girl in the red dress *"Here"* I said *"It's her birthday, buy her a drink"*.

He moved aside towards the bar with Krista, and proceeded to get the birthday girl a drink. That's when I locked eyes with *him*.

Jack.

About six feet away there was Jack, sipping a drink, wearing a black baseball hat so low I could barely see his eyes. His focus was locked on me. It was a pretty intense stare, one I remember very clearly even after all these years.

Very gently, he approached me and said *"Would you like a drink?"* I very quickly responded with *"No"*. He then proceeded to ask me *"Why not?"* And I simply answered with *"because I'm not thirsty"*. Now any normal guy would probably take that as a hint and walk away. But not Jack. He then proceeded to ask me again, well *tell* me, *"Let me buy you a damn drink"*. I caved. And as I rolled my eyes I said *"ok fine, order me a drink then… double Jack and diet… short glass … extra lime… Thanks…"*

At this point in my life I had been around various types of men. A lot of different men; big men, small men, brave men, not so brave men, tall men – the list goes on. Yet for the entire time I was living where I was, I can honestly say there was never any other man besides my husband who ever really caught my eye. Although my husband and I had dysfunctions within our marriage, issues surrounding trust or loyalty were never something we had to deal with. We were always faithful to one another, even at the worst of times. Being faithful comes easy for me. Very easy. My husband was the same.

So here I was standing at the bar with this complete stranger who for some reason felt the need to buy me a drink. Looking back I was not warm, nor was I friendly towards him. It still to this day boggles my mind as to why he was so persistent in talking with me. We were standing side by side and I had my entire body facing the bar, with my right arm up on the counter completely blocking him off, only leaning in towards him just enough so I could be polite and actually hear whatever it was he was trying to talk to me about. The music was loud and it was pretty dark, but my eyes fell completely in line with his lips - his mouth. I watched almost each word as he spoke it. He began telling me what it was he was doing in New Brunswick, and also what it was that he did in the military.

I assumed he was in the Infantry, simply because of his physique, and the other guys who were with him. So right off the bat, this guy didn't have a lot going for him in terms of impressing me. But when he started to tell me a little bit more about himself, I began to learn that he was only in New Brunswick for about five months on a military course. He was a member of the Special Forces. So, I can't lie, I was intrigued. Only for a moment though, because as quickly as he slightly impressed me, my brick walls that surrounded my heart weren't budging. They were probably *re-mortaring* themselves as our conversation continued to become a bit more personal.

But then he did something incredibly sweet. I'm a pretty emotional girl (shocking) so it really doesn't take much to make me melt over something. He pulled his phone out to check the time, and on the home screen of his iPhone was a picture of the sweetest, most adorable little girl I had ever seen. It was his daughter. And she had just turned three years old two days prior. You could see the shift in his eyes when he took his phone out to check the time. His attention was now off me, and he was all of a sudden missing his little girl. He then went on to tell me that he lived in Petawawa, but his daughter and ex-wife lived a few hours away from him. He had the handsome, solid as a stone, *"special forces - I'm super bad ass. I've done really cool shit"* persona down to a tee. However, missing his little girl was the bigger identity he was wearing. It was so clear.

So here I was standing beside a man who most likely had a very skilled and impressive resume; really, any girl's dream man. A true super hero in our country's military. But in that moment he was just a father who was missing his little girl. And that was the part that I was going to love about him the most.

I immediately began to see the softness behind his eyes, his eyes that I could barely see because of his hat. But by this point even I was becoming a little softer. I remember thinking to myself, *"Ok...maybe this guy has something to offer, and maybe he's not a total dick face"*.

He rested his hand on my lower back as we continued to talk, and although here I was standing at this bar, beside a perfect stranger, for some very odd reason the moment he placed his hand on my back I felt at ease. There was something about his touch that made me comfortable. As if I could finally exhale the hundreds of short breaths that had been sitting in my chest ever since my marriage ended. I was still very cautious. Not much was going to fool me anymore. But a big part of me wanted to enjoy whatever it was he was helping me feel.

Comfortable.

Safe.

Breathing. (breathing, super key)

His hands were heavy, but gentle. They had *time* written all over them. He had been many places. Done many things. And seen many things. He had been through heartbreak. He had loved, and lost. Without a doubt this was a man who knew what it felt like to lose something. In that moment I couldn't comprehend all the emotions I was feeling. I kept thinking *"Is this really happening? Am I picking up a guy at the bar? A super hot guy who's probably a winning lottery ticket in the bedroom?"*

Just kidding.

However, I was definitely in a state of *"I think I just picked up a total bad ass… and I like him. And I didn't even have to try, like… at all. So this is what this feels like. Neat"*.

He wanted to go for a cigarette before the bar closed, so with a firm grip I grabbed him by his hand as I lead the way towards the patio. He stopped me, and I turned around as if to say *"Um… hello buddy, do you want to smoke or not?"* And this is when he blew my world apart. This is when he figured me out.

It had nothing to do with the black leather knee boots I was wearing, or my size minus-double-zero mini skirt I had on. He saw through every inch of my armour. As if his eyes were some kind of *Special Forces Eye Ball Edition* with laser beams. Because all my efforts to be *mysterious* were total fails. (no surprise there)

It only took him a few short words to make me shake in my boots; something I was unknowingly going to experience with him in the days to come. He whipped me around by my one hand he was holding so I was all of a sudden facing him; he looked at me dead in the eyes and said *"You don't have to always be so strong, do you know that?"*

And just like that he called me out. He didn't know my story, he probably barely remembered my name, but he saw right through every single wall I had put up. I tried so hard, *so* hard, to appear as tough and strong as I could on the outside.

The moment he said those words, I could barely speak. I hadn't had someone ever be that honest with me.

The words hit me like a tonne of bricks.

And I wasn't ready for it.

The end of the night was just around the corner and it was time to go home. He wanted to come back to my house with me, but I knew better. *"Like hell you're coming over. We just met"*. I said. He looked a little disappointed, but I really didn't care. If he wanted to see me again, he would, and that would be that.

He gave me his number, and we would end up talking the next morning. I was actually surprised when I sent him a text message and he responded. It was the very first message I would receive from him. And I had no idea that eventually thousands would follow.

"Hey, it's Vicki". An hour goes by… *"It's Jack"*.

I was excited. I had plans the following night to attend a wedding. I was going with a friend of mine as his date, but I knew the wedding would be over by 10 or 11, and I thought to myself, *"maybe I could leave the wedding early and invite Jack back to my house? Have a drink, sit on the couch, and actually get to know one another?"*

I felt a little bad about pretty much ditching my wedding date early, but my head was wrapped around Jack.

There was something there.

He called me out on my "persona" i.e, he called me out on my bullshit. So damn right I was curious as to *just exactly* who this guy thought he was.

It was about 9:30 on a Saturday night, and Jack was on his way from the base to pick me up from the wedding hall that I was at. Where I lived was a small town, so everything is close by and very easy to find. I was wearing a little black dress, with a cute pair of sparkly high heels. I had a very little black leather jacket on, and a purse filled with some of the free goodies from the wedding. Of course I took extra. Having an on-going supply of treats and candies in my purse is the usual, and Jack would soon learn this about me, that I'm a candy whore.

I was waiting outside the wedding hall as I saw his headlights coming towards me. I was pretty nervous. I remembered what he looked like, but because the bar was so loud, I couldn't put a tone to his voice. For some reason I couldn't remember what the guy sounded like.

As I open the car door, about to get in, I hear *"How's it going gorgeous"* in this extremely deep, stern voice. It was actually very intimidating. Within the first minute of getting into his car and putting my seatbelt on, I immediately said *"Look what I got! Freebies from the wedding! Bubble blowers!"*

I was so nervous. I absolutely came across as an air head, for sure I did. Here I was, twenty five years old, getting excited over toys made for a six year old. Right after I spoke about my excitement regarding the bubble blowers, I thought to myself *"Good one Vic, this man who's probably in his thirty's for sure thinks you're a tool"*.

You know when you get into someone's car and it has a certain smell? And you either like it, or it turns you off. I don't know what he had in his car that night, but knowing him as well as I do now, there was probably a lot of extra dirty kit from work, an assortment of papers; work papers and house bills, garbage, plastic water bottles, and empty cigarette packs. But the combination of all that, plus the smell of his cologne, I liked it. I liked it a lot. It was the smell of *a man*. A strong man. Brave man. A *fully trained Special Forces man*. I was into it.

In hein sight, it was actually the smell of a man who was in his mid-thirties on the verge of a total mid-life crisis and I was about to become collateral damage --But we'll talk about that later.

After about a ten minute drive down a dark winding road, we arrive at my house.

Now, periodically throughout the drive to my house, among some innocent chit chat, the thought that I was bringing a very skilled, professional killer who was a complete stranger back to my house where both my roommates were not home, I did fight a couple of those *"What if he's not a good guy?"* thoughts. But then I said to myself, *"Vic, this isn't the time to be a negative Nancy. If I think he won't kill me, he won't kill me. Law of attraction. I got this."*

There were a few things that I noticed that very first night. These are things I don't think I've ever told him either. As soon as we walked into my house, I headed over to the over-sized chair by my window so I could take my painful pair of high heels off. He took his shoes off and ever so gently put them to the side of the front door so they wouldn't be in the way of someone opening the door. I took notice how he did that. Now, these are small things, things people don't really ever notice, but I knew every square inch of my house, after all, I *hand-sanded* and *refinished* every god damn part of it. But I noticed where he put his shoes. *"Out of the way, and to the side of the door? Considerate… he must be considerate… and somewhat of a planner – as in, pre-planning for a possible door opening moment from another human being. Smart… "*

I also took notice to the kind of shoes he was *wearing*. They were a kind of loafer, but not a dorky looking loafer. They looked expensive, as if every contour on his shoes were there for a purpose, designed for *extreme walking conditions*, for an *extreme kind of guy*. I remember I giggled to myself for a second because I thought *"What funny looking shoes! Where does this guy come from?! And where in the fuck does he think he's going with those shoes?!"*

After making our way into the kitchen and pouring a full bottle of wine into two very full wine glasses (learned it from my momma), I proceeded to take him on a tour of my 55 year old yellow house. I was excited to let him see each room. This was after all, my *first house*, and as any new home owner can relate, you're proud.

Little did I know, this man owned his own beautiful home in Petawawa, Ontario. He had a newly renovated kitchen, and new kitchen floors, which he did himself. But I was still excited to show him all my plans for the 77 cracks that you would find on the walls in every room of the house.

Now, I know I can come across flaky, and I also know I can *act* as if I'm not aware of my surroundings. But I actually am *very aware*.

Dangerously aware.

The flaky – space cadet type vibe I roll with is just a tactic. If you appear to not retain much information, or proceed to provide people with an image that you're the type of person who *never really knows what the fuck is ever going on* - people won't bother you for information.

Less questions.

Easier days.

It's also a very effective way to see who the people are in your life who will actually hang themselves with all the loving and *meant-to-be* trusting rope you give them.

I gave Jack a loaded gun, *handed it to him* with the barrel facing my forehead --and silently from my heart asked him to please never pull the trigger.

All these years later, the fall of 2011 would become the date stamp of the last time I would ever give a person that ability.

Pause – wipe tears from my eyes – continue typing –

As I took Jack through my home, I noticed him noticing every small detail. His eyes would lock themselves for a few seconds on almost every picture I had framed. It was as if he was taking mental pictures of the girl in the photographs. *Who she was with, what she was doing.* He was almost studying me.

I didn't know if that should have scared me, or if it flattered me. But it was clear, this man was interested with me.

As I said a few words about each room we would walk into, he would just *watch me*. It was actually very intimidating. Every sentence I managed to put together, as nervous as I was, he was intrigued by me. I had never really felt as if I was that interesting of a woman. But as I would later discover, him and I grew up in such different worlds, so I guess there were a few stories of mine he would find interesting.

We sat down on my over-sized couch in my living room with our wine glasses still very full, and started talking. Exchanging stories. Painting each other a picture of our current life, past life, and the future goals we had for ourselves.

After hours of conversation it had become very clear that we had made a connection. And although I had become so relaxed and comfortable among the company of this man, that little did I know I was sitting cross legged facing him in a mini skirt exposing my entire crotch in hot pink panties. This was one of those moments where I was *not* aware of my surroundings… *not paying attention to detail*, or what my legs we're doing. I had no clue. I was too caught up in the conversation we were having.

In other words, I was getting drunk and flashing my panties for free.

all sass – no class

Anyhoo –

I would later find out that he only thought this was endearing, and that he actually thought it was adorable as to how clueless I was in that moment. There would be a lot more moments like that to come. He was learning that I was layered in terms of my life experiences, as well, for a 110lb blonde girl who became excited over bubble blowers, that I was in fact quite the intellectual thinker.

He would also soon become well versed with my sensationally gifted talent of *all common sense disappears from my brain* moments.

I do feel that I am intelligent in many areas. I *absolutely cannot* calculate the alphabet, or find "Y" in some kind of algebraic looking triangle… but I will nail a lying, cheating, cross-talking human being to the wall months before the clues and minor pieces of evidence ever surface.

So, that's good.

Basic requirements for everyday life – I collapse. But continuing to have a gifted skill set when it comes to navigating non-fantastic totally abusive relationships – *I'm all over it.*

"Do what you're good at and you'll never work a day in your life" they say.

Nice.

Thanks.

So I guess I'll keep getting involved with emotionally unbalanced men with unresolved addiction issues and according to that algorithm, shit should be cool.

(It's not)

How about *"do what your good at and become fully medicated with anger management classes by the age of 30"*

Call me crazy, but I don't see any inspirational quotes with those words flashing across office screen savers.

Moving on -

If you come to me with what you're feeling, whether you're scared, sad or nervous, I can guide you through each and every shitty emotion that you're fighting. Emotions are something I know all too well. But if you needed to know why your computer was acting up, or if you needed help adding a sales tax to an amount of money, I would more than likely respond with *"I don't know? Don't you think we should ask the Google?" or "What's really the big deal with tax, anyway? Cash only"*.

I have a hard time walking through each room of my house without smacking some part of my body off the door frame. And if I'm going to fall on the stair case, it only ever happens when I'm attempting to walk *up* the stairs.

But these are all things that I would soon realize Jack would find endearing. These are the soft parts of me. These are the things that we all have in us -- our little quirks. Regardless of what you go through, who you marry, what kind of life you lead, these are the little things that make us all so different. These are the little things about us that people fall in love with.

After about three hours of talking, Jack would say the one phrase that would end up haunting me for the duration of our situationship. *"I don't want to be in any kind of relationship right now. But I definitely want to keep seeing you"*

And although I too was not looking for a serious relationship, because Jack pretty much did *fall into my lap very un-expectedly*, I would soon learn that by him saying those words to me, that would be what he would resort back to over… and over again. Anytime I wanted to make our *situationship* an actual *relationship*, he would resort back to those words.

The devil is in the details ladies.

The devil is *always* in the details.

You would think in any man's right mind, if he wasn't looking for a relationship with a woman, if he wasn't seeking any kind of commitment or connection with a woman, then Jack would have spent the night, scored some sex, and never call again. Or maybe call the following weekend if he was in the mood for a sweet kiss goodnight. That would probably be what any level headed woman would assume was going to happen, right? I mean, I get it; I've done the booty call thing before. It's easy. It's black and white. Rules are laid out from the beginning, it's crystal clear. There are no emotions to navigate through because it's completely non-emotional.

Well, if Jack wanted no commitment, if he wanted non-emotional, then he should have re-evaluated his plan of action. Because he did the whole *"I don't want a relationship"* thing very wrong.

Based on his actions, his call back time, his sweet and flirty text messages, he was doing this "no-commitment" in the most bizarre way it seemed.

Can I get angry because he wasn't your typical asshole? No, no of course not. Can I be angry for letting it get to where it got, which would eventually lead me to selling my home, spending thousands of dollars and moving across the country?

Yes.

Yes I can get very angry about that.

And I did. On many occasions.

As each day would pass without me even being aware, this man was slowly wrapping his hands around me with a grip that would eventually become almost impossible to leave. He knew exactly what he was doing. He would find sly, and smart ways to say exactly the right thing, at exactly the right moment. I ended up becoming completely victim to it. I couldn't see what was happening at the time, but a certain unhealthy level of control was beginning to take place. This is a man who is skilled at interrogating hostages, capturing the bad guys, reporting in great detail to his Commanding Officer. He has been trained and schooled in the most elite ways this country has to offer. He was a Special Forces Operator. And his years in that position were plenty. I was his easiest target yet.

Hands down, his easiest target.

After making it very clear to one another that we weren't in this for a relationship, we decided to go upstairs and call it a night. Now, I tried, I tried very hard, told myself over and over again, *"Vic, if you take your panties off for this man on the first night you have him over, he will probably never call you again."* So as much as I tried to resist him, I was half a bottle of wine and several Jack Daniels deep, so it was happening. I remember thinking... *"meh, fuck it. He's actually kind of great. So well-travelled, successful, such a super macho hero".*

We began to have sex. And let me tell you something about having sex with a man who's hands do a very important job. This is a man who knows what he can and cannot do, and he's very clear about it. Every single time he would place his hand somewhere on my body, he knew what he was doing to me.

He had already studied every inch of me prior to actually making it up to my bedroom.

I remember being pretty reserved at first, I held back. I was nervous. This was after all a man who was about seven years older than me, and I had never been with someone over the age of 30 at this point, so this was very much new to me. I kept thinking to myself, *"This guy has probably been with an obscene amount of women, women from all over, young, old, experienced, un-experienced. What in the hell am I going to bring to the table?"* I figured if I'm going to give it up the first night, I might as well give it my best shot.

So that's what I did. And it must have worked because the next morning when he was dropping me off at my car back at the wedding hall, he asked me when he was going to see me again. I thought for sure this was going to be one of those *"Ok thanks for coming over, great night, loved the story telling! Hope your coffee wasn't too strong this morning, see ya!"* But I guess after sleeping together in my bed, as well as in the shower… I guess this older, well-travelled, Special Forces guy *did* want to see me again. It must have been the panties… when I had them on… when I took them off… And maybe a little something to do with the connection we had… maybe just a little.

I wasn't prepared for all that was to come while dating this man. And I would soon learn that this man wasn't ready for me.

The Romantical bits of the Romance

After the few weeks that were to follow that first night Jack and I had together at my home, everything was still new enough to have the butterflies, but with knowing the very firm outlines of this *non-relationship* situationship of ours, I decided to proceed with an open heart and let myself have the chance to enjoy something sweet; to allow a man who seemed to have honest intentions with me, allow him close enough into my life where we could be each other's best company through this cold, and damp month of November on the East Coast.

After a couple weeks of hanging out, having supper, and talking, always talking --every single day. On this one particular day, he sent me a text message while I was at school. *"What do you think about going to Moncton this weekend!?"* I remember exactly what I felt when I read that message. *"Moncton? Two nights, and three full days with this man, waking up beside each other, just the two of us… what if things go bad? What if something gets awkward…?"* Moncton is about two hours East of Fredericton. It's a bigger and more entertaining city for us New Brunswickers. A romantic getaway for two so early on made me a little nervous. But he seemed pretty excited about taking a little road trip with me, so I figured, what could possibly go wrong? Maybe it will turn out to be a beautiful weekend.

And it was. It was one of my sweetest memories to this day that I had with Jack.

Friday evening I drove into town, dropped my pupp off at my ex-husbands house, and made my way to the parking lot of the barracks on base where Jack was staying while completing the course he was on. I had about three bags with me. For all the driving I do, and living out my car lifestyle that has become quite the normal for me, I actually don't have any proper luggage. One of my bags, my fuzzy cheetah over-sized purse, which I put all my pairs of panties and bags of make up in; and I had a faux-leather over-the-shoulder bag, which held more glittery pairs of panties, as well as some pants, and probably a shirt or two.

I could always tell how opposite our lifestyles were, Jack's and mine. He was kitted out for the most extreme of circumstances. His gear was top notch. Secret pouches, double zippers. This was a man who could climb a mountain with five minutes' notice. Me on the other hand… well… I could fly into a circus dressing room and have enough make up and glitter products to be a part of the show.

I travel light.

Light enough that I can hop into my car at any given moment and cross the country. Just as long as I had my dog in the passenger seat, a pair of beat up flip flops sliding around somewhere in the back, a minimum of one cheetah print overnight bag, and my debit card. If all that was squared away, I was good to go.

It always seemed to blow his mind how un-prepared I constantly was for the weather, or walking terrain. These are some of those *common sense* things I was referring to earlier.

But I had seat warmers in my Honda, why would I ever need a proper winter jacket? Perspective everyone… perspective.

We packed up his car with our weekend supplies, and away we went. We were headed to Moncton.
Just Jack and I.

While driving the two hour drive, we of course fell right back into good conversation. This was one of those conversations you have after you've been dating a couple weeks, and you haven't scared each other away yet, so you decide to open up a little more… reveal some dark secrets… really start painting that picture of who it is you are, and all the things that lead you to your current place in this world.

We shared *all* our mistakes with each other. I shared some things with him that very quickly allowed him to see that although I may speak sweet words, and I may have a gentle touch, but I wasn't always an angel, and I have in fact travelled down some roads in my life that although I'm not proud of, they have landed me right where I was in that moment, and that was in the passenger seat of a man's car who I unknowingly would grow to completely fall in love with.

It seemed the more I told him about places I worked, personal experiences with substance abuse, un-healthy relationships with food, men, drugs, you know… all the ugly things that some of us women go through when we're trying to figure it all out; it was as if he was beginning to fall for me.
His body language was saying a lot that entire car ride.

They say investing in someone is what attaches you to someone. Whether you invest your time, your feelings, your words, your love… when you begin investing in someone on a daily basis, when your daily routine begins to involve communicating with that person, *seeing* that person, your life begins to change. And before you know it, life is now consisting of yourself, what you do to fill your days, and *that person*; that person who has become a part of it all.

That's exactly what began to happen with Jack and I. Although he made it very clear from the start, that he wasn't ready nor looking for a relationship. Before we knew it, he and I were spending all our free time together.

That night we arrived in our hotel in Moncton, after dropping our bags on the bed, we were both relieved and ready to relax and have a good meal. We decided to go to a seafood restaurant right beside the hotel. This was a restaurant that he either heard of, or has been to before, I can't remember which one it was. Regardless, the food was delicious, and the ambience of the restaurant was beautiful. It wasn't very busy, a lot of candles were lit, and twinkle lights decorated the artificial plants that surrounded the restaurant. It was one of the most beautiful and romantic dinner dates I have ever been on.

After our food was served, Jack and I started falling into those good old conversations him and I tend to have. Throughout that dinner, he shared with me a very personal story of his mum. He had lost his mum to cancer only a couple years prior. He began to really open up to me about the last moments of her life, what it was like; he painted the picture for me.

As he went on with each detail as to how it all felt, I was picturing in my head everything that was happening. Among all the things I had learned about Jack up until this point, one thing I had come very aware of was how close he was to his mum, how the relationship he had with her was one that would be everlasting despite the fact that she had passed; he was still very much connected to her. It was actually a little funny, because with each detail he would share about his mum, she was beginning to sound a lot like my mum.

You could see it, it was written *all over* his face, how fragile this subject was, but it was also bringing this beautiful smile to his face the more in depth he would describe her to me. Her details, all her details… she was this incredibly warm woman. You knew she had a big heart, you could tell quite easily with the amount of warmth that Jack had all on his own, you could just see the kind of woman a man like Jack would have come from. She seemed to have an amazing sense of humor as well, one that aided in shaping the kind of person Jack was. He knew when it was time to be serious, but he also has this really sharp sense of humor. Cut and dry really. But I was hardly ever offended by it, because I can be quite short and straight to the point myself.

When I look back to that night, I can't help but make the connection of Jack to his mum. It was almost as if the woman he was describing was the identity of Jack *pre-Special Forces.* He often spoke about how much him and his mum had in common, and I always wondered if he went back to those memories as a sense of relief, or for a sense of momentary peace.
I really do believe he spoke about her with such love not only because *she was love,* but because behind each word he spoke about her it *gave him love.* It brought him peace.

Which was something he hadn't had in a very long time.

I felt happy to be sitting here at this seafood restaurant with this man sitting across from me, letting down some of his own walls, sharing a few more of his secrets and allowing me to put the pieces together in my mind to understand what kind of world he came from, and how his mum had played such a huge role in everything that he had grown up to be.

By the end of dinner, him and I had squared away one very key element; that we were both hopeful for the happily-ever-after, the home filled with love and family, a big vegetable garden, animals, and the ultimate - finding that life-long companion to have all those beautiful things with.

When we got back to the hotel room, he did something that nobody (besides my own mother) has ever done for me. He drew me a bath, *with bubbles.* We turned down the lights, lit candles, and laid in the Jacuzzi tub together.

This was literally a scene out of a movie. I actually couldn't believe that after the summer that I had, after all the nights filled with tears and anger from my marriage, that I was actually being treated like a Queen. It was all starting to feel like a fairy tale.

He poured us two glasses of wine, and I laid on my back and let myself fall comfortably into his arms. It was complete relaxation.

On the last day of our mini-vacation, as we were driving, Jack had asked me a pretty straight forward and direct question, one that nobody has ever asked me. All my family and childhood friends all lived in Ontario. The only reason I was in New Brunswick to begin with was because the army had put me there.

But now that I was no longer in the military, I could move home if I wanted to. Nothing was tying me down. I no longer had a husband, I was done with my two, and hopefully *final* hip surgeries by the surgeon who worked in Fredericton, and I was currently on my way to getting my second College education. So by the spring if I wanted, I was *free to go.*

Sure, I had my house, but you can buy and sell those whenever you want, so if there's no real connection keeping me locked down in New Brunswick, why would I stay? Right?

At this point, I was actually happy living where I was living. Of course I missed my family from time to time, but we kept in touch, and usually twice a year I would fly or drive home to visit them.

But I loved my home, I loved my yard, I loved how bright the stars were outside my bedroom window.
I loved it there. That house is where I single-handedly mended my broken heart. Any woman will tell you that the place you reside (spiritually or physically) where you re-build yourself after a failed relationship – that location is *fucking sacred.*

I was single, independent, I was proud of who it was that I was becoming. I had my girlfriends there and my very good guy friends from the army. These were my friends, this town had become my home. Why would I get rid of it all to go back to a place that I tried so hard to leave?

Well for one, the idea of being able to see my family more often, *of course* that was appealing. Of course there were moments that I was missing. My cousins, Easter and Thanksgiving dinners at our family farm. I was missing those moments.

My closest girlfriends from childhood were succeeding in their lives, they had finished their university degrees, and they were buying homes, enjoying their relationships, celebrating birthdays ever year that I was missing out on.

And last but not least, *Jack.*

Jack lived in Ontario.

Could this be the right move?

"Vic, can I ask you something? What are you doing in New Brunswick?"
And for a few minutes I put my head down, I was staring at the floor mats in his car, and I remember that moment of clarity..

"I don't know… this is where I live. I love it here. This is my home, Jack".

So now, the thought process begins. All of a sudden, I'm forgetting about the fact that I'm going to be mortgage free by the age of 41 if I stay living in my sweet yellow house, I'm not thinking about the quiet, country nights that I get to experience every night on my front porch, and the *most important*, well, *difficult* decision that goes along with the entire idea of moving home was that I wouldn't be able to bring my dog with me. He was an American Staffordshire terrier, a Pit Bull.

Ontario had them out lawed. There was no possible way I could have brought him home with me and if I did, I was risking him being taken away from me if any neighbour complained, or if any blue collar street cop noticed him he could potentially have been euthanized. I could never, never in a million years put my baby's life in jeopardy. I didn't have enough cash available to buy a large property North of Toronto where I could live and my dog would go un-detected. If that was the case, moving home would have been easy.

Could I give my dog up? Find him a home? He was my best friend. This dog remained by my side through every dark night that I sat alone in that yellow house of mine while trying to get through the memories from the night of June 3rd. My dog never did anything to deserve getting left behind.

Anyone who has a dog will understand this. There was no person in my life during that time that came to my aid the way my dog did. The thought of life without him made me sick to my stomach.
But what was best *for me?* My life was changing. It was soon going to be a new year, my college course would soon be over, and I was almost a full year out of the military. I had changed; *a lot of things* had changed. Maybe it was time to go home?

It wasn't.

All the Right Ideas, for All the Wrong Reasons

After returning home from a really sweet weekend getaway, I was excited to pick up my dog from his weekend with his brother and my ex-husband, return home, and catch up with the girls.

I was always relieved when pulling into my driveway and seeing Angele's SUV. We would sit in the kitchen on the bar stools and catch each other up on how our weekend was. This was usually done over a glass of wine, something delicious and healthy she was making boiling on the stove top, and through all girl talk and wine, I would always manage to get a batch of muffins into the oven. She was excited to hear how my weekend went, and I was even *more* excited to tell her. *"It was perfect Angele; this man couldn't be more amazing"*.

Angele: *"How do you think it's going to be when he leaves in February? When his course ends, are you going to be able to end this mini relationship?"*

That's right… the deadline… *that* deadline… the February 15th deadline when all "this" is going to be over.

I went from being a complete stranger with this man, to talking to him every day, seeing each other multiple times throughout the week, cooking him suppers, having movie nights, sleepovers… the list goes on. How the hell do you just end all that? I was a bit nervous about it all. But I couldn't think about it. I was trying my hardest to focus on the moment, enjoy the ride, tell myself *what will be will be*… and all that other crap people say who have never experienced gut wrenching heartbreaks.

When you're hanging onto something that you think you're falling in love with, something that makes you happy, *of course* you're going to be scared to lose it.

Before I knew it, Christmas was right around the corner. Jack was to return home to Petawawa for three weeks to enjoy the holidays and see his daughter, and I as well was flying home back to my family for about a week. After spending six days out of seven together every week since we first met, of course I wasn't looking forward to the break, but back when I was married, my husband and I had spent months upon months apart for training purposes which was a part of both our jobs, so really, three weeks wasn't that big of a deal.

However, before I would know it, I would be right back with him, and it would be in less than three weeks.

I remember the morning he was leaving to do the twelve hour drive home from Fredericton to Petawawa, Ontario.

He had spent the night at my house. I was very on top of my baking, so he had an entire tubberware filled with fresh muffins for the drive. At 5:45 that morning, as he blew me one last kiss through my kitchen door window, I sat on my bar stool, blew him a kiss back, and tried to hold back my tears while eating my cup of oatmeal.

I knew I would hear from him multiple times throughout the day. Not only did Jack always keep in touch, but he never let me out of his sight. Even when he wasn't around me to actually *have eyes on me*, he always knew where I was, what I was doing, and who I was with. Although this may be too much to handle for some women, I actually didn't mind this at all. It didn't bother me because in my eyes I felt cared about. But when I look back, it sort of rattles me. I'm actually not sure if this was love. I'm thinking this may have been borderline control. Control with a *side dish of love*.

But during that time Jack was my guy; he was who I was becoming more and more intimate with as each day went by, so *absolutely* he could know my every move. It made me feel important to him. Growing up and never really having to report to anyone, having the ability and lack of supervision to run as wild as I pleased, when Jack walked into my life and wanted to know all my moves, as well as be there by my side as a constant support when I would have bad days, he was turning into my best friend. He was very slowly beginning to be very connected to me.

I knew what was happening, I was falling for this man. But I was going to take a chance with it. I also knew that it could all end badly and I could end up with my face back on the hardwood floors with a bottle of Jimmy Beam. But I didn't care, I was going in head first, all my eggs-1 basket. *(In the months to follow, by the way, I did in fact find myself face down back on those hardwood floors… my dearest friend Neisha can attest to that).*

The lesson – keep some eggs out of that questionable looking basket. Keep A LOT of your eggs out of the basket. Hide some of them under your sofa, your bed, your fucking neighbour's house – anywhere. Just do yourself a big favour, and do not fill that big basket with every single one of your eggs.

Now, in the future, I'm not so sure I will ever do this again, because by doing this (mindlessly putting all your eggs in one basket – a basket with large unanswered holes) it may take a lot of guts, the reality is - it can come back and burn you in the end. You can remain as hopeful as any person could be, but at the end of the day when reality sets in, sometimes no matter how sweet your relationship is with that person, due to life circumstances, timing, priorities, or (in my case) a complete mid-life crisis, sometimes things just don't work out.

Saying Goodbye to my Sweetest Lullaby

Christmas had come and gone, and before I knew it I was back on a plane back to New Brunswick.
I wish I could say Christmas of 2011 was a good one, but it honestly wasn't, it wasn't at all. I was in the middle of another big transition, and throughout the holidays while staying at my mum and step dad's house, I spent the majority of my time feeling pretty alone.

I had decided to put my house on the market come January 1st, and I was going to complete my schooling in New Brunswick and head home to Ontario by the Spring.

This big decision came with an even bigger sacrifice. I would need to find my dog a new home. I was devastated. But above all, I was angry, so angry that I couldn't bring him home with me. Giving him to my ex-husband wasn't an option, as much as he wanted to keep him, he was about to leave to Afghanistan for a nine month tour and he was needing to find our older dog a nine month long babysitter.

People say that you should never live with regrets. And even though I always thought I was one of those people who attested to that, I have come to realize that regrets are actually quite normal. They are very much a very normal part of life. The day we can all take that huge expectation off our shoulders of *"live with no regrets"* the sooner we can have easier transitions in coping with our fuck ups.

All of those unrealistic Internet quotes that preach the whole "regret nothing" bullshit needs to go. Regrets are a normal. Having regrets simply means we made a mistake, and we *absolutely* are aware of that mistake, and we hate that it happened. Call me crazy, but I believe having a regret or two makes us non-sociopathic. So have regrets. Be angry with yourself that you made a bad decision.

　　　--It's ok – I promise –

Once January came around, Jack was back in New Brunswick for only a few more weeks to finish his course, and then that was it, he would be packing up and heading home to his real home in Petawawa. Having Jack back was wonderful. Of course it was. We had become close, and I was going through quite a few of my own personal changes while having him by my side. At this point in time, I was starting to ask myself if I was falling in love with him. I was still not very sure what that was actually supposed to feel like with him, but what better way to find out than saying *"I love you"* to the person to see if they say it back.

After a few times of telling someone you love them, and then you just don't ever hear it back, you start to take note, and you stop saying it.

But here was the kicker to the whole "love" thing, back in November, he was supposed to come over to my house for the night to relax and watch a movie. But something had happened back at the shacks on the base. And from what he told me, he had a very long phone call with his dad. He didn't go into many details about it, only that it was emotional and difficult for him to communicate with his dad. Around midnight or so, after waiting a few hours in my living room, (yep… I waited for well over two hours in my living room) he finally sent me a text message. *"Can you come here? I've had drinks, I can't drive"*. I was pretty pissed off to say the least. I should have ignored the text message and gone upstairs and went to bed. When I look back at how I just sat there in my living room and waited staring at the front door, I actually feel bad for who I was in that moment. Fast forward to being 32 years old, that's something (waiting, hoping, staring at a door) that would never happen.

Self love, ladies.
Self respect.
Took about 10 years to finally figure it out, but better late than never!

As upset as I was, because of who I was back then (extra-forgiving, emotionally unaware of acceptable treatment from someone versus selfish treatment) I put on some jeans and a baseball hat, got into my truck and headed onto base to see what his issue was.

When I pulled in, I could see him walking towards my truck to come and meet me. He looked as if he had a couple drinks in him, but before I could even say two words to him, he reached his hand out to mine, took me by the hand and lead me to his room. I laid down on his bed, and he laid himself directly on top of me. We were just lying there, talking, and as the conversation kept moving, he slowly began to open up to me. Some of the best confessions that have come out of Jack's mouth have been after he's had a few drinks… surprise surprise. But I was all ears. I wanted to listen. I could tell he had a lot on his mind. While in conversation, he referred to me as *"honey";* and then he caught himself, and began to say how he doesn't call anyone *"honey"* or hasn't called anyone honey in a very long time.

He would eventually take his eyes from starring across the room at the window curtains and lock them into mine, and then he would say it, the one thing that probably got me into the most trouble; *"I'm starting to fall in love with you Vic".*

And there it was.

You tell any woman that, especially if she's starting to feel the same way in return, there's a pretty good chance you'll end up with a woman slightly more attached to you. Those are the magic words. I remember being taken back by it; I don't think I was prepared to hear him say it. And to be honest, to this very day, I really don't even think he remembers even saying it to me.

Which is the most un-romantic yet best part about it. Imagine telling your girlfriends, *"He told me he's starting to fall in love with me! But I can't really be sure, because he was drunk, I don't even think he remembers saying it, but he said it at least!"*

Tip… if he says it when he's drunk, and then never mentions it again, he probably didn't really mean it. Stop – getting – excited – over – mediocre – moments –

And then pick your brain up *off the floor* and gently place it back into your empty head.

By the time January hit, it was a bit of a stressful time for me because my house was now for sale, my one roommate Krista had moved out before the Christmas holiday, and Angele and I had only one plan; if my house sold before May (when my schooling was over) her and I would move back into the house that I shared with my ex-husband, because come March 1st, he was leaving for Afghanistan for nine months.

Selling my house wasn't what really had me stressed out, it was my dog. It was finding my sweet pupp a new home, a family strong enough, and tolerant enough, to take on the responsibility of my soon to be three year old dog.

My dog had an unforgiving amount of energy. He required a lot of attention and a strong handler. He absolutely loved his squeaky toys, and what made him happiest above everything was to go for rides in the truck with me. I've said it before and I'll say it again, this dog was my best friend. He brought so much happiness into my life. Each night at bed time he would usually end up sleeping right under the covers, pressed up against my legs. He would always snuggle his way right down towards my feet, plunk his body down, and start snoring.

Raising him wasn't always an easy day. Unfortunately, for whatever reason, he had some behavior issues. I'm well aware that by having two male dogs in your house, there is the possibility for dog fights. This can happen with any breed. One dog is always going to try to be the Alpha male.

Back when my husband and I were together, after a few too many dog fights between our boys, we decided to hire a very well-known dog trainer in the area who worked with many dogs who had aggression issues. After about three months of training and a few hundred dollars later, my husband and I were pretty on top of the dog fights. We loved our dogs, they were our boys.

My husband had his dog for almost 12 years; that was his baby. When I brought our new pupp home in the summer of 2009, he was the sweetest addition to our family. Our older dog treated him like the puppy he was. They became each other's best friends. They were so goofy together. We have countless videos of them playing in the backyard. My husband and I would sit sometimes all evening on the back porch and watch them play. Those two dogs brought him and I much needed comic relief when everything else between us was falling apart.

Unfortunately, even after months of good behaviour, my pupp would have the odd bad day and attack our older dog. My husband and I became pretty good at predicting his behaviour. Like any parents, you get to know your kids. We both knew we would never give up on those dogs. And when I ended up moving out and buying my house, it was actually a great thing for the pupps, because they had less opportunity to get into fights.

Anytime I would drop my pupp off at my ex's house to spend "sleepover weekends", by the end of the weekend my ex-husband would always have good news to report- zero fights. It was all cuddles and play. I would come to pick up him up only to find him, our older dog, and my ex-husband wrapped up in blankets together on the over-sized L-couch, all smiles and watching movies. This always made me happy and relieved. We both thought that maybe his "angry" phase was over, or even better, maybe our older dog finally let him become the alpha, so there was no more to fight about in the animal kingdom.

But little did we know, the worst was yet to come. And this time, it was all going to end very badly.

During the early days of April 2011, my house had sold, and Angele and I had packed my truck up, multiple times, and moved ourselves into my old house.

My ex-husband was now gone overseas, and I was living in the spare bedroom of the house I once shared with him while we were married. The majority of my belongings were locked away in a storage unit in town. It was a bit of a reality check at first, to be back at this house, with nothing more than my mattress on the floor, some clothes in a suitcase, and one of Angele's lamps as my décor.

But this was only temporary. It was an affordable situation, and it was only for a few months until I would make the big move back to Ontario.

During this time with Jack being back in Petawawa and travelling to a few different countries for work, I wasn't feeling very connected to him. We were usually in two different time zones due to him being overseas or somewhere in the states, and the chances we would get to chat over text message never felt quite the same as they used to.

I knew he had to dis-connect from me; he started doing it back in February before he was about to leave. But when two people separate due to circumstances, not emotion, it's a hard thing to wrap your mind around. It's hurtful, whether if you mean it to be or not, you get hurt by it. The feelings I had for him never went away, there was no "big fight" to make me hate him, or not want to see him ever again.

It just… ended.

I spent a lot of my free time with Angele. She and I would go on hikes, bike rides, driving adventures. I just needed to keep my mind off things. I missed Jack, all the time, and I honestly didn't have a clue when the next time would be that I would see him. I can't even count the amount of times I would lay in bed at night and cry, I would cry like a baby. It felt like the shittiest break up, and even worse, I really had no clue how he was doing with it all. Was it easier for him? Did he find cute girls to flirt with to keep his mind off me? Did he even really think about me all that much?
This man came into my life and brought so many beautiful things, yet it all had to end, on a relationship level, and we had to somehow be "just friends".

He did a very good job at being friendly, and kind to me, but it wasn't the same. A woman knows when someone is letting go of them. And it's an awful feeling.

Before he left in February, he promised me we would visit each other once I was settled in Ontario. He promised me that what he wanted for me, was the *best for me*. He was proud of a few personal things I had overcome while dating him, and he wanted me to move forward with my life and experience all the new things a person can experience when creating a fresh start. As sweet as his words were, I hated hearing them.

I hated that he wanted me to "move on". That hurt me. It made me angry because the more he pushed me away from him, the more I started to feel that everything we had shared was nothing more than a time capsule. As if I was nothing more than a warm blanket and some good home cooking for him while he was away from his actual home for six months and stuck on the East Coast during a cold and damp winter.

It made me second guess almost everything, and I started becoming very sad about all of it.

After months of falling asleep in his arms and waking up with him bringing me a cup of coffee to my bedside, now all that was gone. And I was alone. And very soon, I wouldn't even have my dog to fall asleep with at night.

It was a beautiful sunny day in April. I had woken up early, gone to the gym that morning, and took my pupp for a good run in the field across from my house. I had planned to bake some muffins, do a little cleaning, and head over to my storage unit that afternoon to go through some things.

The dogs were in the living room, snuggling on the couch like usual. Angele was out for the day, so it was just me in the house. Something caught my pupp's eye out front, so naturally he jumped up to see what was outside. The moment the older dog lifted his head to take notice to the people outside, it set something off in my pupp because he snapped. He went from zero to ten in a blink.

Within seconds of them locking jaws on each other, I jumped into the middle of them knowing very well that I could get a pretty bad a bite or two, but that never stopped me before. My only priority was breaking them up before they would literally tear each other's faces off.

I knew my dogs very well, and I knew that if I got my hands on my pupp I could order the older dog to back down and he would. I shoved my one hand right into my pupps mouth. It was the only way I could win against the strength of his jaw. I ripped him off of the older dog and yelled at him to get on the couch and lay down, and he did immediately. I then took my pupp by his jaw and forced him onto his side on the hardwood floor. I remember my hand and forearm had no feeling in them. It was probably a mix of adrenaline and muscle or nerve damage from his teeth being lodged in a few places. He needed to cool down. He needed to come out of his red-zone.

After about five minutes of laying on top of him with my hand still in his mouth, he started to slow his breathing and release my hand from his grip. His tail slowly started to wag, almost as if he was coming out of his rage-fit and returning back to his normal personality. I slowly slid my body off of him thinking he was calm and ready to chill out and make amends with our older dog. But I was wrong. My judgement completely failed me.

He was still seeing red.

Through the many fights my husband and I have had to break up between these dogs, never once, never once *ever,* has either of them ever attacked one of us or any other person for that matter. We had no reason to fear our dogs. They loved people. Anyone who came into our home was only greeted by two very excited dogs wanting nothing more than to kiss them and get their bum scratches.

After my pupp stood up, he tilted his head and locked his eyes on me. I knew all too well that look. He was coming for me.

Within seconds I put my completely numb forearm out in front of me, and he tore right into it. I couldn't believe what was happening, my sweet baby… my best friend was turning on me.

In that moment I felt no pain. The feeling of my heart breaking in my chest outweighed any other pain that was taking place. His teeth were in my wrist, but I did exactly what I knew I had to do and took my arm that he was focused on ripping apart, and drove it straight into the ground. I knew he wouldn't release his grip, so if my arm was going to the ground, so was he. I immediately threw myself on top of him again and became dead weight so I had him pinned on the floor.

For about ten minutes I just laid there with my arm in his mouth and listened to him growl the most angry, horrible growl I have ever heard come out of him. I was crying. Silently. But my eyes were filled with tears. He eventually snapped out of it, he released his jaw from my arm, and ever so slowly started to relax. As I opened my eyes, all I could see was how much of my blood was all over the floor. He was licking his lips. It was as if he was my happy little boy again wanting to give me kisses. My arm felt paralyzed from having my forearm muscles torn by his teeth for so long that I knew I had to get him outside because I was now in no position to win a second fight. At this point he was now pretty much unpredictable.

My ex-husband and I had built a fence in our backyard when we first moved in and I was twelve feet away from the back door. I grabbed him by his lower jaw, still laying on top of him and slowly, ever so gently moved my baby across the floor with the weight of my body. Once I got to the back door, I opened it and out he went. I slammed the door behind him, collapsed onto the staircase and started crying.

My mind was made up. My mind was made up the moment he locked his eyes on me with that mindless stare.

He attacked the wrong person.

He pulled his last trick that day.

I hated myself for knowing it was now his time to go to sleep forever, but I knew this wasn't a dog I could ever be successful in re-homing.

I knew that if I put him in my truck and went for one of our very much loved truck rides through the woods; I knew that his last moments would be beautiful. He would be happy. He would be in his favourite place in the world, in mummy's truck in the woods.

At this point the least I could do was make his final days at least beautiful ones.

I knew after all was said and done, I was going to need somewhere to bury him. I called one of my dearest girlfriends from basic training. Her and her husband lived not too far away from me, and the moment I told her over the phone what was going on, without a second hesitation she said *"Sweetheart you can bury your baby in our backyard, I have the perfect spot in our garden."*

I threw on my jacket, went out back, put his leash on him, and said to him one last time…"*Come on baby, time to go for a truck ride with mummy*". He was so excited. He came right to me, sat ever so gently and let me put his leash on. We got into my truck and went for a peaceful truck ride right until dusk. We went to all our favourite spots. Collecting sticks, twigs, branches laying on the ground. He loved collecting any type of old tree branch or stick.

A few days later the day had come when he would now be going to sleep forever. We sat together in the vet clinic, just him and I. My hand and forearm were still quite swollen from the attack, but none of that mattered. I kissed him on his nose, he was looking up at me, wagging his tail. I just stared at him, I held his face gently in my hands while giving him the last few kisses I'd ever be able to give him. I looked into his big brown eyes one last time. I kept telling him that I loved him over and over again; but it was time.

He was now gone. On April 14th 2012 he took his last breath. He would have been 3 years old June 1st.

In years to follow April 14th would eventually become a date I would face again.

I began wrapping him up in his favourite over-sized white blanket. I remember looking right into his eyes as he lay there completely gone. He was my baby, and for whatever reason I didn't raise him quite right. Maybe I loved him too much and didn't discipline him enough. Maybe I was too laid back with him, and cuddled him when I should have been more strict with him.

Once he was wrapped up, I picked up my 80lb baby and walked out of the vet clinic. I laid him down as softly as I could in my truck. On the way back to my girlfriend's house where we he was to be buried, I remember the emptiness that was filling my entire body. I don't even remember how I was able to drive. I was in a completely different place. Mentally, I was gone. I had just lost the one thing that I loved the most. I made that call, that final decision. And despite what anyone says, whether or not it was the "right thing to do" due to his unpredictable anger, I still to this very day regret the entire thing.

It's an unbelievably large pain that I can still feel no matter where I am or what I'm doing. And I still hate that part of myself that made the decision to end his life.

2012
I Wish it came with a "How to" Guide

So far this year was bringing me more low's then high's. I felt as if I was making the right choice with leaving New Brunswick and moving back to Ontario. It was time for me to be closer to my family. I just think I did it all much too fast. Nothing could have truly prepared me for the cultural shock I was going to slide myself directly into.

I knew in my right mind that the job market back in Toronto would be much better then small town Fredericton, there was simply more opportunity to be found in a city as big as Toronto.

I have a tendency to act very quickly once I make my mind up with something. But this - I should have taken my time with this move. I was slowly coming to terms with the death of my dog. Knowing he was buried in a safe place among loving friends gave me a bit of closure. But it still didn't take away from how badly my heart would ache for him every day that passed. Coming home at the end of the day and not having him greet me at the door was going to take some getting used to. Almost every day as I lay in my bed at night, I still look over towards the door way and imagine him coming up into my bed for bedtime. I can still see his face clear as day, wagging his tail, getting ready for sleeps. I thought I was a lot stronger, I thought I was ready to do what I actually did. But I wasn't. And his loss was about to hit me like a ton of a bricks in the months to follow.

I was now very empty handed. All the things that I had worked so hard for, the career, a marriage, a new home that had become my safe haven, a potential chance at love with an unexpected new relationship, and the love that I had built with my dog who was no longer here. It felt as if overnight all of that had been stripped away.

I thought I knew what I was working towards. Looking back, I truly thought I had my head wrapped around what I wanted. But I was wrong. I was set to move into an apartment in the city with my older sister. I thought it would all be ok, I thought it would all work out. But again, I was wrong. I was very, very wrong.

Jack was always there, in the background, he was always cheering me on, and getting excited for me as the "moving home" day got closer. But with each day that passed as Jack and I remained separated, I could feel parts of myself shutting down. I just didn't want to miss him anymore. I was sick and tired of missing someone. If people are meant to be in your life, they will find a way. I really believe that. And if they don't show up, it's a crystal clear answer for me.

I really did have pictured in my head that I would move home to the city I grew up in, get settled, find a job, and re-connect with my friends. I had no expectations to continue having the relationship with Jack that we shared while in New Brunswick, but I really thought at minimum we would still have visits once in a while.

It was getting very close to the day of packing up my car and heading west, back to Ontario. With the weeks leading up to departure day, I remember very clearly a few times Jack would call me. And I was always surprised when I would see his name pop up on my phone screen. The one time that surprised me the most was when I was just on my way out for a run. By this point he and I were no longer talking every day, and when we would, it was usually him reaching out to me. I had shut down quite a bit. I had to. Between Jack leaving my life and saying my final good bye to my dog, I was emotionally done. I'm almost positive for the last few weeks I spent in New Brunswick, I was merely coasting. I was in survival mode. I didn't want to feel anything; I didn't want to love anything. Which wasn't overly hard as I really had nothing around me to love anymore.

All of it had disappeared.

When Jack called me that day, hearing his voice on the other end of the phone line put a smile on my face. I didn't want to hear his voice, because I knew it would only remind me of how close we once were, but just hearing him tell me the simplicity of how his day was, I missed that. I missed it more then he probably knew.

Jack accepted everything that I was. From that very first night he had met me. He only wanted to keep learning more and keep digging through the layers of very un-organized thoughts that filled my head. He always let me talk about whatever it was I wanted to talk about. And even better, he listened. He would actually hear me.

Something very few people can do.

Moving day was fast approaching, but there would be one last event to take place. Nine days before I was set to make the big move I was unknowingly about to suffer a huge concussion, bruise the left side of my face and destroy my entire car.

It was a Friday night, around one in the morning, maybe two o'clock. I was fast asleep on the mattress on the floor of the spare room of my *used-to-be* home. My blackberry rang. It was a friend of mine. He was very drunk and needed a ride home from the bar. I didn't have an overly huge group of friends that I was keeping in touch with the last month I was still in New Brunswick, however this was one of my good buddy's from the army. I knew if I called him in the middle of the night he would definitely get in his car and come give me that ride home. I got out of bed, put my jeans on, my sports bra and a T-shirt. Got in my car and made my way down the highway into downtown Fredericton. I didn't drink that night, wasn't playing around on my phone while driving, not even touching the radio station. Nothing. I was just driving. Looking straight ahead at the road in front of me. When I look back to this night, I'm not overly surprised at what had happened. My headspace that entire last month was completely gone. I was gone. I had isolated myself so badly that I wasn't functioning like a normal human being anymore.

Before I knew it I was starring directly at the wheel well of a white car making its way through the intersection.

I was running a red light. Going about 80 kms. Not overly fast, but fast enough to completely wreck your car, that's a sure thing. I remember driving straight into this car. Then all of a sudden I was driving into a steel pole that held up the traffic lights.

The air bags blew up, my body and lap was covered in this cold Windex smelling fluid, and my windshield was basically in my lap. Apparently they make cars with shatter-proof windows.

My car wasn't one of those cars.

Nope.

Out of the entire 15 seconds that it took where my mind was apparently not operating a vehicle, *after* I had successfully T-boned another car and crushed my entire front end, I was seeing as clear as day!

"Better put my car in park and turn off the ignition" I thought to myself.

I looked down at my right hand, shifted into Park, and then ever so carefully turned my car off. I mean, *I was now parked.* That's what you do after you park, right? Whether you park at the mall, in your driveway, or after slamming into a traffic light, you shift your car into park!

The next thing I remember is waking up with two very large thighs on either side of my head. I was surrounded by firefighters while lying on the road. I remember how loud it was. The sirens, people on the sidewalk. It was this huge crowd of on lookers. It took me a few minutes to come-to, then it all started to hit me. *"Did I kill someone? Where is the other driver? Is that person ok?"* I was completely panicking. Then one of the firefighters said the best words I had heard in months *"She's ok, she walked away. The other driver is completely fine".*

I then started to breathe a bit more normally. I remember thanking God inside my mind. At that point I thought I was for sure going to jail. *"What kind of traffic ticket do you get for this I wonder?"* I'm still laying on the ground while the firefighters cut open my jeans to see where the bleeding is coming from.
There was so much glass, I had cuts everywhere it seemed.

They kept trying to have me follow their fingers while performing a bunch of other *"how hard did you hit your head"* activities.

I don't remember a whole lot after this. There's a black spot in my memory between leaving my comfortable place on the road to being in the ambulance. I do however remember waking up *while in* the ambulance. There was about five or six paramedics and firefighters with me during that ride to the hospital. Or maybe there was only three or four… and heads were just blurring together. Either way, there were a lot of hands doing a lot of things with tubes and pumps and other things that go "beep".

My eyes were now back open, but I couldn't talk for some reason. I then started to go into shock. *This* I remember very well. My body started shaking and my breath was becoming shallow. This one paramedic, a female, was all of a sudden very up close with my face. I remember she placed her hands on the sides of my head and was saying something to me. I could see her perfectly, but couldn't hear a thing she was saying. I remember looking down and could see my legs shaking as if I was laying on some vibrating bed. It was almost impossible to move anything other than my eyes because they strapped one of those metal halo's around my head just in case I had any breaks in my back or neck. At some point later my body started to relax, the shaking was now stopping and I was able to communicate again.

Miraculously, one of the firefighters had my cell phone. I guess they grabbed it from my car so they would be able to call someone from my phone. I told him to call Jack. I had no passcode of any kind on my phone. And I knew if Jack was called, he would be able to contact my Dad. Looking back, you would think I would have told them to call my mum or my dad directly. But I guess something in me just knew Jack would handle it all. And he did. He got a hold of my dad within moments of getting the call from the fire fighter.

Once arriving at the hospital, I was wheeled through a bunch of hallways. I must have lost consciousness again because all of a sudden I was awake and no longer moving and starring at a ceiling with painfully bright hospital lights.

I just wanted to go home. My entire body was in a whole different level of pain, but I just wanted to be in my bed and away from all the chaos. I was still strapped to the wooden spine board. The staff had my arms and legs strapped tight and my head was still attached to this halo. It's a very similar feeling to when you're on your way into the psych ward. They must do similar schooling for intake procedures.

I laid there until dawn. I was moved a few times to have various chest x-rays, as well, they x-rayed my metal implants in my hip and leg to ensure nothing moved. They did a cat scan of my head and neck. You name it. They did just about everything other than pay my hydro bill. I remember after being pulled out of the cat scan machine I asked the nurse if she had any visual on my actual brain really existing.

I was so fucked up.

But I guess I joke my way through trauma. Or at least I did during that moment. Whether that's a great thing or not, I was definitely full of jokes during those early morning hours. My brain or emotional stability as a whole has never been all that fantastic in my life, so now after this car accident I thought to myself going forward… *"I might be really screwed now!"*

Moving Day

One modest insurance cheque and a *new-to-me* Honda Accord later, May 8th, 2012 had finally come. I had packed this new-ish car the night before, my truck had been picked up a week earlier by the freight hauler to be shipped over to Ontario and delivered to the family farm near my mum's house.

I remember thinking I was ready to leave New Brunswick behind. I was still very emotionally shut down. The weeks to follow after my dog's death consisted of an unbelievably hard time falling asleep at night. I would lay in my bed and be flooded with his memories. The headaches from my car accident weren't letting up very easily either.

For the first time in years I was going through something heartbreaking but I had nothing to hold onto come night fall. Pouring myself a glass of whisky and sitting on the back porch just sipping myself to sleep became the healthiest way I could cope with it all. Falling into addictions or bad habits has always been an easy task for me, but I decided years prior that after my second hip surgery that I was going to do everything in my power to save what I could in terms of my bone health and my mental health. No more bad habits.

I started using fitness as my outlet. It had become my saving grace.

After all, I had lost my career, my marriage, I somehow wasn't able to raise a healthy minded dog. I felt as if I was running out of things I was good at. The moments of criticism from my husband during our married years made me break down in ways I never thought I would. I never felt good enough in his eyes, and I ended up forgetting about the things I was actually good at. The back-to-back losing periods that had taken place so far weren't very much help in terms of helping me hold my head high.

But fitness, I was good at that. I knew a lot about it. I knew a lot about food and everything good and bad it can do for you. Shaping my body into the exact physique I wanted was never really that challenging for me. With school being over and no real home, animals or man to care for, I put all my energy into working out. It was my only real release. Even when I would run, I never knew where I was running to, or what I was running from, but I was running, I was going somewhere. And during those moments of "going somewhere", it was enough to help me get through the lonely days that had seemed to become my life.

I was about to leave the little town that I had grown comfortable in, grew to love, to drive a thirteen hour drive straight across two provinces to arrive in Toronto. Driving was something I did quite a bit; it was a comfortable place for me. All I needed was some good music, maybe a couple cigarettes, and I could drive for hours. It was my safe place. Some of my best thinking and ideas have all come to mind when I've been in the driver's seat of my car on a long straight road heading Lord knows where.

I was nervous about this drive though, thirteen hours and alone at that. For the most part the route was pretty direct, pretty easy, except Montreal. But I had a GPS, written directions and Angele on speed dial. So I felt confident.

After about nine hours with only two quick stops, I cross into Ontario and I'm now on the 401. I made it. And Montreal didn't swallow me up and have me doing circles! I made it through in one shot, and I was pretty proud. You have to understand, that I can be given the most basic directions to get somewhere, I can be equipped with a GPS, a map, hand written directions, a god damn satellite tracking device strapped to my head and I can almost guarantee you that I will mess up somewhere and it will probably be at the easiest part of the drive.

After a few days of arriving, I'm getting settled into my apartment in Toronto. None of my belongings had arrived from the East Coast yet via the moving company, so I was sleeping on my bed sheets doubled up on the hardwood floors in the corner of my room in the apartment.

Toronto was more of a cultural shock then I was prepared for. Yes, I knew the city very well, yes I grew up in parts of it when my dad lived in certain areas, and yes - college, my years at the club, I knew that city *well*.

But what I soon came to realize was that although being a born and raised Toronto girl, I had left that city for a lot of reasons. When I had left and lived on the East Coast, four years had gone by. And within those four years a lot had happened to me. I grew a lot, learned a lot, loved some, and lost some. I was returning home a very different women then the little girl I was when I left that city in the early summer of 2008.

I was a little hardened.

And deep down, more than anything I was just alone I think. I may have now had easy access to family and child hood friends, but I felt very alone. There was a big space inside me that remained quite empty, and just… cold.

The plan? Find work, adapt to my surroundings and emotionally start over; rebuild.

The reality? None of that was happening.

I applied to many job ads, a *tonne* actually. Very few bites; only a couple of interviews. I wasn't happy in the area I was living in. It was loud, the people were not like the East Coast-friendly people I had been surrounded by, and traffic was crazy. It was a far cry from the small town and kind community that I had been living in for the past four years. I tried pretty hard to let my guard down and try to fit in, but I couldn't. People were constantly brushing by you on the sidewalk with their cell phones stuck to their ears. I would hold the door open at a café and let a lady or man walk in in front of me, there were hardly ever any thank you's, or any notions of kindness. I was surrounded by assholes it seemed.

In reality, were they all "assholes", most likely no. I'm sure most were normal, wonderful people. But while out on the streets everyone seemed too busy to even have basic manners, at minimum. But it was the hustle and bustle of the big city that I wasn't used to anymore. And I wasn't *getting* used to it either. What I knew for sure at that time is that I did not want to remain there. It just wasn't for me.
As each day passed, I just felt more and more out of place.

By the end of May, after about three weeks of living in Toronto, Jack and I were talking a little bit more. I hadn't lost all hope in what Jack and I shared, but it had been about three months since we had last seen one another. A lot had changed for me. Sure I missed him, but my mind was focused on more *me things*. I wasn't transitioning well in the city. Everyone had their lives pretty well established. I was starting from ground zero. Instead if reaching outwards for support, I kept to myself and tried to map out how I was going to re-create a happy life for myself.

The night time tears for my pupp started to happen only twice a week, versus every night. But I think the only reason that was happening was simply because I wasn't allowing myself to think about him anymore. I was trying not to remember him. It was too painful.

One afternoon while I was sitting in the apartment on my lap top job hunting, I receive a text:

"Vic... I miss you!" says Jack. He wanted to see me. He lived a quick four hour drive just North of Toronto.

We made plans for a visit that coming week. He told me he would have his daughter with him, and asked if that was ok. Of course it was ok. I had only been hearing about his little girl for the entire duration of our situationship. I had seen so many photos and I always remembered how Jack's face would light up every time he would talk about her.

A few days later I was on my way up to Petawawa. As excited as I was, I was also nervous. How would it be when we see each other? Would he fly down to the front door, wrap his arms around me and give me the biggest kiss ever? Would he lean in for a "friendly" hug and go about being the "friends" that we were? Would he give me a high five? Or one of those god awful hugs while patting you on the back.

After a nearly five hour drive, (I took a few wrong turns) I'm pulling onto his street. My knees we're shaking. I felt like a little girl on her first day of school. I could have really used some Ativan.

I open the front door, and there he was; standing at the top of the stairs that separated the entrance way from the main living area. He was wearing a light blue t-shirt and jeans. He had a fresh haircut, and my god… did he look good. He looked healthy, his face, his complexion, he looked good. His arms looked a little more defined, his chest appeared bigger, and I stood no chance. Jack had always looked good in my eyes, from the moment I first saw him, but today? I don't know if it was the five hour car ride or feeling a little cabin fever from living in a shoebox apartment surrounded by concrete buildings, but Jack looked good. The trees even looked good, the fresh air felt fresh.

I could breath.

He had his daughter right there by his side, she was holding onto his hand as I walked through the door. She was even cuter in real life. I had seen so many photos, but a photo can't capture the spirit of a happy little girl. She was like a magnet for happiness. Now I knew… now it was all coming together why this man was so taken back, was so affected by the sweetness of his daughter. I had barely been in that house for 15 seconds, and his daughter was already putting a bigger smile on my face then Jack was. She was a diamond. She *is a diamond.*

After a few minutes of sitting on the couch and letting his daughter show me all the ways she knew how to do summersaults, it was time for her to get ready for bed.

Let me tell you something about watching a man parent a little girl. Jack is a man who has done very *non-gentle* things in his life. His job alone proved that. And even in his life outside of work, his hands are tough; they are thick, solid, and strong. He is very hands on with everything he does, and this included parenting.

As I sat on the couch and watched him explain to his daughter that it was now time for bed, and all the bedtime steps that go along with putting a three year old in bed, I sat there and watched how patient he was with her, how calm and gentle he was with her. I saw more parenting skills in those five minutes then I had experience in my own life of growing up as a little girl. He was patient with her. He would look in her eyes and let her put her words together, and then gently correct her in how something was supposed to sound, or be put together in a sentence.

From what I knew, from all that I had learned through spending the winter with Jack, it was that he never felt that he was doing a good enough job being a father to his daughter. But my goodness was he wrong, was he ever wrong. If he could have seen himself through my eyes in that moment, he would have thought different too.

While sitting there in his living room I was no longer nervous, I was starting to relax. Everything about being out of the city and back into a small town felt like heaven for me. I didn't want to leave. Can you blame me? What was I going back to anyways? A city that I wanted no part in? Neighbours who gave me funny looks when I would sit outside with my morning cup of coffee in my pyjamas? I really felt as if I had no business going back there.

While in the kitchen washing my hands in the sink, Jack was busy putting his daughter to bed. I was standing there, kind of zoning out just staring out the window that sat over the sink, letting the water run over my hands. I was staring into his backyard. He had a good sized yard. Tall, beautiful trees, and lots of them. At this point I'm still not sure whether or not we are going to make peanut butter sandwiches and sit and talk, or if there's any life remaining to the romantic aspects of what we shared.

Before I knew it I felt him come up behind me. He placed his hands on my sides, and slowly let them slide down to the front of my lower stomach. He pressed himself right up against me and started ever so gently to kiss my neck. I melted. At first I didn't react, I just stood there and let him have me. I needed this. My shoulders had been cold, so cold, for many months. I needed his warmth. My heart was so shut down and on "survival" mode from the emotional disaster I had put myself through by putting down my pupp, and distancing myself from society as a whole.

I just needed a piece of love.

After sitting at his patio table for a little bit and talking about our day, I could see that he was exhausted. His work schedule had been so crazy for some reason that week, and he looked ready for bed.

That night as we laid in his bed, this had been the first time in months we had the chance to be together. I couldn't wait to just shut my mind off, close my eyes, and actually sleep through an entire night.

When everything in your world seems to be at odds, whether you're going through a transition, the end of a relationship, loss of job, new job, whatever it may be, if you're lucky, you have someone there to help you move through that change. You have your support. And although Jack would always tell me over and over again that he was there for me or that he stood by and supported me, so many parts of me had shut down that I was unknowingly existing as a some-what broken person.

I was shutting people out, isolating myself through the process. I don't know why I do this, or *where I learned to do it*, but for as long as I can remember, this is how I dealt with things. I will keep myself completely alone through some of the hardest times in my life, and maybe it's because I want to know I can conquer the worst? With nothing more than my own two hands? Lord knows. But for whatever reason, I don't make any effort to ask for help.

This has hindered me during the process of healing while at the same time ultimately has made me quite strong as I sit here alone today telling you all of this.

Now, don't get me wrong, I have people in my life who support me. I will never be *homeless*, to put it that way. But from a very early age my perspective on men never had a chance to really develop in a normal or healthy way. I had to figure it out for myself for the most part. And naturally, I made a lot of wrong turns while trying to find love in some very wrong places.

I thought I had made a pretty good choice when I married my husband, and although *now* he and I are peaceful towards one another, the damage had already been done. I still have the odd night terrors from the memories of that night in June, and I still to this very day question myself the odd time on my abilities, or if what I'm doing is good enough.

I am by far my biggest critic.

I will never forget the first time I cooked for Jack. He *loved* my cooking. I remember thinking *"Really?"* Anytime I used to cook for my husband, he would more times than not tell me why the meal wasn't all that great. So I started to believe I was bad at making just about anything. But after taking myself away from that, I soon began to realize that I was in fact pretty good in the kitchen.

Jack helped restore a lot of my confidence. He really did help turn my negative thinking patterns into more positive ones.

As we curled into bed that night, within a matter of seconds his hands began to fall all over me.
When Jack came into my life, I didn't really know how to be emotional with someone while having sex with them. My husband and I did have great sex, he was fantastic in the bedroom, but I think I never really knew enough about myself during those years to really be authentic in those moments. I had spent two years prior mastering the art of having a new identity every night in front of multiple strangers, so tapping into who "Vic was" wasn't easy for me. I struggled with that, and for a long time.

After Jack and I started sleeping together, the more open and comfortable I was becoming with simply being no one other than myself.

While lying in his bed that night he started un-buttoning my shirt, and like usual, he was very gentle about it. I had lost a few pounds since seeing him last. Between moving, fighting through the thoughts of my pupp that always made me feel sick to my stomach, and spending half my days inside a gym, I had definitely gotten smaller since he had held me last.

And although he knew I was probably somewhat fragile, he tried his best not to say anything, because he knew like any right-minded man, a woman's physique can be a touchy matter.

Now, the bittersweet factor to all of it was this; Jack didn't want a relationship, remember? He didn't want commitment. His work had him travelling, always travelling, his house was already too much to maintain. Between house renovations, giving his work all that he could, and most importantly, trying to be the best, most loving and hands-on father that he could be, I got it. I got the picture loud and clear.

Jack wanted to be single.

I thought long and hard about my options. I could continue our *situationship*, let the *chips fall where they fall,* or I could make the choice to simply move on. It's not like my life was in any way stable or "in a good place" to start a relationship with someone. I was almost certain I was going to move from Toronto. I was still jobless, and honestly, had really not much of a concrete direction. The only direction I had was that I wanted to re-build my life. Forget starting with short-term, realistic goals. I was aiming to go from zero to hero in a matter of weeks it seemed.

I wanted a life back.

I wanted *my* life back.

My Sweet as Pie Summer

Well, being as hopeful as I am, even in the most hopeless of times, and also being a dreamer, I decided to follow my heart. And my goodness, what a fucking mistake that was.

But didn't shit work out for Cinderella? And that girl mopped floors, but shit worked out for her, right?
She scrubbed floors all the way to a crown on her head.

So before I begin to tell the story about my summertime *sweet times*, let me say this first:

Always remember the facts. Facts will not fuck with you. They will just be there, *never changing*. Reliable as ever. You can even look back to them, and they'll *still be there*, looking all *fact-like*.
Just starring at you in your fact-less face.
Being all *"we're facts, what the hell do you have. Dreams? Oh, that's cute"*

So – before I started drinking Jack Daniels at lunch time, here's some cute-ish moments that took place before I hit rock bottom while giving a lap dance to a Middle Eastern oil tycoon in a high-end Ottawa hotel who apparently has issues with Canada's national security and was deported in 2014.

--Jazz Hands--

Jack and I spent a lot of time together the summer of 2012. Because I wasn't having any luck with finding a job, and I was spending all my free time up in Petawawa anyways, I decided to make a move. Now, I knew very well that the job market in Petawawa wasn't one worthy of moving four and a half hours North for. But there had to be somewhere else I could live.
Somewhere else I could plant my feet and start re-building my life again. It would have to be a city big enough for opportunity, but small enough where I would be able to see the stars at night and feel somewhat comfortable.

Before I made any decisions, I decided to take the opportunity of time and travel. Get in my car and drive. Visit towns, other communities, see what was out there, what I liked. I knew the realities of living in the GTA --it was expensive. Even in the little town where most of my mum's side of the family lived, where my truck was parked at the family farm, Stouffville. Real estate was on the rise, and I was never quite sure if I would ever manage to land a high paying job. And when your resume consists of an Artillery soldier, ex-stripper, and Beauty School candidate… things start to look a little scary.

But in my eyes, no matter where I lived, no matter what I was doing for my paychecks, as long as I was surrounded by kind people, had access to my family, and for the *most part*, enjoyed my job, I could be happy. I really believed this.

No matter what I was doing for work, I wanted to be around people who made me happy. And I was having a hard time re-establishing that back in Toronto. There was such a huge part of me that was still searching for that. There are a lot of things—emotions and certain self-taught securities that you should have before you consider having a stable relationship with a person. And even though stability was what I was looking for, it's never been something I've been overly good at. I can create the nicely painted four walls that are supposed to house it - and have those routine-like flowing pay cheques sustain it, but inside my checklist created life, I'm usually just a hamster in one of those clear plastic hamster balls.

Wheeling around in circles just bumping into shit.

I swear to God my life is all smoke in mirrors.
At this point with four beautiful homes and many career successes, I don't
know if I should now consider it an actual talent? Or a mental illness.

Either way, I'm usually doing pretty well up here in shit creek but with *a
tonne* of paddles it seems.

I put a crazy amount of kilometers on my car that summer. I drove here,
there, down over there; to the left up there. I drove everywhere. I had been
to Ottawa a few times, checking it out, doing job searches on the internet for
different cities. Ultimately trying to get a grasp on which cities had more
opportunity. I drove to Quebec many times for modeling jobs. Weekend
photoshoots that paid cash on site. I was trying to just get by. I have walked
through many *bad-idea door ways* to do "photoshoots" with
"photographers".

My photos were always published. Some were in print. Some were actually in really cool Monster Truck 4X4 magazines. I did a few really fun shoots with some well-known tattoo models. You could also find me in odd outfits with bizarre make up and terrible hair on various internet websites.

With each click, I'd get a hit. (A hit means I'd get paid, usually 0.05 cents per click) But at thousands of clicks per day, why the hell not!

Some were even short black and white movies that played on various cable streams I could never pronounce in very exotic cities, like Pakistan.

For an easy credit card payment of $4.99 you could rent me all day!

My name was Molly. I sat in a window with nothing on but an over-sized white T-shirt while speaking French to a camera

That was it. That tiny film sent me about 300 bucks every month for a three year period.

I didn't really know what I was saying, but I sure looked cute while saying it! At least the Pakistani's thought so.

I'm not proud, but I'm not ashamed at what I did to make cash in hopes of being able to re-furnish a new cute bachelorette pad somewhere in a trendy Ottawa neighbourhood.

I found a very small apartment right along the Rideau Canal. It was beautiful. It was a bachelorette with a very sweet balcony that was covered with shade by this huge, luscious tree that stood very tall in front of the three story house that this apartment was in.

And of course, because I was spending as much time as I was in Petawawa during that time, Ottawa was an easy hour and a half drive South East of where Jack lived. I really thought I would find a nice job in that city, an office job, some type of secretary work. Something had to come up.

For the two months that I lived in this apartment, I would wake up every morning, go for a run along the canal, and pick up a coffee in one of the many coffee shops that lined the town street I was closest to.

I tried very hard with the job search. Again, here I was, in an apartment, an apartment located in a much more peaceful spot mind you, but the job search that I had hoped for wasn't really giving me anything that great. A lot of minimum-wage job adds. I couldn't understand why I was getting pretty much zero call backs for an interview.

I put that resume together when I was in college in Fredericton. My professors had proof-red, edited, and approved it, so I was certain it was up to standard.

At least I thought.

For those two months, I spent a lot of time alone. A lot of nights on that balcony listening to some music, and usually scanning the web for more Quebec gigs for fast cash.

I was picked up with a local Modeling Agency. I met with the owner over a dinner at a really nice restaurant right in downtown Ottawa. Between her and her colleague, they wanted me to sign a six month contract with them. My body was cute and in really good shape, and with my various tattoos they were confident they could use me a lot in the alternative modeling world gigs.

I have never been the model-type. For one, I have a million insecurities about my face. And for two, I just never really cared to be in front of a camera having my pictures taken. But after a two hour business dinner and the opportunity for various cash projects they seemed to already have lined up for me, I signed on.

After almost four months of still no permanent job offer, I was beginning to lose hope, I was getting scared.

For the majority of the summer, three days out of seven would be spent sleeping in Jack's bed. We began falling back into a very familiar routine. A routine that provided me with much comfort, and it was where I was happy. We would wake up, he would get ready for work, I would feed the animals, put the coffee on, and get ready to go for my usual morning work outs at the gym on base, followed by a long day of job hunting.

More days than others, I would come home from the gym and take his dog for a walk around the neighbourhood. I started falling in love with his puppy as if he was my own. I missed having a dog. I missed having one to walk and simply take care of. To nurture something has always given me comfort in even the worst of times.

Each day that passed that I spent there in his town, I began to feel more and more at home. I started to feel as if I was finding my happiness again. I was trying to navigate my way through these never ending night-terrors that Jack came to know all too well. It seemed anytime I would wake up in the middle of the night from a bad dream, almost *immediately* I would feel his hand on my back or my hip.

He was always right there, trying to sooth me, trying to bring me down from a pretty scarred and confused state of mind. It was as if he was an outsider, and he had his mind wrapped around all too well what it was that was going on, but his heart was too big to kick away my crutches and watch me stumble on my own. He wanted me to find my happiness as much as I wanted to find it for myself.

In that time period of my life, Jack was my crutch. Regardless of what was to come of our union in the end, during that time he was a man who simply gave me love when I had seemed to very successfully run from any other form of it.

 And although I did my very best not to let the lines become blurred with Jack, it was hard. It felt as if we were a couple, it felt real.

During this time he was spending almost all his free time in his garage working on re-building his jeep. Jack had put so many hours into this jeep. He was learning so many things along the way as well. I have never seen a man work so hard and for so many hours.

I was really proud of him. That summer we slept together, ate together, laughed together, there was a never ending supply of hugs and kisses, and movie night cuddles, weekends with his daughter.
It was truly wonderful. I started to develop a relationship with his daughter, and she, *all on her own,* brought so much happiness into my life.
Everywhere she went, she brought with her this amazing amount of happiness. It's a happiness that we somehow forget to have as we grow older and "adult" ourselves.

Before I knew it, I had jumped in with both feet into something that only had a question mark at the end of it. That one statement, that one statement that I hated thinking about more than ever, one of the most vital points that I tried to remind myself of from time to time, "*I'm not looking for any kind of relationship right now*". That's right, Jack didn't want a relationship… so let me ask myself again, what was it that I was doing? Why I applied so much energy, time and love into something that had more risk *than anything* versus any type of long-term gain is something I never did end up ever doing again.

Looking back – treating that situationship as a stock share is how I should have navigated it.
Was Jack Coca Cola? Something with a guaranteed return?
No.
Not really.

Jack was more along the lines of something like a... start up IT Company. Incredibly risky. And hard to understand.

Date the Coca Cola's; ladies.
Not even the Pepsi's.
Find those Coca Cola's.

The Coca Cola type-men are a guaranteed return on your investment.

Summer was nearing an end, and I was growing restless. Come October, it would have been a year since we had first started this whole adventure with one another.

As time went on, it started to become very real what all this was. He wasn't going to let me go, even when I would try and leave. He would always, always call me, tell me to come back, come back and stay the night. The thought of me moving on and actually being with a man who would give me what I deserved, he hated that thought. Despite not being in a place where a traditional relationship was what he was looking for, the fact was simple - He loved many parts of me. There were many things he saw as special, and I knew he was always aware that the quirky things about me he loved so much were things he'd never find in any other woman.

It was time for me to make a choice. I would either get commitment from him, or I was going to have to put an end to everything. I couldn't be "just friends" with him. It was all or nothing. I can't navigate the grey zone.

Some nights I would pray for some kind of higher power to help me move on with my life.

We'd have moments of breaking up, or me "leaving", but those moments never lasted all that long.

Anytime I would come back to him, he would be there with open arms for me. So yes, I would always end up falling right back into the emotional fish bowl I was trying so hard to swim out of.

By the end of the summer, his jeep was close to being done. About a week before I left on what would be a much needed road trip with my dearest girlfriend Neisha back to the land we love, New Brunswick, I decided I really wanted to give Jack a present for all the hard work and very late nights he had put in with his jeep.

The jeep was actually amazing. Off road deluxe. It was completely done by the hands of Jack and a couple of his good friends. As the project was nearing the end, Jack kept running into a lot of problems, parts weren't the right parts, things weren't fitting. He was exhausted, and I don't blame him. He was working really hard.

I remember about a month earlier he had been on a website looking at these really high end watches. These watches did everything. I don't know a lot of technical things, but from the website, these were the Rolex of watches in the Special Forces world. They were big, black, tough, impressive watches. They were water proof. Space proof. Woman proof. Everything. I knew there was one in particular that he really loved. It was the most expensive one.

Not only did this relationship come with no real commitment, it also came with financial funding on things like… my credit card.

Self-love/respect rating at this time – still 2. Not even climbing near the 3. Still remaining unaware of the much larger issue at hand which was the complete inability to recognize I was in fucking la la land.

"Hi my name is Victoria, its 2012, I'm 26 years old and I score a 2 out of 10 in emotional self-awareness. Nice to meet you all."

I knew the price of the watch, but I could afford it at the time (shout out to all my fans in Pakistan). I just kept picturing the look on his face if I was to actually get this for him and surprise him with it. I was after all very proud of him for all the hard work he had put into his jeep. Looking back, when I did click that button on the website "Yes, I *would* like to order this crazy expensive watch for a man who cheated on me and un-knowingly manipulated me," I wish someone could have been there to be like *"Hey! You dumb asshole! Pack up this shitty apartment, stop dating this dude, and head home to Toronto where you clearly have some deep rooted shit you need to work out with your family!"* But unfortunately for me nobody was there to say that. Just the ever so subtle "ping!" notifications from my lap top anytime I'd receive a hit on one of my many totally fucking bizarre internet photos.

About a week later via FedEx the watch arrived at the apartment. After opening the cardboard box it was in, I'll admit, this was a pretty amazing watch. I inspected it thoroughly, ensuring all was as it should be. Wrapped it back up and planned on hiding it somewhere Jack would frequent often within his home.

Like the washroom linen closet.

"Yes" I thought to myself "I'll hide it between a stack of bath towels. He'll find it in no time!"

Petawawa, Ontario

I was set to move to Petawawa, (still holding steady at a 2 out of 10 in emotional self-awareness, by the way) so I packed up my little apartment in Ottawa and decided to move in with one of my best girlfriends from the Army. It all happened rather quickly. I wasn't in the greatest state of mind after returning home from a one-week road trip back to New Brunswick with Neisha.

Just before we left for the East coast, I had cut ties with Jack. I was done.

That was it. It was time to rein myself back in; it was time to toughen up. Suck it up buttercup, move on. If the man misses you, I'm sure I will hear from him. And if I don't hear from him? Well, hardwood floors... Jack Daniels… etc. I'll get through it.

As beautiful as it was being back out on the East coast, I was about to go through some serious emotions, and I was so happy, *so* happy, that while going through these feelings of a "break up" that I was in the middle of nowhere to do it.

Seriously, I was.

Neisha and I were in a trailer in the woods. Thank god for that. No cell phone reception, and no internet connection. This was a blessing in disguise because I could only imagine the emotional garbage I would have regrettably put onto Facebook that week. Break up memes galore. I'd be all about it.

During day two of being out in the woods, Neisha and I were driving around in the mule. A mule is kind of like a golf cart, but a jacked up version. Bigger tires, thicker treads. It's for camp sites and off roading mostly. As we were driving down the main mud trail that separated our camp site from the main road, I began holding my own two hands very tightly. I was completely freezing up. Neish slowed down and said *"Vic what's going on, you ok?"*

I wasn't. I was panicking. You know that awful feeling of panic that comes over your body when you think you're really losing someone for good? I was panicking. *"Are you having an NB? (Nervous Breakdown) Vic let me know if you're having an NB and we'll pull over"*

"No... no" I said, *"Keep driving... I'm ok... I got this"*.

Before I left for the East Coast, I had told Jack that I needed space, I needed time and space away from him, and I didn't want him contacting me. And reality was starting to sit in. But I knew I had to be strong. *"No going back"* I'd keep saying to myself. *"Not going back to this type of situation, ever again"*.

After a few much needed days in the woods, Neish and I headed back to her parents farm. It was quiet, which was also in the middle of nowhere, *the whole town* was sort of in the middle of nowhere. It was perfect. It was what I needed.

One night while being halfway through the duration of the trip, I woke up to a missed call and a voicemail. It was Jack. I was very surprised, and of course I had to listen to the message he had left. It was late, it was around one in the morning. What was he doing awake this late on a work night?

The second I listened to the voice mail I could tell he had a couple drinks in him, *not drunk*, but maybe three or four beers. His tone always changes a bit. He said in the message that he wanted to know how I was doing, *what I was doing*, and that he wanted to hear from me.

Now, very carefully, I had to divide this into two separate thoughts in my head. Although, as emotional as I am, I do have these rare (very rare) moments of logic, and this was one of them. Was he simply calling because he missed me and just wanted to talk? Or, was he calling because he was worried he was going to lose me, was he roping me back in…

After this night we ended up having small talk over txt for a couple days while I was still out there. He was getting ready to leave very soon for a work trip way up North where he would barely have any cell phone reception himself. We wouldn't both be back in Petawawa until the end of the month.

But I was happy about that. The more distance between him and I, the better.

After ending our trip back to New Brunswick and arriving back into Ontario, I was really starting to feel the effects of losing my best friend.

I was starting to head down a dark road. One that wasn't necessarily new to me.
I still had no legit day job. My personal life was a total mess, and empty at that. And even though I wasn't on any type of bad terms with most of my family, I was so out of touch with them during this time in my life. If I wanted expert insight, or some words of wisdom from people who could probably help me turn things a little bit around, you would have thought I would have fell into the arms of my family.

Divorce has happened everywhere in my family. Almost everyone has done it. Most of us nowadays can laugh at our wrong doings that led to it. I had people who loved me who could be there for me, but for whatever reason I deprived myself from ever raising the white flag and stating *"Ok fam, I'm pretty tired, feeling a little discouraged, scared for my future, I need some help"*. But I never really reached out.

On the occasions I would reach for my phone, my dad was usually the lucky winner in receiving my tearful phone calls. He would always listen to the pain I was carrying, but his advice usually remained the same *"If a man is dealing with regret from his past relationship or past marriage, stay as far away from that as possible. You will be nothing more than collateral damage"*.

And he was right. He was usually pretty bang on when it came to seeing the bigger picture.

Mid-September of 2012 was a very low point for me. I had seemed to step into a dark closet and I wasn't really sure how I was going to get out of it.

I wasn't myself. I started doubting all the choices that I had made that year.

I have had nothing but doors shutting on my face. Ontario wasn't working out for me. Although there were some sweet moments I had experienced that year, 2012 was overall becoming one of my most challenging years, ever.

Now that I had shut the door on Jack, I was left in the hands of my own devices. (Super dangerous place to be)

I couldn't trust myself.

When you start re-thinking all the turns you took, and you're standing there looking at where they basically got you. *"Should I have stayed in New Brunswick?"* It was the small town where I had found a sense of peace. It had become my home.

I was angry. So angry at everything I had given up.

I stripped it all away, and for absolutely nothing in return.

I had finally awoken, but I had awoken with deep, deep regret. I had done it all so fast. Re-planting myself in Ontario in hopes of a better future. But I just kept hitting walls. I barely even recognized who it was I saw in the mirror anymore.

By leaving the Toronto apartment I was staying in with my sister for those few short weeks before moving to Ottawa, we suffered a major falling out with one another. (Sister fight) So although Melissa and I are such different women, as much as I won't admit it, she does know parts of me that only a sister can know. After all, we did experience life as we knew it growing up as two little girls seeing and experiencing things that we weren't necessarily ready for.

She may not have been up to date with some pretty serious things that took place in my life while I was living out East those four years, but all that required was a few hours sitting down together and exchanging a few stories. I'm sure she would have understood better where my head was at and why I didn't feel happy living in that city.

But I burned a very big bridge with her. We are both pretty stubborn, so admitting mistakes or apologizing for harsh words wasn't something her nor I would easily budge to make happen. The new life I was trying to create for myself wasn't happening. I was unemployable. Felt completely unlovable. But mostly, I felt alone.

There were a few fights Jack and I had endured while being together. Most of them erupted due to him over-drinking and becoming paranoid of me leaving him, or cheating on him. (None of which were ever happening, until I finally *did* leave him) However, the few nights where it was more than just yelling at one another had without a doubt done a good enough amount of damage on me. The man never raised his fist to me, but I almost wish he would have versus the psychological games he played on me. By the end of our relationship, besides being completely torn up about it, feeling *screwed up* was a much bigger burn I was going to carry away from that experience.

One cold day that fall I walked into an Ottawa strip club. I took a seat and asked the bartender if any girls were around to dance a couple songs (it was 2:00 o'clock in the afternoon) there was a girl, a French girl, worked in Ottawa, but lived in Quebec. So onto the pole she went. I ordered a Jack and Diet, and just watched her dance.

I sat there for about an hour, maybe more; I don't really remember to be honest. But she was doing a good job. I tipped her, asked her dance some more, and she did.

Sitting there, just me and the stripper, I knew I had to make a huge change in how I was doing things.

I started going through this imaginary checklist in my head while sitting at the base of the stage.

-Don't put all my eggs in one basket – Check
-Don't give a person your all when they are an emotionally confused person – Check
-Don't even get involved with someone who is emotionally confused – Check
-<u>Don't even txt a guy back</u> who is emotionally confused – Check Check Check!
-Tip this stripper again, she's not half bad – Check
-Get a proper day job – Trying*
-Find somewhere to live – On a scale from one to ten, this was a pretty important 10.
-Aim to not look like an ex-stripper when showing up to interviews for these so called 'day jobs' – LIGHT BULB moment
-Find out what the initials R-S-P in my bank account profile stands for and figure out how to compound interest the hell out of the number inside that account – Again, a level 10 with regards to importance.

And lastly,

-He was 5'7 – Stop crying - **Check**

This whole time I thought I was following my heart. But following your heart can come with a level of fantasy, a crazy basket of hope, and *complete* un-realistic expectations in the romance department. We need to stop doing this to ourselves.

We don't chase love.

Love is *in us*.

And when you allow the right people to surround you, *love shows' up.*

I had let myself become completely involved with a man who had a lot of his own deep dark demons. He saw my soft heart as one he wanted to hold tight in his hands. He had me buckle at my knees night after night when he would keep me awake until four in the morning on those kitchen chairs of his. He would lecture me, and almost interrogate me it seemed.

I regretted ever telling Jack about my life before the military, because he used every weakness I had in me, *completely against me*. There is any easy way to tell if a man is a true born and bred asshole. Tell them you were once an exotic dancer. They'll either *not give a single damn about it* and still treat you as the human being you are, or, they will take *any* and *every* opportunity they have to use those moments of your life against you.

There was a time Jack and I were fighting, and I had locked myself in his bathroom. This was one of those nights where he was drunk to the point where it wasn't even him anymore. I remember sitting on his bathroom floor wondering how or when I would leave. Fighting with him wasn't in me. And locking myself in his bathroom seemed to be the only room in the house where he wouldn't be able to get to me. Within a few minutes he slid a two dollar coin under the bathroom door. *"I know that will make you move"* he said to me.

Gaining clarity of everything that had taken place with that man was what I needed most. And when that day of clarity comes, although it's a much needed wake up call, it really hurts. You're ashamed of yourself and embarrassed all at the same time for the simple fact that you loved yourself *so little* to actually stick around and endure that type of pain for as long as you did. I can't speak for anyone else, but for me this was a big part of the reason I probably had a hard time going back to my family in my hometown after him and I split.

I think I was mostly embarrassed above all.

But the beauty in this train wreck of a year, both personally and career wise, is that things eventually began to look up.

I now lived in a house back in Petawawa with two of the craziest ladies that have ever lived, and my God, do we laugh, every day we laugh. And laughter is so important, *girlfriends* are so important.

"Vic, you need to be writing. You could get a serving job, or an office job and it would be ok. It wouldn't be very challenging for you though, but it would be something to fill your time. You need to write. Use your words, Vic. That is what helps you remember. That's what you need to be doing"
Says Julia.

One of my most favourite women on this planet, my high school partner in crime, *Jewels*.

So that's what I did. Sitting there in my 8x10 living space, the smallest bedroom in this 3 bedroom house on a military base in quiet little Petawawa.

I started over.

The Endings Always Bring about a New Beginning

Early in 2013 I started working for the Government in Ottawa. All my job searching had finally paid off and I received a phone call to work within a branch of the Government where I would find the most wonderful co-workers who would no doubt watch me crumble through those early weeks of the major heart break that was to come.

It was a snowy evening. And you guessed it… Jack and I had still not *completely ended.* The last few months of any relationship can be messy, blurred lines you could call it. I was at Jack's house. Supper was in the oven, I was sipping a glass of wine while waiting for him to get home from work. We weren't "back together" or anything of that nature, I think we were just doing what felt natural. And regardless of the crap I had gone through with him, something inside of me just wasn't done I guess.

My daily commute was almost two hours one way to my new job in Ottawa, so I knew within months to come, I was going to need to move closer to the city. My gas bill for my drive to work would soon catch up to me.

Although he and I appeared to be in a *somewhat good* place with one another, I couldn't help but have these uncomforting suspicions. For the entire year we had been seeing one another I always thought I was the only girl sleeping in his bed at night, because with as much time as I had spent there, there's no way there could have been other women. There was just no way.

But during the beginning of our relationship? The first 6-7 months? With all the separation we had between us… could he have slept with other girls behind my back? Well, yes, yes he absolutely could have. But with all the attention he always gave me I never saw that as ever being something that would be happening.

Well ladies, if a man doesn't commit, and seems like he's on this never ending journey on "finding himself" (even though he's 33 years old, has a full time career, a beautiful child, divorce behind him), I had discovered that evening that he in fact *had cheated on me - was cheating on me - did cheat on me.*

Multiple times.

When your gut is speaking to you – listen.

Eighteen.

That's how many different women there were.

And that was only what I was able to count.

Now, I could only *prove* he was sleeping with maybe six or seven of them, but eighteen email addresses in total of completely inappropriate conversations that had been going on since the first day I met him.

Reading through the emails made me feel as if I hadn't even existed in any part of his life. It was one of the most gut wrenching experiences I have ever felt with a man. It's the ultimate slap across your face.

A combination of feeling completely embarrassed, idiotic, repulsed, and really fucking angry all during the same few seconds.

You throw those emotions onto a young woman who's not the most emotionally-balanced to begin with and you're asking for an arson job.

Just saying'

I had noticed earlier he had left his lap top open on the coffee table in the basement. Knowing he was still a little ways from home, my gut feelings had me chomping at the bit. It was the best but also *worst* thing I could have done.

Opening this man's lap top was like opening a whole other world of forbidden secrets. The photos, the emails, the Facebook messages that filled his inbox. I swear, if one more glass of wine had been flowing through my veins, this lap top would have seen the asphalt of the driveway in which all these women parked their cars on during the nights I wasn't there.

This man wasn't *"finding himself"*, Jack wasn't *"soul searching"*. How the hell could he of been? Any free time he had while I wasn't around he would be enjoying himself with some other lady friend in the freshly washed bed sheets I had put on the bed the day before.

Looking back, it's not rocket science. The man was a cheater. Through and through.
He had stumbled across me, unexpectedly cared for ways he never imagined he would have, wanted me to be just "his" and nobody else's.

During those moments, of reading each email, noticing the date in which the email or sexual act took place, my stomach dropped. It was the hardest pill I have ever had to swallow.

It was awful.

And the worst part was, I thought I had loved this man. How the hell was I so blind?
Right there, I realized that although I always knew people were capable of all things, good and bad, *this* was a serious wake up call, that within weeks to follow, would turn into one of the most transforming times in my life.

So thank you Jack.

Thank you.

Not only did I find emails with all the evidence a girl would ever need to finally walk away, I also came across emails between him and his ex-wife.

That alone blew my mind.

All the things he told me about her had me believing she was a controlling, no-fun, hard to live with type woman. Anytime he spoke of her, the one thing he would always be sure to mention was that she was an amazing mum. But in terms of a good match for him? He had me convinced they were oil and water.

On the outside - here we were, spending some truly peaceful, quality time together during our evenings after our work days. Ordering in, watching Netflix, we even started renovating his bathroom together.

Don't ever start renovating a man's bathroom with/for him until the dollar amount of marble counter tops he's putting in is equivalent to the diamond he has already placed on your fourth finger, left hand.

There I was – like a love struck idiot in my free time on my hard-earned weekends… I was taking shopping trips to the Home Depot and painting the ceiling of this man's bathroom… just me and the paint roller.

I hate that he has a beautifully painted bathroom.

If I had any worry that the success of this book wasn't going to bring me good fortunes, I'd be sending you an invoice back-dated to 2013 for labour services.

You practically paid prostitutes, surely you'd pay for a bathroom reno' team of 1

I still might fire off that invoice. Keep your eyes on your mail box.

Not only was he having someone to keep him company through the on-going nights of him trying to *find himself*, he got free labour out of it too.

Manipulation they call it; a trait that I have now developed a sixth sense for.

What I took away from this experience that I want all you ladies to know – is this:

When a person is completely on top of the world (ie. in receipt of great sex, un-limited supply of female attention, the Friday nights with the boys & enjoying various party additives all the while receiving unconditional and devoted love from you) – is that his train will *one thousand percent* de-rail at some point.

Life is nothing more than a bunch of giant boomerangs being flung out into the universe by every thought and action we create.

When people do things that cause a person pain – that pain will come back and smack them in their pain-causing face. They get a 100% return on their investment.

It's a guarantee.

So when a person does you wrong – *so wrong* that it actually breaks you into what feels like a million pieces, pick your heart up off the floor, pack as much of your shit as you can, and walk away.

*Just like that**

Save your words.

Never mind writing him a *"you seriously did me wrong, you'll regret this"* letter.

Because regardless of how hard you try to make them understand how they did you wrong, they won't hear a single word you're saying.

When a person sleeps so soundly while committing such hurtful actions behind your back, trust me, they have years of shit to work out before they'll come to terms with how screwed up their thinking was.

So walk away.

And merely leave them *dumbfounded* as to how you did it with such grace.

Grace trumps crazy.

Let their brains have a moment of confusion for once.

Because you're done with being confused.

Don't be the crazy girl. If you ever get the urge, call me. I'll hammer down the crazy girl part in a heartbeat if it means helping another woman get that last moment of grace in front of the person who made her *feel like a disgrace.*

The biggest burn behind the early months of 2013? The secret email conversations with his ex-wife.
I knew the other women meant nothing. I knew he cheated mostly because he was in a bad place during that time overall.

But the ex-wife? That hurt. That hurt because there was, or *used to be,* something very real between them. But what he didn't know, that I instinctively *already knew* is that the *re-uniting of love* between those two would never work to begin with. It would end before it would have ever gotten a chance to begin.

You see, I was once married too. It's natural to question yourself as well as your decision as to why your marriage ended. And having a child with that person would no doubt make you ponder even harder about wanting to possibly try in making it work again.

I'll never forget the day I called my dad.

It was one of the best phone calls I've ever had with him. My dad remains one of the first and only people I really go to for major relationship advice. After all, he's been married and divorced three times, and two of those marriages involved children.

My dad had some very helpful and encouraging advice for me.

"Sweetheart, if you're with a man who is contemplating going back to his marriage, you need to stay as far away as you can from that man; as he is very confused. He may think returning to his wife is the answer, but I can guarantee you whatever he thinks will work out between him and his ex-wife... trust me, it will not."

"Stay away" My dad said.

And I trusted him.

Upon letting Jack know I was now informed about his cheating ways, (I'll leave the details of how that conversation went up to your imagination) as well as his conversations between his ex-wife and him behind my back, I told him we were done.

It was done.

The next day I came home from work. I was in tears all morning just knowing my things were still in his house and that I still had to return to his home and face him before gathering my things and leaving. The ironic thing about all of this, is during the time he was having heart felt conversations with his ex-wife about re-uniting and being a family, I was still there in his arms every night as he would deceit his ex-wife, word for word. As far as she was concerned I was barely in the picture anymore.

There were multiple, *multiple moments* where I was so tempted to contact her... and let her know what was really going on. There was such a mess to be made between the two of them, and I was armed with so many words that she needed to hear.

But I didn't.

I let fate play out the way I knew it would. And here was my prediction...

I would pack my things and demand Jack to never contact me again. (Even though I knew he would)

Within moments of me leaving his home, he would reach out to his ex-wife (this was a man who I truly believe during this time in his life could not be alone)

And he did, he actually told her he was "helping a buddy" when in fact he was filling my truck up with gas and helping me move my things from his place to mine. He fed her lies, day after day. But I knew she was smart… and I also knew she would wake up and remember the reasons why they were no longer a married couple.

They would email back and forth for a few weeks and become "excited" about re-uniting.

Then, karma would make a visit to the little town of Petawawa, and Jack would eventually receive an email from his ex-wife letting him know that her heart was no-longer wanting to re-unite, and on top of it, that she had met someone else.

Jack would now be alone. Without the company of his speed-dial whores, the woman who loved him unconditionally (me), or his ex-wife.

Sit with that for a minute… what do you suppose happens next?

Bingo.

In come the emails... *to me.*

"I miss you. I made a mistake. Why can't we go back to the way things were! Just you and me, hanging out, being together! I'm ready to move forward with you! A home together, a family, anything you want, I'm ready!"

Reading those emails come the spring of 2013 made me sick to my stomach. Because it was so damn predictable.

I told him no. Over and over again. But the emails didn't let up for a few weeks.

I won't lie, it was hard. And for a few moments throughout my days working in Ottawa, I would ponder… go back and forth in my head, if returning to my relationship with him would be a good idea. Has he changed? Did he realize what he had lost? Was he ready to love me the way I deserved to be loved?

Ladies - these are the moments when you need to listen to your girlfriends. Because although a few months may have passed since the initial painful break up, you are still not thinking straight. So, when your closest girlfriends look you dead in the eyes, and tell you *"No friggen way are you going back to that man".*

Believe them.

The Calm after the Storm

I'm not going to sit here and sound all tough as if it didn't hurt. Although as I sit here now and tell you all this, it's easy to look back and with ease, put these words onto the screen of my computer. It's easy because I've healed. All of us, we *always* heal. Some pains stay with you forever, but in very big ways, we overall reach a more peaceful place with whatever it was that broke us. As in love as I was with this man, once finally having the weight of all the worry and stress from that un-healthy partnership I once referred to as a "relationship", the chips began to fall into place again.

There was this over-whelming feeling of calm. You know that feeling of realizing you have just survived a heartbreak? I had that moment. And it was mine for the taking.

I was in the kitchen at Neisha's, I had just gotten home from work, it was early April, and I received a text message from him. Thinking back, I honestly have no idea what the message read, but as soon as I saw his name show up on my screen, my immediate reaction was *"oh god, what does he want"*.

YES! I thought. YES! That is victory. That feeling? That *"oh god...it's him..."* that feeling that comes with the words *"what the hell does he want now?"*

What a feeling.

I knew then, it was time to move forward and consider the possibility of opening up my heart again.

You would think after a year and a half of a relationship so filled of deceit and heart break that I would have sworn off men all together. Although I was bitter, I wasn't going to let the temporary pains caused by that man interfere with my grand plan of true love and a family.

Jack had a big ego during those times, and he definitely caused a big hurt in me, but it certainly was not big enough to steer me off course. I believe in love. And I believe in love after heart break. And when I looked towards my future I still had my dreams of being with an amazing person.

Through all the ups and downs with that man, there was always one person in particular who stayed in the shadows; who was there for me unconditionally through any and every rainy day. And that was my piece of heaven New Brunswick. Let's call him Chevy for short.

Chevy would prove to be there for me anytime I felt alone and needed to hear some reassurance. Whether I needed someone to lift my spirits, advice on an outfit, someone to vent to. Or simply someone who I knew could remind me of what exactly it was that I deserved from a relationship.

No matter how silly the questions that I asked, or how many times I repeated myself during our talks, like a brick wall built by God himself, he was there for me. Strong as ever.

He was after all usually the first person to wish me a happy birthday every February 28th. *"Happy Birthday Beautiful"* would be the message I would see at 6:30 am on my blackberry the day I turned 26. I'll always remember that.

He never judged, just understood.

As time went on, Chevy and I became even greater of friends. With more phone conversations then actual real-life face time with each other, no matter which province we were in, he was always just a phone call away. When I think back, it was him who brought me a lot of comfort during times where I felt so alone. He was usually the only person who could calm my storm. And more times than not, he was the only person I would turn to for help.

We would flirt, we brought smiles to each other's faces, but that's as far as it ever went. I think we both knew what we had was rare. The odd time he would open up to me about a girl problem he was having, or we'd just talk about relationships and how tricky they can be at times. I was always able to completely be myself with him. Whether I'd say something stupid, or cry over some asshole, he would always be there on the other end of the phone. I could always tell without seeing his face when he'd be rolling his eyes at me, or wanting to tell me to smarten up and remember my worth. Chevy has this perfect way of giving advice that not every girl wants to hear, *but needs to*, yet he always knew to be gentle in the delivery of it.

Chevy had a few love stories of his own, but none that ever ended up getting too serious. So when he finally retired his bachelor ways and settled down with a beautiful Nurse who *absolutely adored him*, nothing could have made me happier. I never met her. Nor do I think she even knows I exist, however, I know enough about her from Chevy, and when he speaks of all her beautiful qualities, I couldn't think of a more perfect person for him.

Despite being all tied down, he still remains fiercely independent. He moves to the beat of his own drum. He wakes, he works, and he works hard to play hard. Anytime he wants something he makes it happen for himself. He never waits on anyone to give him the green light, he just goes and gets it when he wants it. Something I have always related to and respected him for. Since leaving the military, I have done whatever necessary to remain financially on my own.

We may have failed enormously as a "dating couple" but this friendship we have developed over the years is a friendship I have never had with any man. About seven years I believe. The very few men I have trusted over the past ten years turned out to hurt me in ways that I was so far from ever being ready for. I'm almost positive that half the reason why I love and will always love Chevy is because he is one of the few people who I have completely let my guard down with, and he has never once, *not ever*, used my weaknesses against me.

He has never hurt me.

And I don't know if he'll ever know just how much that really does mean to me.

Throughout the spring, I began thinking more about moving on.

"Let's give this whole love thing another shot" I told myself.

Now, with my work schedule, my daily commute to Ottawa, as well as the low-key Netflix lifestyle Neisha and I lived, I knew the only way of meeting a guy would have to be online… unfortunately.

Although I had been an on-line dater before, and the only person who I have in my life from online dating is Chevy, who has indeed been a blessing, I just had my reservations about the whole thing.
But I also knew that if I was going to meet a man outside of this little Petawawa town, I was going to need to make an online profile and start the search.

My profile was quite bland, and pretty inaccurate as well. With fears that Jack would no doubt look me up and try to give me some form of grief about dating, I knew I couldn't post a profile photo of myself, as well, the details about me had to be altered.

Birthday, age, likes, interests, all of it, had to be fake. I was there for strictly business. One reason and one reason only, to see what was out there.

What was out there? In this beautiful Ottawa valley that linked together small town Petawawa and our country's capital city, Ottawa. There was after all, two hours of highway separating the two places. I thought for sure there had to be a good hearted man somewhere in that bush.

And there was.

Sunsets with the Cowboy

It was one evening in April, I had gotten home from work, had a bubble bath, was fixing some supper, when I decided to make my dating profile. *"Here I go"* I thought. *"May as well light this baby up".*

Within a few minutes of being all set up and "active", I began scrolling through some fellow online-dater's in my age group.

There were lots of photos to search through, but nothing was catching my eye. I wasn't looking for a six pack and muscles, nor was I interested in a super hero-saver of the world job description. I was looking for heart, I was looking for family. Values and morals; kindness. I wasn't in the market for getting my heart torn apart again, nor was I interested in some wild hog chase. *I just wanted somebody who wanted me – and just me.* And I wanted that somebody to be a good person, to be honest, and to be faithful.

I knew what encompassed the heart of a monster; I knew all too well what those eyes looked like in a man. So when I came across this one particular profile photo, what drew me in first was the expression on his face, and the kindness in his eyes, and that smirk, that sexy, but sweet smile he had.

Everything else was kind of a blur, what he did for work didn't mean anything to me, or what his hobbies were became irrelevant. After reading his profile, the word that stood out to me the most, was how many times he mentioned "family".

He was a single father. He had become a dad quite young. He was twenty five going on twenty six in a few short weeks, with a son who was turning five that fall.

His story was not anything un-heard of in this day and age. He had gotten his girlfriend pregnant very early on in their relationship, things moved too quickly, they were young, and it crashed and burned. But that seemed pretty normal to me. Doing anything in your early twenties usually ends badly, let alone attempting to raise a child together after dating barely a year. I was married and divorced faster than you could pour a cup of coffee. And I liked that he was a father. I knew that it was the feeling of a family that I was ultimately searching for deep down.

He drove a loader for work. A very big piece of equipment with a shovel on it to move materials. He had been working steady for a construction company in the Ottawa Valley for almost ten years. He was very good at his job, and he took pride in what he did.

After the relationship ended with the mother of his child, he had sold the house they once lived in together and moved home back to his family farm. He would see his son on the weekends like most single dads who work full time, put the pieces back together for himself and try and move forward.

A couple years had passed since that had happened when I would come into his life.

Let me tell you what it was like, what those first moments were like while meeting this man.

Let's call him John.

John had been busy after moving back home with the family. He decided to start his welding business, as well as continuing to work full time at his construction job. With the help of his family, he had built a huge, very impressive garage on the property of the family farm. This would be the starting grounds for his welding shop. But not only was this his shop, he had a trailer as well. He was branding himself as a portable welder, where he could bring the welding repairs to you, and work on site wherever the client needed him to be.

He's always been a smart man. As well, he seemed driven to make something of himself.
He was honest, and hardworking. He knew the surroundings in which he was raised quite well.

We talked over the phone for about three weeks before we actually met. The more I spent time talking to him at night as I lay in bed, the more I began to like this guy. My heart had been through a lot, and although there are worse things than break ups, I was still so guarded, and rightfully so.

I'll never forget that first night we stopped text messaging, and actually heard each other's voices on the phone. I knew he was *backwoods country* through and through, but that first night I heard him speak, it was the sweetest and most gentle voice I had heard in a long time.

He was becoming my sunset after the hurricane.

Super cheesy – yes, I know. But I was beyond screwed up and exhausted after my *situationship* with Jack. So yes, this boy was my sunset after the damn hurricane.

Let's continue:

The first day we decided to meet he invited me down to the farm. It was a Saturday and was quite over cast that day. April 27th, 2013 it was. I will forever, *forever* remember this day.

I woke up bright and early, had a really good work out at the gym, I wanted to look "energized" and "fresh" and all those other things that crying through your previous heartbreak on a stair master helps you achieve. I came home and put on my cutest pair of jeans, with a little faux-leather jacket. I remember this morning I was feeling all kinds of things. I was finally going to meet the man in the pictures, and so far all seemed to be going well.

Unlike Chevy, I hadn't sent him running for the hills quite yet.

About fifty five minutes south of Petawawa, down the highway headed towards Ottawa, lays the little town of Arnprior. In the quiet back woods of Arnprior was the farm where John and his family lived. He invited me down for the day to go skeet shooting, and of course, to finally meet one another.

As I pulled onto the property, I immediately saw his brand new fully-loaded Dodge Ram. Although I am a tried and true Chevy girl, I can still admire a nice looking truck, especially if it's sitting on 35 or bigger inch tires. My jaw drops every time. Well built, lifted 4x4 trucks on a good all-terrain or off-road tire, is like the Louis Vuitton of purses. A well put-together truck rattles me just' right.

Pulling in I decided to park beside the farm house, as I figured John would be waiting for me inside. But to my surprise he was in his garage, wearing his work boots, coveralls, and an old sweater. Hardly the typical *first date* look, but I would come to learn very quickly that he was a true simple man, through and through. Something I knew I always admired in men, but it was also something I had learned to truly love and appreciate in a person because of him.

As I got out of my car and made my way up the stairs of the front porch, I heard a yell come from the barn yard *"Hey"* he yelled. I turned around to see this harmless looking young man with his casual farmer/working man attire. At that point I had absolutely no idea the adventures I was about to embark on with him over the course of our summer together. My moments with him are some of my most special memories of a love that was truly as sweet as the pie we would eat after Sunday family suppers at the farm.

I began walking towards him, with the friendly greetings of the family farm dog, Sniper, walking beside me wagging his tail; there he stood. With his hands in his pockets, his baseball cap on, and a pair of sunglasses, that smile… that kind, *warm* smile, there it was, watching me, and getting bigger as I walked towards him.

We immediately greeted each other with a hug. He stands about 5'11, maybe 5'10, a body as beautiful as a hard working farm boys could be. His hands were like bear paws. They were thick and strong. My hands were so little while in his, and I loved that. His voice while talking to me was soft, *always soft*. He was just gentle all together. Compared to what I had been through, I think I decided to send him a message over that dating website because something in my heart sensed that this wasn't a man who would hurt me. Isn't that what we "damaged girls" go for? A man who we secretly know can't hurt us. Or *won't hurt us*. And we do this because our self-esteem has been so *overly tampered with* that we go for the path of least resistance.

The path that will allow us to some-what heal. When I look back on my time with John, I always refer to it as my *pink oven-mit relationship*. John didn't bake, or wear the colour pink. But he was my soft, recovery relationship. I don't want to say he was any kind of rebound, but when I look back, maybe he was?

Either way, no matter how hard someone flings a pink oven-mit at you, it's not going to hurt you.

You're safe.

If it's you and a pink oven-mit locked in a room, chances are, *you'll be ok.*

That day, that first day on the farm, felt like a fairy tale. He took me through the barns where there were baby sheep, as well as five beautiful horses in the pastures. He gently led me around the property as we continued to talk and actually let ourselves nervously enjoy one another's company.

I would learn that his mom was a woman with more heart than anyone on this side of the river. A truly giving, and accepting woman. She was so hard working, always doing things for others.

Her needs were the last thing on her mind, as her family was her world, and you could see how that farm, where John's mum and dad lived, was the heartbeat of their family. It was the gathering place for Sunday suppers, it was a second home to all the kids. I knew how much that farm meant to John. With John being the only son, I knew from early on he felt a certain sense of responsibility, as well as pressure, to continue working on that property, and to be there to help his dad out whenever he could.

Before I knew it John was starting up his big old Red Dodge Ram to take us out back to shoot some guns. As I walked towards the passenger side of the truck, to my surprise, John was already at the door waiting for me, as he opened the truck door, my jaw *dropped.*

"Seriously?!" I thought to myself. Pure gentlemen charm. This boy was doing all the right things.

By the time we got to the back field and shot a few skeets, John asked me if I was thirsty. I guess before I came over he had already packed some gingerale in the cooler in the back of his truck, along with some little glasses to pour it in. This man wasn't trying to booze me up or get me "loose" with a beer, it was gingerale. Probably the most innocent and sincere gesture I have ever received from someone. Deep down I remember thinking to myself *"really would prefer a couple stiff double Jacks after shooting these guns... but I'll sip Gingerale... first time drinking this stuff since my 8th birthday party... but when in Rome, I guess".*

Not once throughout that day did John make me feel uncomfortable, or disrespected. He was a true gentlemen for the entire nine hours or so that I was there. It was refreshing. It really did feel nice.

I remember throughout that afternoon in the field how many times we made each other smile.

I guess you could say after a day that felt like a country western fairy tale, I knew this was someone who was going to give me enough reason not to run. As each sweet morning text message would go by between our visits, I started feeling more and more comfortable and excited about maybe being his girl.

Before I knew it, it was going to be our differences that would end up drawing us into one another. I had never been with a man quite like him. He hasn't seen a lot of bad things in this world, and I liked seeing the world through his eyes. It gave me this ability to see the soft things this world has to offer. For so many years before I had been surrounded by a lot of change, loss, constant mountains of hurt that varied in size. For John, with the life he lead, it felt as if it was going to be a way I could see the world through rose coloured glasses again.

He was always doing work on the farm, as well as all the repairs he did in his garage to the four wheelers, tractor, trucks in the yard - you name it, he fixed it. But as rough as his hands were, they were always gentle when holding mine.

For those first few months of that summer I would go to work every day, only to count down the hours until I would be home at the farm with him again. My life began to become quite routine:

-Work
-Gym
-Groceries for some lunch materials for his lunch box
-My apartment
-Quick bubble bath
-John's farm.

As boring as a routine like that can get, I never minded it. I certainly could have done less driving between my apartment and his farm during my nights after work, but I was beginning to feel happy being at the farm every night.

I loved making him things for his lunch, making him big fruit smoothies to have every day. He wasn't perfect; Lord knows none of us are, but to me during that time, he was becoming really important to me.

There is something very amazing about how a woman falls in love. We all do it a little differently. And with each relationship, it always happens a little differently. I didn't have a beautiful past with men. I never had a man who would day in and day out work at showing his love for me. But little did I know, this time in my life was going to once again be an experience that was going to teach me a different kind of love.

I think this love was supposed to teach me that a heart hungry for *simply love* isn't necessarily going to point you towards finding it within a *person*, or a *situation*, like a relationship. A hungry heart that isn't sure of what it's missing will find it in all the wrong places. A bad relationship. A drug, or liquor. I believe a hungry heart is an addictions favourite thing to prey on. Because I can tell you, when your chest feels empty, and your life feels cold even during the hottest summer months, that place in you that hasn't been adequately fed is going to love anything that will promise to love it back.

So when people encourage you to find or further pursue your passions, do it. Because it stands very true - that when you sink yourself into something that fills your bones with love, purpose and pure happiness, things that want to hurt you don't stand a chance at getting close enough to burn you.

The more time that passed, things began to slowly become a little less rose coloured. There would be days I felt this huge space of disconnect between John and I. As if he didn't understand who I was deep down, or maybe he never wanted to quite know who Victoria really was, *all of her,* and I don't really blame him. I know he loved me, but some days I felt that he loved my outside, which I worked hard at keeping polished and pretty, more than the experiences actually beneath my skin. I don't think he ever wanted to hear about, or believe that the dark places I had in my mind ever existed.

I tried to never let that disconnect between us become something that could eat away at the respect we had for one another. But I feared it might. When there's a part about you, regardless of how small or irrelevant those memories are to your life the way it is now – if your partner refuses to accept them or even care to learn about them, there will be a part of you that will always feel not fully loved, accepted, or even *approved* by them. And before you know it, that tiny part of you that your partner may refuse to believe exists will eventually become the biggest elephant in the room.

John worked hard at his job, he worked hard with welding, and he worked hard with me. And despite him not wanting to really understand what made me tick, there is no other man I have known who had ever worked so hard to be "enough" for me.

He made me countless promises of how much he loved me. We spoke of the future, and what we wanted it to look like almost every other day. We both saw the same dream.
And as we would sit on the swinging white bench in the yard, our legs intertwined, him holding me in his arms, we would speak with such excitement as if he finally found that one person who he was going to build a life with.

I was beginning to believe that John was going to be my happily ever after. That I would take one last walk down the aisle in a beautiful white lace wedding dress, (ok, off-white, cream, whatever) sunflowers in my hands, with John at the end of that walk.

And that come hell or high water, this man would never leave me. Loyal to a fault. Commitment didn't scare him, he yearned for that connection. It was all the security in the world a woman could have ever needed, and here it was, right in front of me.

We had our share fare of fights, like most couples, you're always going to butt heads about one thing or another, but come the fall, it was as if every other sentence out of his mouth or mine would start an argument. I was beginning to become unhappy with driving an hour to work each day. I was also beginning to become worn out from waking up as early as we did (4:30 am or so) putting in a full day's work in a very busy office, then coming home and never truly giving myself that time to really unwind and relax. I devoted almost all my free time to being by John's side.

His son was no longer just this little boy. He was now a little boy who I was grocery shopping for. Without even thinking I would grab his favourite chocolate granola bars while in aisle 4, or a Kinder Surprise Egg when I was in the check-out line. His runny nose or scrape on his knee were now my concerns. Making sure he had an extra sweater in the back of the truck if we were on our way out, or if he had enough sun screen on his little arms and back of his neck during John's baseball tournaments. My maternal instincts were at an all-time high.

Regardless of our silly fights, or different views on things, or the fact that my past was more colourful then a rainbow, once I started removing all the barriers from my mind that stood in our way, I started to think he was the man for my future.

*Note – once you reach a point where you need to remove a handful of valid facts that clearly outline how starting a family won't work with this person, this is not the type of relationship you should aim for when family planning. This is a relationship that possibly offers you the right place, surroundings and time – to start a family. However, the actual person you choose to play the role of **daddy** – super key point not to overlook merely because everything else is looking pretty decent.*

Sometimes our desire to just *make it happen* begins to blur the lines between *sound* - and *unsound* decisions.

I can't even count how many young women I've seen push their men into marriage and kids just because the women were practically screaming for it to happen. All so their "time line" could stay on track and they could pin wedding dress ideas to their Pinterest pin board.

They rush into it.

Then they have money problems.

Then they resent each other.

And separate by 35.

Don't smoke cigarettes just because the cool kids do it.

Same logic applies to getting married and having kids.

Don't do it just because all your besties are doing it.

With a show of hands, how many people do we know who are either:

   a)   Stuck in unhappy, no longer fulfilling relationships due to mortgage payments and kids. Where the husband has an on-going subscription to Porn Hub.

Or, the opposite:

   b)   Broke as hell because the men's (or woman's) pay cheques are being reduced by good percentages to finance the life they *used to have* with their partner and kids.

And the only thing they can do with their Tinder dates besides swiping right on their faces is invite them over for a night of Netflix and Chill.

On their buddy's couch from Leon's, while sitting in the basement they're renting.

Because they're broke.

And made *emotionally driven* life choices when mistaking *lust and young-adult confusion* for *love, partnership and long term goals.*

Insane and *sane* aren't just different shelves pills sit on at a pharmacy.

They are actually excellent points of reference to look to when making huge fucking decisions.

As we know, my two ex's were both military men. Big, strong men. I believe John would compare himself to them. He struggled with his insecurities, but fixing that should have never been my job.

If you weren't going to feel confident with the pasture your cow walked out of, you should have been searching different pastures. Maybe pastures closer to a Church.

Lord if I know.

As days went on, we started falling apart. I started to become angry, I started to feel as if I was being taken for granted by him.

I put myself out there on this silver platter, doing everything that I knew how to do. I worked hard at my job, I worked hard at keeping my appearance at a certain standard, (*for you superficial type, I was a dime '69 at age 27*) and I worked hard at being a girlfriend who could still get all her errands done in time so she could devote the evenings to the man she loved. My whole idea of balance was completely out of whack. My whole idea of who I was becoming as a woman was entirely backyards.

Being that it's the end of 2018 as I write this, if you were to tell me that my future as a woman would involve tending to the needs or comfort of a man six nights a week, I'd probably look at you twice and ask if you were drunk. I could not imagine living that nightmare.

Drunk and/or blind.

Wonder Woman *does not exist*, even though I thought I could maybe be her, and be all things for John - career woman, supportive girlfriend, weekend step mummy, the list goes on.

That reality couldn't have been further from my truth.

I wasn't put here to uphold a perfect silhouette with the only job titles as: *Supportive Woman* in someone else's life.

I was getting tired, and the thank you's from John were becoming less and less, if any.

Come the fall, late September, with the weather starting to change, my hip would ache during the cool nights. Ever since 2008 when I first broke it, once the cool weather starts to set in the aches and pains intensify for a few weeks. This wasn't anything new for me. But it was new for John, as we had only met very early in May.

I had some pain pills at my apartment. Anytime I've had my surgeries I've never taken the recommended dose of prescription pills; I barely took any of them. They always made me light headed and zombie-like. Everything about them just disagreed with my body. So I had extra bottles under my bathroom sink at all times, just in case come night time I'd have some on hand when the dull, deep aches would become painful enough that I wouldn't be able to fall asleep.

Throughout that September I remember taking a pill or two almost every other night. For whatever reason during the fall of 2013 my hip was really struggling come night fall.

Never once did it cross my mind to consider the effects these pills would have on my birth control. With my work schedule and busy evenings, trying to stay on track with vitamins, birth control, grocery lists, bills, baseball games, my head was already filled to the brim with "things to remember".

There are quite a few narcotics out there that can defer the way your body absorbs the birth control pill. I came to learn this after going onto Google one morning at work.

Since I had been pregnant once before, I knew all too well the slight changes in my mood, my food aversions, and my sleep patterns. I can pretty much clock my body right down to the very last minute of what's going on with it and *why*.

About a week before the Thanksgiving weekend, I was driving down to John's farm one night after work. I knew the moment I woke up that morning that we had conceived. I just knew. For a few days before this day my dreams were wild; so vivid. I was even more sensitive during those days then I usually am. It wasn't too hard to figure out what was going on.

For that entire day at work the brief moments between each pay transaction I would process, or each phone call I would take, my body kept that very real fact right at the forefront of my eyes; *I was pregnant.* How, and when would I tell John?

He already had a five year old, and although we were beginning to plan a future together, a future that included babies of my own, at this point, we had only been dating for five months. Sure, things moved sorta fast with us, but this was *way too fast*.

I got married within five months of meeting my husband. And we all know how that ended.

So getting pregnant with a *boyfriend of five months*?

"Shit"

"Big shit"

When you don't learn a love lesson once, the universe brings it back to you, just with a different face. Same bad credit with the banks -- but different face.

If you can't keep your train on the tracks, you'll derail.

So you can cry, and feel like a victim, or drive your train.

Drive your train ladies. Always choose to drive your train.

The formula was simple. I was taking narcotics for pain that in turn disabled the effectiveness of my birth control. And continued having un-protected sex.

Sometimes... that results in a baby being formed.

Now to be honest, to be *very very* honest, I was twenty seven and working for the Government at a Corporate Headquarters in Ottawa. I had no debt that needed to be paid off. Between Jack's little girl and John's son, I had been playing "step mum" for the past two years. I felt ready to be a mum. I felt ready to be a mum since I was twenty three years old when married to my husband.

But was John ready to be a dad? Again? I had a feeling this news for him would not go over well.

I mean, a part of me thought *"well, we care about each other, I truly don't believe in my heart that he is going to bail, or be non-supportive"*.

Those are the actual thoughts I was telling myself. Aside from the odd *"he still technically lives with his parents, and I think he might secretly be poor or hugely in heavy financial debt"* thoughts. Not exactly favourable baby daddy qualities, but where has thinking negatively ever gotten any of us.

*Negatively is actually code for <u>clearly.</u> Thinking clearly gets us <u>everywhere.</u>

As much as I was never in a million years expecting him to jump up and down with joy, the actual reaction I got from him was pretty heartbreaking. That moment, that absolutely crucial moment when you first break the news to them… his cold silence immediately made me take two steps back from him and the realization of *"it's me and my baby… no daddy"* hit me.

As I pulled into the driveway that evening, I could see him and his son in the garage sitting on a lawn chair together. He had been busy working away getting his chores done that night so by the time I got there we could all relax and enjoy the evening together.

As I walked towards him I could feel the nervousness filling my entire body. Part of me was so unbelievably happy, because I was a very new mummy that day, and just knowing that nine months from then that by June 18th or so, we'd be welcoming a sweet baby into this world for the very first time. That thought alone brought such an incredible sense of purpose to my life.

As I stood just a few feet away from him, his son ran off to go and play. John sat there. He knew I had something to talk to him about, and due to the things that were going on with my body that week, he already had the thought in his head that pregnancy was the news.

I looked right at him, and I said *"I'm pregnant"*. He asked me if I had taken a test. *"No"* I replied. I hadn't taken a test because I hadn't missed my period yet, so the test would probably give a negative result anyways. But I just knew. I didn't need a test. And I think because John knew how aware I was with my body, by him hearing those words come out of my mouth, it scared the shit out of him. I could see it in his eyes. He knew that if I had *that feeling*, my feeling was more than likely right.

He continued to sit there, he didn't say anything, his eyes just wandered to the scenery behind me. He looked over at his son playing in the yard not too far away, then his eyes found their way back to me.

"Do you want to talk about our options?"

Those were the first words that came out of his mouth. I stood there, completely numb.

"Options?" I said to him. *"What options are you referring to?"*

Almost all my respect for him shattered on the ground right then and there.

For any and all women who have had that moment, it forever changes the way you now see and feel about that man. I think we could all probably agree.

He had a three second window to say the right thing, to make the right move, and he fucked up.

He fucked up, and I never got over that for the remainder of our relationship.

I looked right at him and stated the reasons as to why *other options* wouldn't be necessary. If sixteen year olds working at Tim Horton's and living in one bedroom apartments can raise a few kids, I was pretty sure between him and I, plus both our families, we would be more than ok.

I stood firm on the very fact that this baby was here to stay. I knew it was early and that within the first three months I could miss-carry. But I wasn't going to let my mind wander down that road. Why on earth would I?

While standing in front of John feeling more alone in this game then I ever have, something must have occurred to him, or maybe his loving side that I knew he had within him started coming through, because he must have realized he better warm up or put his arms around me. Something.

Anything.

I never did forget what that day felt like.

Feeling unloved, unwanted, as if someone is quitting on you.

Being alone.

On that day the way I now saw John was different. He had left me on the curb, cold and alone that day. His promises now meant nothing. His words held little value. And as each day passed, my mind no longer praised him for being a good man. My heart became very detached from everything and anything that had to do with "us".

As the days passed, I became more and more aware of the simple fact that I was indeed pregnant and I couldn't ignore the fact that I was no longer seeing John through rose coloured glasses. This was supposed to be the most incredible time of my life. This was supposed to be the happiest and most exciting first early days of a pregnancy.

I was falling asleep by 8:00 o'clock almost every night. Getting up in the mornings at 4:30 for work seemed impossible. Not only was my morning sickness awful, but only drinking a tiny cup of coffee versus my usual large wasn't helping my all day sleepiness. But I was doing everything I possibly could to make sure my baby was getting all that she needed.

I just knew it was going to be a little girl. She only wanted toast with garlic butter for breakfast, and scrambled eggs for supper. I went out to the drug store and got the best of the best pre-natal vitamins that were available. I even kept my work outs light, being sure to not raise my heart rate too high while at the gym.

This was it. This was my time. This was my baby. And I was going to do everything in my power to give her the best start that I could. I knew in the back of my mind that there was a big chance I would end up doing this solo. I figured having an unhappy partner would only make everything about having a new born that much more difficult.

During the month of October I spent more nights at my apartment then at the farm. I was too tired to be making the trip down to John's place after work. And to be honest, my morning sickness would usually ease off by 11:00-12:00, but by 6:30-7:00 in the evening it would be back in full swing. There were some nights I would be so sick that I'd be in my bed, showered and in pyjamas from 5:30 onward.

For most of those nights, I spent them alone.

There were many nights of fighting, as I would send John a text message telling him I wanted him to be with me. And believe me, I've never *needed* a man for anything, but there were two or three times that month that I asked him if he could come up to my place for the night and pick up a McDonalds McFlurry for me, or some ginger ale. My nausea was so bad, and I felt so awful, I just wanted my man with me. I didn't want to be alone going through my pregnancy woes.

He showed zero interest in coming to my apartment. It was like pulling teeth getting him to put the tools down by 8:00 o'clock, wash up, grab some snacks, and come to his pregnant girlfriends place.

There was one night he came. After we had a horrible fight over the phone.
I had been in bed since 5:30 that evening, sick as ever. I had barely any food
in my apartment, and I hadn't eaten since lunch. I asked, pretty much *begged*
for him to come up for the night. I told him I needed him. He replied with
"I'm eating supper with my mom".

I was in dis-belief. I couldn't believe the shit that was becoming my life.
All those nights I rushed around town to get groceries, make his lunch,
spending $80.00 a week on organic frozen fruit to make his damn fruit
smoothies for work, and this was how he was returning the favour?

And people wonder why I'm as independent as I am today.

*(This man-serving way of doing things didn't pan out to be my thing -
apologies to the traditional husbands seeking traditional wives – I'm not
your type)*

I started to really dislike John. I started to lose even more respect for him
than I already had. If things kept up the way they were, I sure as hell wasn't
building a home or investing a single penny of my savings into a life with
someone who'd be busy eating dinner with his mom.

I deserved more than that.

During the first few weeks of my pregnancy John became *more than distant.*
He would be out in his garage until 10:00 o'clock at night, pretty much every
night. He had no interest in touching me or holding me while we'd lay in bed
together. Mentally, he checked out. He completely shut down.

He was letting the small things completely stress him out. He worried about
finances, even though I reassured him over and over again that we would be
more than fine, he still continued to worry about having to sell his new truck,
or sell his snowmobile.

The more he would open up to me and vent about his concerns, the more I
wanted to tell him to stop talking, because if selling his snowmobile, or
trading in his truck for something more reasonable in price was a nightmare
scenario for him, then he truly was letting his cards show. And the cards he
was throwing down were revealing how much of a jack ass he was.

He placed more value and concern on his material possessions than anything
else.

I started to find this very soft, quiet place within me.

It was as if I was beginning to take steps backwards in time. I started seeing the life that lay ahead of me. It no longer seemed to be the picture I could once visualize within my mind. My future with John no longer seemed in anyway ideal for me. For pretty clear reasons. My mind slowly started to go into over drive. I was panicking. I no longer knew where it was I was supposed to be.

I began to realize that John was not going to be the man I would lay down in bed with every night for the rest of my life. It hit me like a wave, I just knew I had to get out of the life I had started with him. I needed out of that small, empty town, and I needed out of the relationship that was in no way serving me anything except stress, sadness, and loneliness.

I worked hard for my income. I worked hard to support myself, and I put my heart and soul into taking care of John any which way that I could. But the way in which he returned the favour, never amounted up to much. He was too wrapped up in himself and his own worries that he left me out to dry most days.

I was drained by this point. In so many ways. And I was scared about what my future would be like.

I wanted a happy home. A safe home. A home with bedtime snuggles and feet rubs as my angels would fall asleep each night.

This future - I knew would never happen by staying here with John. He was too selfish. He was too consumed with his small time concerns. He needed to mature in so many ways.

In early November, a few days after the birthday of John's son who just turned five, we got in my car and drove downtown into Ottawa.

I had made the decision to terminate my pregnancy. This decision did not come easy, as for the nine weeks my angel was inside me, I was preparing - doing everything necessary to ensure my sweet baby would be off to an amazing and healthy start. But the moment I mentioned to John that I thought we should put this to bed, he agreed; he agreed *immediately*. It was as if I had just given him a winning lottery ticket. I have never heard a man sound as relieved as John was the moment I suggested an abortion.

I take full responsibility for what I decided to do, however, I didn't opt for that choice because I was in a happy and loving relationship. I was in a night mare of a union with a guy that was going nowhere with me and getting worse day by day. There was no way I could bring a baby into that. There was no way I would raise a baby and have to deal with a father like him. It's not that he was a monster of a person, but he wasn't the person I could have spent the rest of my life with. He had a lot of blessings right in front of him yet he was the last person to see them.

The day we came home from the clinic in the city I went straight home to my apartment.
I was in so much pain and still so nauseous from the drugs. I wanted to be alone and I was in no shape to be around him or anyone. I had just done something that tore a piece of my heart away from me that I will never get back. As I lay on the table in that clinic I said goodbye to something I had fallen so deeply in love with.

I know many women who have had abortions in their lives. Some of my closest friends who are hands down – outstanding women have had an abortion at some point in their life. There is no wrong or right. It's completely your decision, and I don't think any part of making that decision is easy for any of us who've been there. As much as I was torn in half about what I was deciding to do, I ultimately knew this was the right decision for my life. I hated that the right decision felt as gut wrenching as it was, but a part of me also knew there was no numbing this out. A part of me also knew that emotionally I was more than likely going to flat line after this.

And I did.

In a way I wasn't prepared for.

When I got home to my apartment I ran straight into the bathroom. I could feel my underwear filling with blood. My stomach was in immense pain. I didn't even make it onto the toilet to change the hospital pad they gave me. The moment I got my pants off in the bathroom, blood was everywhere. I climbed into my bath tub, turned on the shower and cried harder than I have ever cried in my 27 years of life. I fell to my knees and had my face on the bottom of my bath tub watching the blood stream down into the drain.

I wanted my baby back.

I cried for hours for my baby to be placed back into me.

What I had just done was now hitting me. Everything was *very* real. What I felt about John - none of that mattered. What I felt about my future, *none of that mattered.*

All that mattered was my love for my baby; and how she was now gone.

And I did that.

I chose that.

Whether right or wrong, or the smart choice for my future, none of those things held any importance. I was now a woman with a hole so big in her heart. An emptiness colder, more still, more heavy then any emptiness I have ever felt. My baby was on her way to the heavens and there was nothing I could do to bring her back.

There was nothing I could do to turn back time.

Time, ladies. Something we don't get back.

Each portion of our lives are the direct results of every single decision we have made up until that point – and *continue* to make.

On that day - my life was a black hole of pure hell because of the decision I made.

I hated myself. With every ounce of hate that my body was capable of producing, I used it on nobody other than myself.

After about an hour of laying in my tub the water coming down from the shower began to turn cold. I turned off the faucet, grabbed a towel, slowly climbed out, and sat on my bathroom floor. I looked up to the white ceiling and I prayed to God to take care of my sweet angel. I told him I was sorry. I told him how evil I felt, and how much I hated myself. I asked for his forgiveness even though I knew I deserved none of it.

I'm not sure what kind of answers I was hoping for, I think just to calm my own heart, even if it was just for a moment. The blood of this was on my hands. And the stains would always be visible to my eyes for the rest of my life.

And they still are.

As I stood up and looked in the mirror at myself I saw nothing but regret. I saw nobody except a broken and tired woman who made the wrong decision.

I took one solid strike at that mirror and with my fist I smashed the entire thing off the wall. I didn't want to look at myself.

I had so much shame that I told the girls at work, and even some of my family members, that it was a miscarriage. I could barely look at myself and come to terms with what I had done, let alone tell other people. I was not secure in my decision. I *thought* I was making the right choice. But now, all I knew is that I was a very empty and angry woman. During this time I was rooted with nothing more than regret and complete self-hate.

Looking at one of your closest co-workers who knows you so well, and who has always been there for you as a shoulder to lean on during your hardest days, and to tell her a lie; to tell her it was a miscarriage. To sit there as she wraps her arms around you and gives you her comfort because her heart is breaking for your pain… I hated myself *even more* for not being honest about what took place. But it was so fresh, and still such a mistake in my eyes, I couldn't come to terms with myself let alone anyone else.

There are going to be things that we are going to make decisions about in life. And in the moment they may be decisions that we are unknowingly going to regret in the future. We can't hold ourselves prisoners with complete shame about these choices we make.

In those moments – when we are making choices on hard matters – if you made a decision while weighing every part of the situation with great care, then despite the outcome or feelings post-decision, we cannot cripple ourselves over it. We cannot shame ourselves.

In a world full of multiple opportunities to make mistakes that we will shame or define ourselves by, don't let this be one of those choices that you add to that list.

You did the best you could – at the time – with what you had.

The pain of a bad decision may never go away, and that's ok. But it's how you live your life *after the fact* while continuing to feel those pains within your heart is what really matters.

Don't be the woman who carries the pain with no mission.
Be the woman who carries the pain with the ability to have empathy and understanding to others fighting through the same conflicting thoughts.

Turn your pieces of pain into places of power within you.

My time in Ottawa was now over. My time with John was over. For good. I needed to be in the only place where I knew my heart could heal, and I could wake up and be surrounded by the smell of that fresh East coast air that made me remember what *being home* felt like.

At this time all I had was the possibility of a one year contract sitting on my desk. All I had to do was sign the dotted line and the Government would move me back out East. All I had to do was say yes. My current position with Health Canada was coming to an end later that year, however I had a job offer from the Head of a different Department in Ottawa, to be his Executive Assistant. I knew that if I took this job and worked directly under a pretty successful man and to remain in Ottawa at that, my career would no doubt continue to rise. Had I been in a better place emotionally, I probably would have stayed. Probably would have chosen career over small town East Coast life. But I knew in my heart I couldn't stay there. At that time it wasn't a certain career position that I needed. It was peace of mind. I had to get myself to a place where I could bare looking at myself in the mirror again.

So I signed. I signed for a job with a different department to work in their Finance and Compensation department, and I was to start the 5th of May, of 2014.
At the time of signing, May was still a few months away so there was some time to be spent alone during the evenings at my apartment in the little town I lived in.

I needed this time more than ever. I needed to somehow make peace with myself; with my heart. For those couple of months before the movers showed up and packed my things, my life was very quiet. I was at work in the city Monday to Friday, and come the evening time, I would spend it at the gym down the road from my apartment, and then bubble bath, pyjamas, and a TV show or some crosswords. I didn't want the hands of any man near me or touching me. My body needed to heal. Everything inside me was still sore. Physically I struggled with the healing. My body was tired. My heart was shut down. My nights were spent alone. But as each day went by I was one day closer to getting back home.

I had no man or love interest waiting for me in New Brunswick. I only had a few girlfriends and a few brothers from the Army as my points of contact. But none of that mattered.

The only thing I needed was to be waking up in the only place on this earth where my heart knows the difference between the morning winds and the night time winds. I needed to be back sitting on my porch with a cup of coffee as the sun would come up, and I'd check to see if the squirrels got the peanuts I would leave out for them the night before.

I needed my home. I needed my friendly neighbours, who no matter where I lived in New Brunswick, all of my neighbours treated me like their daughter. I needed my quiet nights, my bright stars - *my piece of heaven New Brunswick.*

Coming Home

In the early hours of the morning on April 30th, I packed my three kittens in my car (two farm kittens + my Tuxedo cat, Rocky) did my final sweep of the apartment to make sure the movers got everything, left Easter coloured jellybeans and a chocolate bunny from Laura Secord on the kitchen counter for the new tenant, locked the door, and I was headed home.

I have driven back and forth to New Brunswick many times before. I knew the route like the back of my hand. But this was a hard drive for me. Even though I knew deep down, I knew instinctively that John and I had no future, I was still struggling with the pain from how things went so south for us, and so quickly. When you're going through a shit storm of change, hard, *painful* change, the best thing to do is nothing— do nothing. Ride it out; sit tight and do not make any major decisions. When you make *emotionally driven* decisions you will lose every time. Knowing the rational of that, yet being where I was mentally, it was hard for me to find the balance between those lines. I knew within a few months down the road, after getting settled into my new home, I knew I would be *ok* with the choice I made. To leave Ontario again and to hopefully find my forever home here in New Brunswick.

But that morning while I made my way through Ottawa, the outskirts of Montreal, then Quebec, and the never ending part of the Trans-Canada highway between Quebec and the New Brunswick border; I struggled. My heart kept wanting to turn around and run back to John, only to completely break down and let him know how sorry I was, for everything. Regardless of who was right or wrong, or who was the bigger asshole, I just wanted him to know I was sorry. But I kept my hands gripped on that steering wheel. I knew I had to keep my car moving East.

When I look back to that drive, I remember how badly my wrists hurt once I reached Quebec. That's how tight I was holding the steering wheel during the first six hours of the drive.

Looking back to that day, the only thing I was sure of was that I had a new house key to pick up and a new address to report to for work the following Monday. Everything else was a complete blur. I kept breaking into tears during that entire twelve hour drive. The further I was away from Ontario, the closer I was to starting over. But what I didn't plan for were those deep pains from terminating my pregnancy to follow me back to the East Coast.

In my mind I ignorantly thought I could leave that place, leave that small Ontario town, my job in Ottawa, and I would also be leaving the *hurt* behind me. The hurt from Jack, the hurt from John, my sweet angel who was now in the heavens, *everything.*

I was running from myself.

But no matter if you go 100 kms per hour or 200 kms per hour on that Trans-Canada hwy, apparently it's only a matter of time until certain pains catch up with you and they show themselves to you when you least expect it.

The *peeling of the onion* effect.

Like that one sweet onion you keep in your fridge, and only peel parts of it when you need a pinch of onion for your recipe.

Heart break un-peal's itself one layer at a time like an onion.

And during various, very un-planned moments too.

Anytime a person says *"Vic, you realize you can't run from your problems".* I swear to God each time I hear that phrase, I lace up my Nikes as if to say *"Um... want to fucking bet?"*

I'm a runner. In all forms. And it works wonders for some things. But this wasn't going to be one of those successful running stories.

(For the record, running from some of your problems is completely do-able. As long as you map it out properly, be vague when discussing details of your past with your new team of co-workers, change your social media name to something other than your birth name, dying your hair a new colour, maybe some lip injections & a professionally manipulated social insurance number with a difficult to verify T4 payment record – you're good to go)

Anyhoo,

Around 6:00 pm that evening I was approaching the New Brunswick border. After a long day with only two quick gas stops, I was only a couple hours away from putting my car in park.
I opened my car windows (something I always do when I'm minutes away from crossing into New Brunswick) and the moment that air filled my car, my heart was becoming more and more full. I had butterflies in my stomach. I was smiling through my tears. I had made it.

It was now --all healing-- from here on out.

Nobody could touch me, nobody could hurt me.
Those bad memories from a few *not so nice* men were now behind me, and both didn't have my new address or soon to be new phone number, so I was safe.

Everything started to feel calm within me. Even though things in my head were still un-settled, and my heart was still hurting in a way that I knew I would come back from differently, my body started to have this all-over calmness about it.

The grip on my steering wheel started to loosen.

I was home.

I was a few kilometers away from the home that I was to be renting for the next year while working for the new department. I had only seen a couple of photos of the place on the internet, and I spoke to the landlord only once. It was actually one of my New Brunswick girlfriends that had found this house for me.

I was still in Ottawa when I signed my contract for the new job, so I needed to line up a new place to live in time for work on that Monday. (Out-sourced that task)

I gave my girlfriend a few specifics on what I knew I would need.

It was a pretty short list, but the main points where very important:

-small town, no more than a 25 minute drive to work
(I won't live in a city)
-at least two bedrooms
-a window over my kitchen sink
-quiet street
-driveway long enough for my Chevy pick-up & my car
-backyard is a must
-must have a porch on either the front, back or both ends of the house
-enough kitchen cupboards for all my baking supplies

If she could find me that, I knew everything would be fine.
I trusted her judgement.

She knew what I liked. But more importantly, what I needed.

It wasn't until about a week before I was set to leave Ontario that she actually gave me the address of my new place. And the only reason I even got it on the day that I did was because I was booking the movers and I needed to give them an actual location to deliver my furniture.

When she gave me the address over text message, I had to look at it twice. My eyes popped right out of my head. Out of all the house rentals available, (and apparently there weren't too many that would foot my bill) but the little house she had found, not only did it look completely perfect in the photos, but even the name of the street sat well with me.

Then, I looked at the town.

Hampton.

I started quietly laughing..

Hampton, New Brunswick
E5N 5A5

Hampton is a small town. Very small. Which is great news for me because the smaller the town, the bigger the trees, the kinder the people=the safer.

That is a total jack pot in my eyes.

However, this wasn't why I was laughing.

I knew Hampton. I had been there two or three times, *briefly*.
And I had been to their Tim Horton's as well, years prior, because in the early morning's I would leave Chevy's house after one of our nights together, I would head to the Tim Horton's drive through before getting on the highway.

Out of all the ways Chevy had been in my life, for all the times I wished he was sitting next to me, just so I could have one of his hugs, or hear his calming yet stern advice in real life, and after spending more of our friendship separated by provinces, I was now moving to his home town.

That's right.

His home town.

I even went on Google Maps and was able to see by typing in both our addresses' that we were now going to be a mere five kilometers away from each other.

Five.

Just five.

I feel like I can throw a baseball further than that.

My land lord had been paid first & lasts', I was to start my new job in less than a week.

There was no changing this.

I remember not being sure if this was going to be a good thing.
I mean, for one, to have someone nearby in case I ever needed anything, that's always a good thing. Especially when moving to a town you have never lived in, and you are moving there *alone*, it brought me a lot of comfort knowing that Chevy would be a stones' throw away.

However with saying that, there was a flip side to this.

Anytime I would see Chevy, it was natural instinct - I would jump into his arms, or grab his arm and pull it around me if we were lying in bed together. Even if we were sitting on a couch, within seconds I would manage to be sitting pretty much on him, or pressed up right close to him. Not because I wanted to get naked with him, but I just always needed his comfort. He was like a magnet for me. If there was a way I could slide my feet into the socks he was wearing and have my head come out of the neck of his shirt while he was still in it, I'm sure I would make it happen.

Our friendship was easy to see for what it was.

We had very separate lives, but we had a bond. He knew things about me that nobody knew. And I always felt safe with him having those secrets. I was a shit show, more days than not, and he was my rock.

Easy peezy.

It never mattered before where I lived, but I did worry about being so close to him. It was almost as if I didn't want to let myself rely on him. I had some sorting out to be done between myself and I, and I didn't want to drag him into any of that.

My plan:

Unpack, become settled, start work, and stay far, *far away* from men (for a little bit).

The simplicity of knowing Chevy was just down the road was all the comfort I needed to tuck myself into bed every night and focus on my job, my animals, my money—my *plan*.

Hampton, New Brunswick
My Saving Grace

On the early morning of May 1st 2014, I arrived at my *soon to be* home in Hampton. I had only seen a few photos from my girlfriend, so I wasn't sure exactly what I was walking into, but I knew it had the basics that I'd need. When I first walked into the house, to my surprise it was a lot longer and a lot bigger then I had imagined.

But that didn't bother me.

I've never minded cleaning floors. It's always been what's relaxed me, so the more floors to clean, the better.

It was beautiful in Hampton. Truly beautiful. Southern New Brunswick – make it a place you'll visit. It's actually pretty magical. Hidden waterfalls, lush forests. It's God's land.

The people are kind and the trees are big. After what I had been though during my last month living in that small apartment North West of Ottawa, I needed some peace.

This house, this town, it all foot the bill. My job was to start only four days later on the following Monday. At this time I only had what was in my car, as my belongings and furniture were still on the way with the moving company. I emptied my car, let the kittens run free through the house, and started blowing up my air mattress. I didn't have a single thing with me except my toothbrush, a few hair brushes, and a trunk full of clothes. But I've always had an easy time living out of a suitcase, or a car for that matter, then I ever did staying in one spot settled up in a home. So this was an easy go for me until my belongings arrived the following week.

I quickly became friends with the brothers who ran the town convenience store. They were so good to me when I first got there. Anything from buying the right screws to hang my curtains, or where to find laundry soap at ten o'clock at night, they were my go-to guys. They always lended a helping hand, and most importantly, they cracked me right up almost every time I went in to that little store. I was still on edge from the things that had happened in Ottawa, so a smile and a good laugh was honestly the only thing I needed.

After a few weeks had gone by and the rest of my things had arrived from the moving company, I was getting settled. Every day I felt more and more at home. While driving home from my new job there was no other place in the world where I wanted to be driving to. Hampton becoming my saving grace.

That summer I spent most of my weekends tinkering around in my yard; pulling weeds, cutting down dead branches, doing up my flower gardens. I found the perfect spot on the one side of my house to plant my sunflower seeds that my mum had sent me in the mail. This home was small, and the yard was small too, but it had a garden shed out back, which was all I really needed for my lawn mower and flower pots.

I had no interest in meeting men, or dating any. My head and heart just weren't there. At work I was surrounded by some seriously bad ass women. These were good women. Very wise. One lady especially reminded me of an older version of myself. She was close to retiring when I got there, but my goodness did she ever have stories to tell. Between her and I, we almost challenged one another as to who made bigger mistakes in their personal life. *"You had to put your first husband in jail? Me too!"*

She had a lot of very wise and very comforting words that I leaned on more than she probably knew.

Another co-worker very quickly became a sister to me. She was married with two very young, very cute little girls. Her and her husband would eventually see me through many more years to come. Nowadays they are pretty much my family out here. Their home is always a place where I know I'm welcome. And it's something I am incredibly grateful for.

For most of my weekends if I wasn't on the road visiting my girlfriend's and their families, I was here at my rental home in Hampton. I was perfectly content to wake up on my Saturday's and go for a work out at the small gym in town. And on my way home, cruise through some other towns to see if I could find some sturdy old furniture on the side of the road that needed a little TLC.

Anytime I've gotten away from something that was bad for me, I usually end up spending the next six months re-finishing furniture and then putting it online for sale.

I picked up this hobby while in my first house, my yellow house. After leaving my marriage it seemed that keeping myself occupied with hand-sanding furniture was the healthiest and most economical way to keep the bourbon at bay. The simplicity of taking something that needed fixing and making it beautiful again, there's a level of healing in that I suppose. Because with the right shade of wood stain, some of the marks that have aged that piece of furniture can forever be hidden as if to look brand new.

Come early September I was about to meet someone who I never expected to meet in this sweet small town, nor was I even sure of him when I first spoke to him. I was absolutely not looking to date anyone – in any way. Even the idea of texting a man really wasn't appealing to me.

But something, Lord knows what, had me willing to make a friend.

Let's call him Jax.

Jax grew up very close to Hampton. The area in which he grew up is beautiful, and I know this because he took me there. More than a few times.

It was around eight o'clock on a Saturday evening in early September. I was in my pyjamas, I had on a silk night gown, race car pyjama pants, wool slippers, with a decaf Tim Horton's coffee and a rented DVD from the boys at the convenience store.
I had zero plans on leaving my house that night, *zero.*
But I got a message from Jax just a little before then. He said he would do something low key and local with me if I was up for it.

When I read that message, I literally looked at myself in the mirror, took a good hard look at the total loser pyjamas I was wearing and said to myself *"Oh God woman, go for a damn drink, it won't kill ya."*

So I wrote him back and I said, *"I'll stop into your place for a drink if you're up for that?"*
There was no way I was inviting anyone to *my house*, as I have a hard time inviting people in.
Usually they take one look at the trinket collection I have in my bedroom, or once they spot all three cats, that's usually enough to send them running.

I have a habit of collecting special things, sparkly things. They can be junk, or an actual treasure, but sometimes people get the impression that I'm this travelling gypsy, which to be honest, isn't very far from the truth. What nobody really knows is each piece, each treasure, has a story. A very special story. Even my jewelry. Some of it is big and wild, and others are small and simple, but all of it comes from somewhere different, and most of it I never bought brand new. But through experiences, moments, my travels - I've collected a lot. They are my most cherished possessions. I'd hand someone the keys to my car before I'd part with any of my treasures.

Jax had mentioned that his brother would be there and that his house was a bit of a mess because he had only recently moved in. So naturally, I thought to myself, *"Oh good, there's two strong men there to murder me and bury me out back. Perfect."*

But apparently that small negative self-talk didn't stop me. So I thought I better put some different clothes on, brush my teeth, slap on some deodorant, a baseball cap, and give this a shot.

Usually when getting ready for a date, you at least *shower* and do something nice with your hair, maybe a little make up. Not me. Not that night. I had zero expectations. I don't even think I really cared. I made sure my teeth were clean and that my panties were on straight. That was about it. I got in my car and drove on over to his place.

Before I left my house I gave one of my very close girlfriends from work his address. Just in case I went missing she'd know where to look.
My trust was at an all-time zero, so I tried to take all precautions.

When I pulled into his driveway, I could see his truck parked out front, and out of all the things that I could have been thinking about before meeting this stranger, the first thing that honestly came to my mind was *"F150 FX4. Smart man."* I all of a sudden felt a little more sure about him. He made a smart choice in the truck he drove, so we've got to be *somewhat* like-minded. I really didn't know who or what kind of guy I was meeting. We had only spoke a little before he had asked to meet up.

All I really knew was that he was a pipefitter and that he had recently bought the house he was living in. I knew he had lived in this area for all of his life. (Between travelling back and forth out West for work)

I didn't even know his first name now that I think of it. As I approached the door, in my head I was saying to myself *"what the shit do I say? Hi there.... you!"*

I knock on the door, and within a few seconds I can hear his footsteps. When he opened the door I was pleasantly surprised; *very pleasantly surprised.* The first thing I noticed were his teeth. Not sure why, but as soon as he opened the door and had that smirk on his face, I stared right into his teeth. With me, a smile goes a million miles. He had this Denzel Washington type smirk with his teeth. I was into it. I don't care what you do for a living, or what kind of status you may have in your town. But if you have a kind smile, a *warm* smile, you've already scored pretty high with me.

Lots of men have a good smile, pearly white teeth, all that jazz, but very few have that warmth to them. Very few have anything more worth discovering, or looking into. Same goes for women.

I've met shallow men, powerful men, dick head men, rich men, and poor men. All of which had many talents. And so far Jax seemed to be successful in his own right by having his own home and property. But I was also going to soon find out that not only did he have a great job, but that he was passionate about his work, and from what I have learned, quite good at it too; better than your average pipefitter. But on top of it all, I was going to eventually learn that he had a heart that was always in all the right places. A very authentic guy with his intentions.

Some men are born evil. I believe that. Some men and women can do horrible things and sleep just fine at night. I've watched people commit true acts of pure pain to a person they apparently loved, then witness them carry on with their lives without any remorse or guilt.

There's something very un-human about people like that.

Over the years I have learned to recognize that evil in people. Very easily, and *very quickly.*
People often wonder once they get to know me why I double check all the locks on my doors and windows, or why I will run my errands in a baseball cap with a hoody on and baggy track pants. I know too well what it's like to be compromised and trapped in a situation where you don't think you're going to come out the same.

Those memories still burn in my head. At times when I've been driving down the high way I've had to pull over. Like a movie reel, my windshield turns into this giant flash back and I'm unable to see a single thing except that memory of being trapped in that washroom.

I had my reservations about Jax, even though I knew barely anything about him.

Just with my memories alone, the good ones, and the bad ones, a certain part of me had lost faith in having kind hands ever wrap themselves around me.

Hands that were once filled with love and trust had all ended up turning on me and putting bruises on my skin or the absolute worst words inside my head. Scars which I see and words I still hear every time I sit in my bath at night.

Weather it's the memories of the bruises hidden under the roses that I had tattooed onto my wrists, or the words used against me that were used in an attempt to cripple my self-esteem. Ridding your subconscious of things that have deeply hurt you is a very uphill battle. It's comparable to walking to school in the winter time, *uphill and both ways*. Each time you re-visit the memories in an attempt to form a reconciliation, more times than not you end up briefly feeling the pains of opening those doors inside your head – only to quickly shut the doors and say to yourself *"I can't. Not today"*.

But as soon as I walked into Jax's house, as soon as I felt him in real life once he opened that door, I knew nothing of that sort was ever going to happen with him. I just knew.

I was greeted by his brothers beautiful dog, Bruno. He was excited and playful, and since my history is with Pit Bulls, I had not a single fear but to only bend over and try to steal some kisses from this big mastiff-mix boy.

After Bruno let me into the front door, I looked up and looked right into Jax's face.

"Shit". I thought to myself. *"Why didn't I put a little more effort into my appearance?"* I honestly think I hadn't showered since nine o'clock that morning. And that afternoon I had been painting and re-finishing a small coffee table that I was planning on selling. I may not have looked it, but I was dirty, and probably smelled a little like paint thinner to be honest.

His eyes were bright and blue. And his smile, warm.

He was incredibly attractive. A strong jaw line. His shoulders were strong, and sturdy.
His body was solid. Even the way he walked across his kitchen, ever step he took, he was strong. He was a man who was sure of himself.
He had a firm mind and he knew it.

Just within that first five seconds, I had already sized him up in my mind. And knowing the things about him that I know as I sit here and type this out, my initial impression and first thoughts of him were pretty bang on.

He didn't have to tell me that he was a man of old fashion values, I could feel it in the way he spoke.

You could tell he took care of himself physically.
Clean diet, daytime trips to the gym. Which was nice because my lifestyle was pretty much the same.

Then out of nowhere I started to catch a pinch of those flirty girly girl type nerves. So I put my purse down on the kitchen counter, walked through out the living room and sort of gave myself a mini-tour of the main level. I then pulled out my bottle of Jack Daniels from my purse hoping to make a drink to calm my nerves down a bit.
But to my surprise, before I could even pour my own drink, he had opened up his freezer and took out a quart of Jack Daniels, and offered to make me one.

My eyes opened wide.

He knew exactly what I wanted. *"Perfect. We're off to a good start"*.

We sat on his big black leather couch, with drinks in hand, and slowly started to get to know one another. The conversation started to happen pretty naturally. I was weirdly at ease with him. Usually I have a sixth sense with men. I can now feel out a bad egg really quickly. And even when meeting anyone new, there may not be anything wrong with them, not a bad bone in their body. However, I'll still look for something because meeting someone who isn't going to completely hurt me in some way has never been my luck.

After a little bit of time had passed we moved downstairs. He brought out chairs for us to sit on and enjoy the evening outside. Jax also had a Harley Davidson. Between the smart choice in the F150 he had purchased, the beautiful spot up on the hill where his home was, those sharp eyes, warm smile and sharp mind, he had a fucking Harley Davidson. So of course, he started it up for me.

Hearing a Harley Davidson is one of my favourite lullaby's. Just the sheer sound of them makes my heart race. I'd hop onto the back of one of those in nothing but my underwear and ski goggles. *"Let's fucking go"*. I'd say. Being on the back of a motorcycle is like the missing beat to my heart. It's the fastest way to ending a bad day. Because after you get off a bike, you don't even remember what you were upset about in the first place.

If Doctor's could prescribe motorcycles instead of pills, the world would be a better place.

We sat on those two chairs for hours that night. Just sipping our drinks and getting to know a lot about one another. Everything about it was just really nice.

Jax is an assertive man. He is wise with his opinions on things, and he is quick witted and sharp. I've always really liked that in a person. He also has this amazing sense of humor. He can crack me up on the turn of a dime. I've always been a little left field with my ways. I have a dry sense of humor and I'm pretty jaded, so I can laugh at a lot of things most people would find down right offensive. But that's because there hasn't been much that I haven't been through, especially within the past ten years. Some days I wake up and feel as if I have the heart of a sixty five year old woman.

Sitting there that night with Jax, there was nowhere else in the world where I needed to be.
I had no idea what would become of him and I, but I knew I liked him as a person first and foremost. And I don't like too many people.
But I could appreciate the things he would say. I could relate to his perspectives on a lot of things.

"Let them eat the dirt"

Was what we both said at the same time when describing raising kids.
It was odd and funny all at the same time because that's never happened with any man I've had in my life, finishing the same sentence.

During that night I began to feel comfortable with him. I remember thinking to myself that I may have found someone who won't just be any old friend, but who would be someone I would be able to call on down the road if I ever needed something. He had this very calming effect on me. I don't know why, he just did. My mind is always going a million miles an hour. Mostly just memories flooding my vision. I had a hard time learning how to no longer live in the past during most of my twenties. And then there's my to-do list that seems to be non-stop. But being with him, my mind just found this calm place.

It was different.

It was nice.

I spend enough time taking care of myself. I spend enough time on the road, and enough time bringing in the money. When I'm with a man I would hope that it could be my turn to shut my brain off and his turn to give me that security that I've always had to provide for myself. I'll drop my reins. I'll leave my alpha-female mind at the door.

For the right man, I'll be the right woman.

I get my way with a lot of things in my life. I go head to head with any competition for whatever job position I'm fighting for. If I want a vehicle in a certain colour or with certain extra's, I always, *always*, get exactly what I want for the price *I decide on.* Even if I'm in a betting war over something, I'll shoot five grand over asking just to make it mine. Call that stupid or wasteful, but if I want something, I'll tell you this much, *I'll make it mine.* I never accumulate something without a plan as to what I'll be doing with it. Whether I treat it as an investment or achievement, there's purpose to it.

So when I'm with a man and if he lets me have my way with things, I lose interest immediately. They have to instill a level of dominance over me. And if they don't, I automatically realize that I'm the alpha sitting in the room, and if I have to be the alpha 24/7, I'm not interested.

I walked away from a man once. This was a man who never did anything wrong, or hurtful. He was actually quite kind and very gentle. He had a lot of power with his work. He owned a very successful company in Toronto. He had a roster of vehicles. Porsche's, Bentley's, Mercedes. You name it, he had it. Money was not an issue for this man. And giving me anything and everything I could ever dream of, all I had to do was say *"Baby may I".* I met this man while I was working at the club in Toronto before I left for the military. But I decided not to write about him mostly because there wasn't anything overly interesting that came from my time with him. As well our time together was brief, a couple months, not even.

Despite his outward appearance of power and success, behind closed doors, he was a weak man. He knew very little about the simple things in life, the *survival things.* Had I stayed with this man, I would have never had to work a day in my life. I would have private planes fly me to exclusive vacations anywhere in the world. This man was crazy about me. He had this love for me as if he wanted to put me in his pocket and protect me from this big bad world.

But his life wasn't my life. His fancy ways and expensive dinners, that's not who I am.

I mow my lawns in bare feet and my underwear. With a ripped up tank top and some old shitty baseball cap on my head. And I love doing that. That's one of my favourite things to do in the summer time.

Rich or poor, that doesn't hold much weight with me. But if you have a strong set of boundaries, old fashion morals, and you make it clear with nothing more than a look, or a single word out of your mouth that you mean business, you can be damn sure that I won't go anywhere.

I crave that.

-A boundary-

Because growing up, I had none.

I constantly cross the line, *have crossed the line*, and have paid for it too.

That's what I liked about Jax when I first met him. He had that in him. That alpha dominance that I will listen to. He would always make my ears perk up. And they don't perk up for too many people, *ever*.

I'm stubborn, but I will bow down to logic and reason, no matter how emotional or angry I am.

Unless you're an Alpha who I genuinely despise and overall disagree with on all levels, then it will be *World War fucking three*.

Throughout my mid to late twenties I learned how to find my stability amongst my instability. My life has been a whirl wind on so many levels. And realizing before moving to Hampton that I felt more at home in my car on some highway, versus in an actual home, I knew I needed to make a change, to slow down, and give myself some form of security and roots.

I never left Jax's house until about two in the morning. We sat there together and listened to some really great music. We enjoyed the warm evening, and just enjoyed each other's company. It was as simple as that. And I wouldn't have changed a single thing.

Before I started getting my things together to eventually end the night and head back home, he leaned in and grabbed me for a kiss. And it was pretty perfect, I can tell you that.
He tasted good, he felt good. *Everything was good.*

Now, had I not genuinely really given a shit about this guy, I would have never stuck around for an entire evening. And definitely never let him kiss me.

I wouldn't say I'm a picky person when it comes to men, and I most definitely do not have a certain "type" because my ex-husband, as well as my two ex-boyfriends all look very different from one another. It's always been something else, something deeper. They've got to grab my attention. And that's not an easy thing to do.

But Jax was slowly turning the right keys in me, because he had me thinking twice. Most days men don't take up any space in my head. I've always been a goal digger—dream achiever. I've always had this natural hunger for independent success. Doing things my way, one move at a time and putting in the ground work. My instincts to provide and make gains to support myself is how I've always operated the past twelve or so years. Growing up always having a firm understanding of the paths of my dad and step dad – how their success was solely due to hard fucking work, and never losing sight of their vision and their goals. The blue print was always very clear.

Both my fathers were basically raised by just their mothers. My step dad, Ron, he grew up with just him and his mum. His dad didn't stick around to support the family he had created. And my dad, his father died while flying his small plane one night by crashing it into the woods somewhere in Northern Ontario. My dad was just a teenager when this happened.

Everything both my fathers achieved as young men who eventually turned into *extremely successful well-known men,* they made their legacies happen due to nothing more than sheer hard work.

Their formula was simple. If you want something, you can do it. Just work for it, and *don't stop working for it.*

This phrase my dad used to tell Melissa and I any weekend we were little girls having visits with him. And it was usually always in the car when driving us back home to our mums at the end of the weekend visit *"You can do anything you want girls, just put your mind to it".*

I'll never forget being nine years old having my dad explain to us *"before you ever get married or have a serious relationship, you need to rent or buy your own place and have your own pay cheques that cover all your necessary expenses. Until this happens, don't ever let a man build a life with you. Because if the day comes when you need to get out of that situation, you're going to need your own financial resources to successfully do so."*

Nine years old.

Fuck Dora the Explorer.

Move over Barbie.

I was learning about financial independence.

Jax was slowly taking up room in my head and I couldn't figure out why. He was still so brand new. I had nothing invested into him. Maybe it was simply because he gave me something I hadn't felt in a really long time.

A safe and simple place to rest my mind.

Sussex

The next day we had made plans to head out on his Harley. The weather was calling for clear skies and sun. So around 11 or so that morning as I was sitting on my front porch having my coffee after my work out, I received a text message from Jax, *"Hey gorgeous, just on my way home from the gym"*. We had decided that sometime between noon and 1:00 we would head out for a day on the road.

I don't think guys know how special something as small as a text message can be. Maybe some girls don't really care too much, but I always loved the small things.

I loved that he called me gorgeous. I loved that he was texting me and letting me know he was going to be on his way shortly. Those are the small, kind things that have always scored high with me. Mostly because it takes close to no effort. So if a man is too lazy to do the small things, take a guess at how good he'll perform the big things.

After the night we had, I'll admit, I had the butterflies for this guy. I didn't want to admit it to myself, because I knew all too well that once the butterflies come, that means this man is now taking up room in my head. And up until that point I had worked very, *very hard* to remove all those thoughts and feelings from my life. I purposely avoided bars, night clubs and all men the entire summer I was in Hampton. I wasn't interested in anyone's hands touching me or words possibly puzzling me,

Didn't want it one bit.

But this guy, I was excited about him. I'll admit that. I don't vibe with people very easily. I'm guarded, *so guarded* it can get in my way more times than not. But Jax, I wanted to let him in. That realization alone surprised me.

They say the best kind of people you can meet are the ones who will challenge you. The ones who can help you learn things about yourself. The ones who will ask you the tough questions.

Jax challenged me. Sometimes I didn't know when or how to drop the alpha-female in me and be just female anytime I was around him. We could express our points of view and go head to head over something with each other. We would banter. I was still trying to figure out my place with him. Through all these friendship-forming activities I was still navigating my place with him.

Friend, or lover.

Or, friend *and* lover.

If we were to be just friends, then he would get to know a very different version of myself, and my vulnerable side, I would have *never* shown him those parts of me.

I have a lot of weak spots. Nobody needs to remind me. I can see them every time I look in the mirror. There are a lot of sore spots deep down in me. And I don't really know if Jax could see them. Maybe I don't cover them up as well as I think I do. But having people use my weaknesses against me has caused me a lot of pain in my life. Nobody really puts two and two together, why I have opted to live such a solo way of life. Or why I have ultimately chosen to keep myself on the outskirts of a small city in a province far from the province I grew up in. But the one reason I can, *and do* tell people when they ask is simple; I found home here. I found home in New Brunswick.

I think ultimately there are memories or certain heart breaks I experienced growing up, and for whatever reason how I handled those times, I'm ultimately not proud of. I still carry with me an overwhelming sense of guilt with the falling out I had with my older sister the year I moved back to Toronto after the army. That really bad night when we had our fight in the apartment she got for us which led to me packing up and basically fleeing to Ottawa is years behind us, but I still have a lot of shame with the entire thing. I was in such a dark place when I first moved back to Toronto. She would tell me I had a chip on my shoulder, which was an understatement, really. I was not a nice person during that time by any means.

Overall she was just trying to understand the head space her baby sister was in. And I absolutely took her miss-understanding as something entirely different. Over the past few years as I have healed certain pains, the clarity of making things right with the people you love begins to become priority.

Almost every GIC, RSP, one of my investments accounts – all those things are in her name, as my beneficiary. And not because she would ever need those financial accounts because her and my brother-in-law live comfortably, but if I was to leave the world early for whatever reason, I want her, her bubby and my niece and nephew to have it all. They are my number ones.

Later that morning after showering up and getting some jeans on, I went back out to my front porch to wait for Jax. Within minutes I could hear his bike. Without a doubt, one of the best sounds to my ears; a *Harley*.

When he pulled up I remember being really happy to see him. After giving him a mini-tour of my little house, we were on our way through the back country roads headed to the small town of Sussex.

Sussex is the next town over. It's a little bigger than Hampton, and like most Southern New Brunswick places, it has a lot of sweet charm.

We had no destination in mind, we were just going to head out in that general direction and enjoy the day.

This is my kind of day. This is my heaven. On the road on the back of a bike just cruising. Feeling that hot sun, breathing in that clean air. Stopping every now and then to check something out, or grab some food and gas up. Being on that open road that day with his one hand reaching back every so often to touch my thigh, I was a pretty happy, but more importantly, relaxed girl that day.

We drove through some of the most amazing country side. He took me through the parts where he grew up. We even drove right by his parents' house which they still live in today. As we'd drive by certain intersections, or forks in the road, he would turn his head back just enough so I would be able to hear him, and he would tell me a little something about the place we were at. He had grown up in these parts. These were his stomping grounds. And by seeing everything through his eyes that day, it showed me a lot about him.

I have seen a lot of New Brunswick, I have lived here years ago as well. But on that day while being his passenger through those rolling hills, and learning things that only someone who has lived in those parts can tell you, it was total bliss.

I knew I was letting my guard down with him. Even just by leaning into him while walking around the Sussex fair grounds that day, my body will always speak before my mind, and when it does, I pay attention. I knew by leaning on him while walking through the fairgrounds I was probably starting to find my comfort with him. I had a feeling I would be able to someday trust him. Maybe I was already starting to.

When we arrived in Sussex, to our surprise it was the annual hot air balloon festival. And to make things even better, it was a car show as well. There were 1967 Mustangs, 1967 Chevelle's, flawless '57 Chevrolet trucks. My eyes were popping out of my head. If someone could draw a picture of what my "dream date" would look like, it would have looked like that Sunday in Sussex.

Driving in on the back of a Harley, then browsing 50 plus old school muscle cars and classic trucks, that right there is pretty much my heaven on earth. Add in a few sips of Jack Daniels on ice, being held tight and close beside a good man, —I'm all smiles.

I don't know who appreciated browsing those cars more, myself or Jax. It was pretty much a candy shop for us both.

Even though I knew this thing with him and I was new, and I had zero idea of where it would or *would not go* between us, I knew enough to just enjoy every moment of that day.

I needed a day like that.

A day that was simple and loving.

Being there with him I was able to feel beautiful just the way I was. No make-up, no fancy clothes. My ripped jeans and cropped jacket, with some black sunglasses; that's me. Simple. And for the first time ever, I was holding hands with a man who appreciated a simple woman. And it felt amazing. My words could just roll off my tongue, there was no pretending with him. I was relaxed. He took me for exactly who I was.

I loved that he knew almost all the answers to my questions. I'd be confused about a model or an engine in one of the cars, and he was able to break it down for me, and explain to me the difference in torque or power.

I love learning.

I always have a basket of questions when I want to master something. My old Chev has taught me everything I know about vehicles and engines. Just the amount of time I've spent with her. I've been under my truck more times than I've been under my ex-husband. So with Jax being able to explain certain things to me in a way that I could understand, I really appreciated that.

After a really good afternoon of taking in the sights and admiring the really, *really impressive* cars and trucks, we decided to head on back home to Hampton.

The ride home was just as good as the ride out. By this point I was feeling even more comfortable with him, and safe. I think that's the best word to use to describe the overall feeling; safe. I didn't have to think too much with him. Our words flowed pretty easily between one another, and the more times he would take one of his hands off the handle bars and hold onto one of mine, the more I was able to relax.

When we pulled into Hampton I was expecting him to drop me off at my place, maybe a kiss or two good bye, and let that be that for the day. But to my surprise he seemed to have no plans to end our date quite yet. I told him I still had a movie at my place that I never finished watching, and if he wanted to end the night by making it a movie night, that would be ok by me.

He was right on board with that idea. And even still to this very day, looking back, I still don't know exactly why; that from that Saturday evening until the very early morning of the following Monday, he was right by my side. It was pretty much a three day date.

Since that weekend, a lot has happened between him and I. I'm not even sure if it would do me or you any good to write about it, it all sort of feels irrelevant now.

Regardless of what I have learned over the years, and even when I can sit here and realize very clearly that I have not only learned, but survived some truly awful relationships, I guess a part of me can still be naïve. Some days those rose coloured glasses sneak back onto my face.

Falling asleep that Sunday night with him in my bed was great. Of course we kissed, of course we fooled around, but I knew I wasn't going to sleep with him; there was just no way.

For a long time with the few men who have loved me, (this excludes my ex-husband) somewhere along the lines of those broken relationships, I became this sex object to them. There were too many moments where I was used by them for the wrong thing. I wasn't about to let "sex" be my selling point for Jax.

I love sex. And if I'm with someone, I like to have it 5-6 nights a week, Sunday mornings, and twice on Tuesdays. I really love sex. But my trust has been so torn up, and my body has been hurt, my heart has been hurt. I wasn't about to let someone in. Not just yet.

Maybe I needed to make him jump a few hoops before I'd let him that close to me. Not because I didn't trust him, but I think I needed to do that for me. In my mind, I figured if this guy was really interested in me, he would wait if I needed him to.
Right?

Or, maybe by not sleeping with him right away, it would be a pretty basic way to see what his intentions were going to be with me.

The one thing I've learned about Jax since meeting him is that he never had hurtful intentions. He's not someone who is out to hurt you, or to cause you pain. He has a good heart. He does have a strong mind, and a sharp perspective on things, but a mean heart? No. Not even close.

I place a lot of value on people who speak up and speak their mind. People who don't let the opinions or beliefs of others sway their mindset. He is one of those people. That is why despite any of the romantic up and downs of our friendship, he ultimately has always had my respect and my friendship. And he knows that.

That Monday morning when I left for work, I was still in awe of the simple fact that my one and only date since moving to Hampton was still sound asleep in my bed. I had been out of the dating game for a long time, but I guess I still had it.

Around ten in the morning or so on that Monday, while at my office, I receive a text from Jax. He must have just woken up. He thanked me for letting him stay the night, to which my reply was, *"It was really nice having you there"*. And it was.

Any night he spent in my bed, I was happy about it. Put aside the fact that I loved his kisses, his touch, or simply him on top of me making things feel really, *really good*, I liked his arms being completely around me when we slept.

When he would crawl into my bed every early Saturday morning when he'd be coming off of work, he would always slide into my bed as quietly as he could, in order not to wake me.
He would then slowly start to tickle my back, and kiss my shoulders.
It was his way of letting me know he was there.
I'm pretty sure he knew how on edge I was about robbers and break-ins, so he never made any sudden movements anytime he got into my bed.

Over the next few days, we would text a little here and there. Our conversations were usually always pretty simple, short and sweet. Which was ok for me. Because I was always busy with my job and with my home.

Eventually with his work schedule at the Irving refinery, seeing each other was becoming next to impossible. I worked days. He worked nights. I was happy for him that he was getting good work, because I knew he liked to work, but at the same time, I remember thinking what awful timing. Just when you're starting to get to know somebody you want those opportunities to be able to see them. After having a few dates with a person you know if the feeling is fading or if it's turning into something a little more.

During the next few weeks we barely saw one another. He would almost always send me a text message around five or six in the evening, just saying hi and to ask me how my day was before he would have to be starting work. His simple texts more times than not put a smile on my face. During those weeks he began working, the only way we were really able to see one another was on those early Saturday mornings when he would crawl into my bed while I was still asleep.

He would cruise on home in his truck from Saint John, and pull into my driveway just as the sun was coming up.
Those handful of Saturdays we had together were some of my nicest Saturdays when I lived in Hampton.

I'm a go'er. I wake up, *and I go*.

I work out, I run errands, I clean, I bake, I garden, I do laundry.

I Go.

Having this change of pace and getting into some-what of a routine for a little bit of laziness on my Saturdays, this was a much needed change of pace for me.

At this point I still hadn't gave it up with him. I was growing a little tired of our PG 13 mornings. Not that they were completely PG 13, but realistically, enough was enough. It had been about a month, maybe more since meeting him. We had quite a few visits considering our work schedules. So eventually I sort of knew that it was time for the good stuff.

Sex isn't a big deal. I know this. People do it every day all over the world. Lots of the young women in this area seemed to do it so much they even got a cheque per baby from our government to help pay for the all the kids they had.

But for me, it's always more than *just sex.* I don't sleep around.

I don't judge anyone who does. I honestly couldn't care less if you do it for a career or if you decide to join the convent. But for me, I like laying my head down on my pillow at night knowing that I'm not an easy woman.

I'm the furthest thing from easy.
I'm layered. I'm complicated. I have a temper. I can make irrational emotionally driven decisions and be completely unapologetic while doing it. As I've gotten older, the emotionally driven decision making process has finally taken a bit of a back seat.

A giving heart, *yes,* but I'm also sensitive, and sentimental. I cherish things, and usually longer then I should.

I love giving unexpected gifts, or volunteering. When I was a little girl there were so many moments where I wish my momma didn't have to work so hard to make ends meet. I wished I had someone around more. Someone to just help. So now that I am a woman and I have the resources to help, I do.

Whether it's reading to a little girl whose mum can't be there for her, or walking the shelter dogs who have no families on my Friday nights. These are the things that take up my time and fill my heart.

Chasing boys or texting men has really never been my thing.

I can fly off the handle if you piss me off, or if I feel tricked or fooled. That's probably the biggest one.
Once I get the smallest suspicion that I'm being used or possibly being tricked, I fly right off the handle.

I'm easy to become weary of certain things, I suppose.

I can't help but still keep my eye out for a motive when people are eager to come into my life.

But at the end of the day, my good experiences these days far out weight my bad ones. I have worked really hard to re-build that reality.

Nothing is out of my reach, and I know this about myself. That good old quote *"If you can see it in your mind, you can hold it in your hands"*.

My dreams work; because *I work*.
It's as simple as that.

It takes a lot more than a few nice dates and sweet compliments to get my panties to drop.
I have to really like you. And not just like you, but have that *feeling* about you.
And I know that having that feeling about someone usually only happens once every few years for me.

The next Saturday morning that Jax came over was a great Saturday morning.
It was early, with the sun barely rising.
I felt him crawl into my bed before he even did his usual back tickles to wake me up. Within a few minutes he was on top of me, and it was exactly what I needed.

The sex was good. *Really good.* Within the first few minutes I was an exceptionally happy woman.

We did it three times that Saturday.

That was a great Saturday.

We even broke my bed. The one and only time I have ever broke a bed during sex.

Even though by me telling this story, and by the sounds of things, one would think that I should have never had a worry in the world. Doesn't all this sound great?

It sounds great because it was great.

It was laid back between us, I was trusting him. Each time we would sleep together it was more than enough to keep me satisfied, and to keep me loyal. We had never discussed what we "were" exactly.

Any woman who is seeing someone, a woman who actually cares and who isn't sleeping around with other men, it's only natural that she's going to want to know where she stands with a man. It's how we keep things organized in our head. We just want to know.

But come October we began to drift apart. He didn't seem interested in ever really seeing me and the text messages became less and less.

This really hurt me.

Which, I wish it didn't, *but it did.*
The only thing that came to my mind, the only *rational* thing was pretty simple -he just wanted to have sex with me. Once having sex a few times, the guy loses interest and will pursue something else. Whether or not this is accurate, this is how it felt. Eventually I became un-interested in contacting him at all.

Move on.

Maybe there were a few reasons why he no longer was coming around.
Maybe it had nothing to do with his feelings towards me.
But he sure never gave me any kind of explanation. And I wasn't about to ask for one.
Not over a month and half of dealing with a guy. I knew better.

After a few weeks had gone by it was mid-November.
It was five in the morning, and I was lying awake in my bed (I'm a bad sleeper)
Something Jax's visits made easier for me. But with him now not around, I was back to waking up throughout the night.

My phone rings.

I looked twice at my screen, "Jax" was written on the incoming call.
I remember being so confused. Maybe it was a pocket dial?

I pick up, *"Hello"*
"I'm outside your front door" he says.

"What?!" I say to him.

So out of the blue. Completely unexpected.

I get out of bed, put on my robe, and as I looked out my window of my front door, there he was in a black sweater and baseball hat.

And there was his truck, parked in its usual spot on my drive way.

I opened the door and asked him in a *not so friendly manner* why he was here. After over a month of not hearing from him he shows up on my porch at the crack of dawn.

Not ok!

Deep down I was glad he was there, but I was also angry with him.
What makes him think he can just show up unannounced?!

As my brain was telling me to stand my ground and slam the door on his face, the panties I had on under my robe were yelling *"shut up ya old lonely prude, the sex is good, invite him in!"*

Panties won.

I invited him in.

We stood in my entry way for a few minutes, he seemed confused as to why *I was confused.*
All he kept saying was that he just wanted to see me.
The whole thing caught me so off guard. But at the same time, I wasn't born yesterday.
A part of me knew he didn't show up to have pancakes with me before work. There was probably a pretty simple explanation as to why he pulled into my drive way that morning.

Even though in the back of my head I could heard myself saying *"Do not sleep with him. You're angry at him. Be angry at him".*

During those moments when we made our way back to my bedroom and crawled into my bed together, I knew all too well what I wanted.

I had missed him during those weeks, and I wanted more than just a cuddle from him.
Which he happily delivered.

The Tipping Point

That fall was a hard couple months for me. Looking back, it all makes sense now, but while going through those days, I wasn't seeing things clearly. I had my blinders on. Big time.
It was nothing Jax was doing, but the feelings surrounding that whole time did involve him. And as it would turn out his place in my world during those weeks leading up to Christmas would be life changing time for me. And like most of those times in our life, we never understand it until we're through it.

That morning he came over, as confused as I was as to why he showed up so out of the blue, I was still happy he was in my bed and in my home. While I put the coffee on and fed the animals, I remember that feeling of being almost relieved that he was there. I realized this about him since the first moment I met him, which was that he brought me a certain amount of comfort. He brought a *steady-calm* into my world anytime he was around. I can say very truthfully that's something I have a hard time providing for myself. It's always been hard for me to feel secure about my surroundings. Growing up and having no real sense of security, as you become an adult, I think it's hard to recognize just what that should look like.

But when I met Jax, and those mornings waking up beside him, I knew he had it. He provided it. I could feel that sense of safety in my bones anytime he was around.

And it was really nice.

Getting into my car that morning and driving into work, I remember having no clear feelings about him, or whatever it was that we had. I just remember putting on the radio, hearing a Mariah Carey song come on, and I laughed. I laughed right out loud. Because in that moment I really had no care about any relationship or any desire to want to commit or *seek-out* a committed *anything*, with *anyone*. I just had a really great morning with someone who not only meant something to me as a friend, but on top of that, the sex was fantastic. I think it was in that moment when I subconsciously decided that I was no longer going to attach my sense of self *anything* into the actions or *lack of actions* that were shown towards me by a man.

I can't tell you how freeing it was. I can still remember to this very day that during that moment of turning on the radio and hearing Mariah Carey come on, I very briefly thought to myself *"I wonder if he'll find the coffee in the fridge to brew himself a cup in case he feels like a coffee"*. But very quickly my thoughts began to speak loud and clear. And those thoughts said *"who gives a fuck if the guy brews a cup of coffee, let's just hope he remembers to grab all his shit before he leaves because he ain't coming back!"*

I moved to Hampton because I needed to start over. I needed out of Ottawa. I needed to be as far away as possible from Petawawa. I needed a saving grace. And New Brunswick has always been that place for me.

Being in Hampton, where nobody knew me, it was the answer to my prayers. During the summer months the families on my street became my circle of friends. My neighbours to the left of me, the Germans', I had become their unofficial daughter. Sunday home cooked meals, or Saturday mornings helping me chainsaw the branches off the old trees in my yard, *anything and everything,* they were there for me.

I spent my evenings at the town gym. My Saturday's taking care of my home and doing my hobbies; gardening, crosswords, antique shopping, you name it; I kept busy. And I kept myself out of whatever type of "scene" someone could be in.

Although by November, I started feeling un-easy. About everything. About where I was living, the job I was doing, and the emptiness of my home at night. I was on edge at work and it was effecting my relationship with my boss. My boss was an amazing lady. She worked really hard. She was one of those women in the work force who make things happen. If she wants something done, she doesn't stop pushing until she sees through the changes she wants made. I love working for people like that.

I have no use or much respect for people who conform to the extent where they are puppets.

Because I was constantly on edge and unsure of where I would be living come the New Year, any time my boss would ask something of me, or put a deadline on me, I would push back. We had a few words on a few occasions in her office.

It got bad.

The worst part was that in over seven years of being a working woman in the professional world, never once have I had a clash with any of my bosses. I'm a very hard worker. I'm reliable. And I see things through; *every time.* I knew by having these closed-door blow outs with her in her office, I knew this was not me. This was not my character. Something was wrong.

But for whatever reason I guess I began questioning everything. Anytime something happens in my life, I run. I'm a runner. And I know this about myself.
I've become really good at it over the years.
I have my list of phone calls to make when moving towns or switching provinces. I even know the best rates with moving companies between Nova Scotia and Ontario.
I can drive that Trans Canada highway with my eyes closed.

But I didn't want to run anymore. It isn't the cheapest thing in the world to do. Even though no matter where I go that's new, I always find a way to make a good living. I have learned to become really creative with how to save a dollar, or to *flip* a dollar.

When something hurts me, all I want to do is pack up and leave. Sometimes we can't always process the things that happen to us all at once. Sometimes it takes weeks, months, even *years* to come to terms with how something came to be in our life.

But every day spent in our past is a day lost in our future.

The day my marriage ended my entire world changed. It didn't matter that I had grown up fast, or that I had seen and been places during my younger years that took my rose coloured glasses away from me. None of that really mattered. The night my marriage ended I was 24. I was young. I was alone.

Nothing in this world could have prepared me for the outcome of that night. I'm not talking about the discussion that my now ex-husband and I had that made us come to the finalization that our marriage was over, but the night which changed everything. The night he was handcuffed and put into a police car.

I sat in our family room in my bath robe and watched him in his blue jeans and white t-shirt with both hands cuffed behind him. I remember that moment clear as day. My body was full of pains. My eyes were soaked in tears. My trust in a man, *any man*, was destroyed.

The depth of those hurts have travelled with me for a few years too many. And even though I had forgiven him years ago, and my heart has since healed from those years, not a day goes by where I don't remember the events of that night. The flashbacks can still cripple me at times.

My ex-husband and I were set to finalize our divorce on December 20th, 2014. Ironically, December 20th would have been our sixth year wedding anniversary. A few weeks prior to driving up to Fredericton to meet him at the lawyers, I remember I began feeling angry. Not because I was now going to be a divorced twenty eight year old, but I was feeling angry because everything was becoming very real for me.

During that November my days at work were becoming long. They were busy. Stressful. And my nights were stone cold and spent alone. Jax was no longer around. After he showed up that morning on my porch, I didn't hear much from him for a few weeks. Even though I tried to convince myself that I didn't care, because I didn't want a commitment from anyone, it still hurt me. Rejection has this beautiful way of hurting you and strengthening you all at the same time. Viscous process. But no matter what, always worth it once you are through it.

That's just about the only thing you can tell yourself when you're feeling rejected or un-wanted. It sucks to be in that place of pain, but the longer you dwell on it, the longer you'll remain there. So once you decide to move on from it, you'll be much better for it. And moving on from it, despite how hard it may feel at the time, that's a choice we make. Learning to be in charge of your thoughts is the only way you're going to be more powerful than your opponent. Whether your opponent is a person or feeling, you have to make the decision to get over it.

Don't let the temporary relief that the wrong person is giving you fool you into thinking it's the right thing for you. In some way I had been searching for fulfillment from the promises of other people. But the moment I'd reach out for help, nobody would be reaching out for me.

Fastest way to feel hopeless – look to others for a purpose.
Fastest way to feel powerful – look to you. And only you.

If the only colour you're currently seeing right now is black, hang onto the above statement. Remember that easy truth.

Find whatever strength or talent is inside of you, then run with it. Whether it's writing, singing, flipping houses, running a charity or basket weaving. Find what's *meant for you* and give that your love. Once you start loving what's meant for you, the right love will *find you.*

Even though ultimately I felt used by Jax, I told myself not to hold it against him.

It was what it was.

So move on.

With my upcoming divorce finalization around the corner, when I look back I now realize just how much anger was still inside me. I love to love. And I love to have someone in my world who I can do things for, and do things with. It's not about me just wanting to please someone to fill a void, it's truly about the pure want and desire to simply *give love.*

Having a good man somewhere in the picture, having my home, my animals, that is when I am at my best. Sure, I can work the career world. I can go head to head with anyone no matter where I am or what I'm doing. I'd never want to be put up against myself in any aspect of the work world. I'm smart, sharp, and fast. My work ethic will run circles around you. And that's a sure thing.

I've bet my entire independence on it.

So the proof is in the pudding, *gentlemen.*

But where I'm truly happy, where I'm most myself, is in my home and in my kitchen. Cooking and baking and being with my loved ones. I wanted babies. I wanted a little girl who would be momma's little butterfly and daddy's little sweetheart. I wanted to have a son, a son who I would name after his daddy. I wanted to pack their lunches and see them off onto their school bus every morning.

I wanted that life.

In my mind there is nothing more beautiful than the love of a family. I believe in the highest of highs' that a woman can achieve total greatness. But for a woman to raise her babies, to give love to her man, and hold down the home, that's my cup of warm tea. The pure simplicity of being able to lay down at night beside your littles ones and read them they're bedtime story. For me, that would have been my lottery ticket.

The day that I have truly achieved my greatest potential as a woman will be the day where I become a mum. Because that would mean that I had managed to steer my life in a direction that enabled me to be lined up with the right kind of love, the right kind of man. And if I ever got to that place, it would be because I had fully learned how to love myself that way I should have been loving myself all along.

When you finally learn to love yourself in the right ways, you won't accept anything less from anyone else.

As human beings, we spot people's shortcomings faster than we spot or even look for their strengths. So as women if we aren't overly ecstatic about accepting a man's physical shortcoming, why do we accept an emotional short coming. Or a moral short coming.

That is why the very well known *learn to love yourself* mantra has been one of such popularity all these years.

But did any of us really understand what it even meant?

The literal translation, sure. We more than likely understood the general concept surrounding the words.

But I don't think you'll ever really understand those words until you experience that truth in the physical.

I have nothing to prove to anyone. I've already done it. Take five minutes and look into my life. I have vivid memories of my grade 10 Math teacher and grade 11 English teacher letting me know that I had a bland future ahead of me if my marks didn't change. I have been knocked down onto my knees more than once by people who I thought I loved. I have lost people. I have left people. And there have been numerous moments where I have had to work twice as hard as the person beside me in order to be recognized for my abilities.

What I will admit is what I believe to be true. There are certain things in life that are without a doubt tried, tested and true. History does not lie. In fact, if you slow down and take a peek back you will see for yourself. Certain old fashion values were considered values for a reason.

Women hold many talents that men are just not hardwired with. We have the ability to nurture those who are sick, (not that men can't nurture), but we tune into the action a lot faster. And that level of nurturing comes extremely natural. We can tune into our compassionate and empathetic side more easily than our aggressive side.

As a woman I know where my strengths are most useful. My body was not built to build brick houses. My body nor my mind was built to protect my home from intruders. Regardless if I can load a snappy little Beretta and never miss a target. Or shove a few rounds into a 22 and start firing, in my heart, deep down underneath my Sasha Fierce Independent Woman life that I created, I never wanted those responsibilities to be on my list of required duties.

I do believe I was put on this earth to nurture. To provide my love for those *who I love*, and for my support to be available anytime it's needed.

The past ten years of my life I have been walking my path doing the complete opposite. My abilities of strength and independence have been on full display for anyone and everyone to see loud and clear. But as fulfilling as some of those years have been, what most people didn't see were all the moments I was alone and *not feeling strong*.

My shoulders are not big, and bearing the weight of always solely providing for myself does break me down. Walking through the grocery store with perfect strangers looking you up and down, or older men starring at you as if you're shopping alone *just because*, or if you're shopping alone because you *are alone*.

So let nature run its course. If you are lucky to find yourself at night in the arms of a hardworking man who always helps you remember just how beautiful you are, enjoy it. And when you wake up and turn over and see him sleeping there peacefully because he's aware that he found his bliss when he found you, then my only advice to you would be to take that life.

Love it.

And know that you are so blessed to have it.

Know that you have the self-awareness and skill set to be able to do it all, but also know what type of environment you see yourself in in order to be the absolute best version of herself.

By early December, I had come to the conclusion that I wasn't sure if I was going to stay here in New Brunswick anymore. In my mind, I had come out here in the spring, and I needed that, for a multitude of reasons. And it had served me well. But now I was beginning to worry that my need to "escape" out here was a move solely based on panic. And now that the storm had reached its calm, being two provinces away from my family didn't seem realistic anymore.

In the past nine years I have moved fifteen times. I had a very hard time staying anywhere longer than six months before I would pack my things and change postal codes. But after the fall had passed in Hampton, I guess I just felt alone. I was beginning to realize that I needed my sweet, safe and quiet here in Hampton to heal from a few things. And that I needed those early Saturday mornings on my porch with my coffee. That I needed to come *all the way out here*, to do those things. I needed my New Brunswick ocean air. My big tall green New Brunswick trees. My roads. But now I was contemplating the various reasons as to why it wouldn't make much sense to *remain* out here long-term.

I figured I would move back to Ontario come the spring of 2015. Just slightly over a year from the day I got back here.

Looking back, I'm well aware that some of my life choices or moving patterns pretty clearly say *"M-E-N-T-A-L H-E-A-L-T-H I-S-S-U-E-S"*.

But to be perfectly honest, I think I was very lonely. I had the freedom and ability to get up and move as I pleased, so I never saw anything particularly unstable about doing it. But I think if you're in a place in your life where you're happy, or at minimum, content, you don't make drastic moves every 6-8 months. That old quote, *"Happiness isn't a destination, it's a mindset"*.

I was a person who felt incredibly alone, and deep down, I was really sad.

There was a very small moment, a very *specific* conversation I shared with Jax early one Sunday morning in December. And if it wasn't for that conversation on that morning, I wouldn't be sitting where I am right now.

The doors that have opened for me after 2014 came to a close, I would have never dreamed of. So for that, I *thank you Jax*. I was seconds away from making one of the biggest, *truly biggest* mistakes of my life.

I was about to run.

Again.

But this was my tipping point.

And he just happened to be right there, right smack dab in the middle of it. And because he was, whether he knew it or not, he stopped me from leaving my place of grace.

He broke my bad habit.

Not too many people can change my mind once it's made up, *yet he did.* He called out so many parts of me that morning as we sat on his living room couch with coffees.

We had gotten into a conversation about New Brunswick and why we both love it so much. For me, it has become my home in so many ways. Because here in New Brunswick is where I feel safe. It's where I have always come to re-build after any storm.

For Jax, he was born and raised here. It is not only his home because he grew up in these parts, but it's his home because he loves it just as much, *if not more* than I do.

The rolling hills. The amazing hidden waterfalls. The people of the East coast. The clean air. The open roads. The views.

Everything.

Everything and anything.

That Sunday morning in December as I began explaining to Jax that I was thinking about leaving, he looked at me and asked a very simple question; *"Why?".*

I don't like when people ask me *why.* I have a hard time figuring out if they are genuinely curious as to *why something is,* or if they are just looking for secondary information. But the moment he asked me why I thought leaving New Brunswick was a good idea it forced me to sit on that for a moment, and to actually *really think about it.*

I didn't say anything right away. I remember I was sitting on the one side of his couch with my legs crossed underneath me and I looked down at the floor in a blank stare. He then spoke up and began describing all the beautiful things about New Brunswick. And that each and every time he would be away out West for work for months and months at a time in the oil fields, he reminded me in great detail *how* and *why* coming home to New Brunswick was so important to him. He looked right at me and spoke about the rolling hills that can only be found out here in NB. He went on about all the beautiful reasons why New Brunswick is home.

During our conversation that morning, I couldn't help but remember that Sunday back in September on his bike. How beautiful it was. How healing it was for me, for *so many reasons*. He was still unaware of all the pains that were inside the girl on his bike that day. But something in me knew that *he knew* he had helped me in some way.

At this point in time Jax and I were not a couple in any way. We were very rarely seeing one another, maybe once every couple of weeks. But that morning he spoke directly to my heart whether he knew it or not. It was his words and *his words only* that helped me remember where my heart truly was.

It was not in Ontario.

The idea of moving back there was simply a reflection of my *run away* habits. When I get uncomfortable – *I just go.*

The idea of Ontario was not a true reflection on where I wanted to go or where I wanted to be at that time. Moving provinces was not going to solve my problems. It was not going to erase the pains and regrets I was still holding onto. It was simply an old bad habit that was starting to become really expensive.

During those few hours of much needed conversation that morning, putting aside the failed dating attempts, or blow outs that I had with him over something as silly as feeling insecure on whether we were dating or not, that morning there were no more questions for me. It was like he had turned a new page in my mind. Maybe he knew deep down and could see through my fog of confusion that I was on the edge of making a big mistake.

Or maybe he didn't see any of that. Maybe he was simply sharing his love of this place with me in hopes that I would agree, and not pack up and simply disappear. Whatever it was, I am grateful to him for that morning. He parted the clouds and removed a layer of fog that was keeping me blind. By the simplicity of his true and direct words he broke my six year running habit.

Just like that.

Home Sweet Titusville

Come the New Year, during the first week of January 2015, I was at my office in Saint John extra early for some reason that morning. While going through my work emails I opened the real estate listings on my computer, *just to take a peek*. With all the details of Jax and I behind me, I was ready to get on with things and possibly make a move, but not a far one. I was still living in my little rental house right in the town of Hampton. I was happy there, and comfortable. But with the $1000.00 monthly rental fee, financially, continuing to rent wasn't making sense anymore.

The house had served its purpose. It was a great little crash pad. But now it was time for another mortgage. This would be the second home I was purchasing solo during my twenties. But moving was something I had become so well versed in that finding the home, the realtor, landing a lawyer for a minute to sign paperwork wasn't something that ever overwhelmed me. If it was smart financially to purchase and line up a move, then I would do it. Taking care of the details would just be additional *things to handle* that I would add into my day.

I opened the realtor webpage, typed in my price range, chose my location, and there it was—My Home Sweet Home, *Titusville.*

Picture the most beautiful story book farm house.

White siding, black shingled roof, deep red front porch that lined the entire front of the house. Surrounded by acres upon acres of tall grass and peaceful woods. A long gravel driveway with three 100 year old poppler trees lighting the way to the main *side door* of the home.

It was beautiful.

The house itself was 105 years old. The structural soundness to the home didn't worry me one bit. Back in those days houses like this were framed by two by six's. A tornado could blow through Titusville, and that house would still be standing.

The inside of this house was even more beautiful than the outside it seemed. Natural pine hardwood throughout. The kitchen had beautiful, light natural tone coloured tile floors. Beautiful solid wood kitchen cabinets with the perfect farm house window above the sink with a view of all the land. Green, fresh, beautiful land that I would own if I decided to purchase this property. Tall ceilings. Thick, Victorian era trim and door frames. It was old, but my Lord was it ever beautiful. Of course like any home over the age of 50, if you let a marble roll loose on the floors, that marble will roll forever. But if you could get over the wonky floors, you were in for a treat. The foundation was stone with a four foot width. This home was here to stand for another 100 years.

It had been on the market for about one year, completely vacant. It was a bank repo. Which was great news for me as I would be able to purchase this home for the tiny price of $103,000.00 dollars.

Yes, you read that right. This was a 2,200 square foot, four bedroom two bathroom home with a sale price of 100 grand. Even if this wasn't a bank repo, the listing price would only be maybe twenty grand more. One of the perks of living in Atlantic Canada is the real estate. A home like this just on the outskirts of Toronto would easily run you $600,000.00, maybe even more. But in Titusville, sweet little Titusville, it was nothing more than the cost of two SUV's.

Titusville is a tiny little town just ten minutes outside of Hampton. Each home having its own few acres, some that had more. And each home seemed to be occupied by the most kind, loving families. People would ask me all the time why I chose to move out there. Besides the famous *Titusville General Store*, there was nothing out there. Just green fields, older homes, one street light, and the most amazing sky full of stars each night the sun would set.

I think a part of me was still healing. A part of me was still hurting.

Seclusion. Alone time. Serenity. Titusville is all those things.

And what could possibly be more peaceful than a neighbour who was 65 years old and spoke with a Southern New Brunswick accent so thick, even his *cows* had a hard time understanding what he was saying.

But this is where I would buy my dream home.

As I sit here and write this portion of the story, I am no longer living in my Titusville dream home, although the home I now sit in is quite sweet, very cute and small, it's not Titusville. And I'm reminded of that every time I walk into my small, commercially built non-unique bathroom. A far cry from my floor to ceiling beautifully tiled *extra deep soaker tub* Titusville bathroom.

By 4:30 pm that very same day I made arrangements to meet the listing realtor to view this house. Prior to being able to see it, due to it being practically in the middle of nowhere, the realtor said that unfortunately due to so many people seeing this home out of pure interest, but not having their financing lined up, she would only show this home if I had proof of financing.

I told the realtor "*No problem. Give me an hour*".

I called my accountant, gave her the MLS ID#, and within the hour she faxed me a letter from my bank stating approval to purchase.

I left my office at 4:00 pm and headed straight to Titusville. When I got there the realtor was only minutes behind me. I immediately did a walk around the home. Examined the outside, the roof (which needed replacing) the overall structure of the home. You can usually tell a lot by just the outside of a home. I looked at every area of exposed stone foundation, the windows, whether or not structural lines were straight, and the porch, *all of it*. So far, no major concerns. No deal breakers.

Upon entering the house, you walked into this great spacious mud room which had a dark wood flooring, fresh white trim, and a huge bench to sit on that ran across the extra-large window. In this mud room was an over-sized closet and a glass farm house interior door that opened up into the main living area of the home. The wall colours were beautiful. Pale greens, warm beige's. It was pure, rustic country warmth. The floor boards in the next room were a rustic laminate. It was so natural looking and appeared thick, it had grey tones more than warm pine tones, but it was stunning.

Then came the kitchen. Unlimited cabinet space with extra-large tiles in a pale pink/beige that covered the entire floor. The counter tops were done in tile that looked like marble. An updated coriander sink which was later finished off with an antique looking faucet that Jax had installed for me late on a Sunday night.

The rest of the home was pine hardwood. The stair case needed a little TLC, but it was nothing an electric hand sander and a few coats of stain wouldn't fix. I re-did my staircase in my sweet as pie yellow house, so I would follow suit in Titusville.

The upstairs bathroom had an antique vanity. Anyone who enjoys Pinterest will know exactly how I felt when I walked into this over-sized renovated master bathroom that had an oak vanity. It had the most detailed carvings on the knobs, the legs, and the drawers. It was finished with a deep mahogany-like stain. The counter top was tile (again that looked like marble) with an equally elegant backsplash that went about 6 inches up the wall. A black rustic faucet with an aged Victorian style white porcelain sink.

After spending about one hour in the home, while the realtor was doing her job explaining how cute each room would look with the right curtains or lounge chairs, I was more focused on the important things. Some of the plumbing had been re-done, was is it done properly? It looked good. But I knew I'd have Jax come and look over it all just to be sure.

Electric panel updated? Yep. How many amps? 100. Should be 200, but if it's just me living there, 100 will be fine.

Roof--Needs replacing. If I find the right guy, it could be done for five or six thousand. A new roof is never a deal breaker. It's to be expected when you're looking at older homes.

Foundation. Am I going to sink? Well, with the six steel jack posts all on two by two concrete pads, not to mention the huge tree log running through the center of the house with a diameter wider than the trees on Vancouver Island, this home was solid. There were no signs of rotting floor boards that I could see while in the basement. At this point there was nothing stopping me from making an offer.

But -- the septic tank. With bank repo homes nothing is disclosed. No history of the home, no history of flooding, or plumbing issues. That's the risk you take for the bargain price you're getting the home for. If the septic tank was steel, it would most likely be rotting by now and in need of replacing within a few years or sooner. The price to have a new septic done on your land? Between excavating and the current price of concrete for the new concrete tank, you could be up against fifteen thousand or so. I told myself that unless I somehow found a way to get information about that septic tank, I couldn't blindly walk into purchasing this home.

While driving home after spending about an hour at the house, I decided to call up Chevy. He grew up just down the road from this house, so maybe he had some information on any of the previous owners. And most importantly, whether or not the septic had been re-done. And just like usual, the man came through. He had the name of the young man who owned the home just two years before me. I was assuming this was probably the last person who owned the place before it ultimately became property of the bank. Within minutes I was able to track down the young guy from the internet. I sent him a message with a small introduction that I was basically wondering if he had any knowledge about the septic tank. By the next morning I had gotten a response from him. *"Hey! Ya, I lived in that house for a couple years. The septic was re-done by the neighbour, the farmer. It was done in 2009. It's concrete".*

Within a few short minutes I called the listing agent and told her I was ready to put in an offer. However, she had some news that made me a little nervous. *"Well, there's another offer on the table. A young guy. Works for the Irving's. His financing was approved. He's ready to purchase"*

"Shit". I said to myself. *"Ok, well, obviously highest bidder wins, so my offer is full price. Full listing price"*

Due to how the real estate game works here in New Brunswick, everyone comes in a little bit under asking. No over-bidding takes place out in these parts. So with the insanely low price of the home to begin with, I wasn't going to miss out of not getting it over missing the bid by four or five grand.

The very next morning the listing agent called me *"Congratulations Victoria, the house is yours!"*

I was over the moon excited. I knew the other bidder wouldn't have come in at full asking price. My best guess was he would have thrown out $95,000.00 or $98,000.00. And I was right. His offer was just in that area. From owning a home before, I knew that ultimately five grand more would only make a difference of maybe forty bucks on my bi-weekly mortgage payment. So in my eyes, there was no bidding war to be had.

That house was built to be mine.

Period.

The Real Adventure Begins

February 13th, 2015, on an extra cold, extra snow filled Friday morning, the moving company arrives to my completely packed up rental home in Hampton. They were to load the truck and travel fifteen minutes down the road to my dream home, Home Sweet Titusville.

Only a few weeks earlier I had seen an ad on the internet about a litter of puppies. But these weren't any regular, wildly known dogs, these were Presa Canario's. I'll let you to the *Google Image search* these beauties. I knew with moving into my farm house, I was definitely ready to have another big heart beat with me again. After the years of instability due to a bad relationship and constantly moving, having a dog wasn't in the cards. And to be honest, after the death of my pupp, I was never quite ready to love another dog until this time frame.

I sent an email to the man who had bred the Presa puppies. I knew he was sure to be receiving hundreds of emails from all kinds of people all throughout the Maritimes, and with his connections, other parts of the world. I was sure to explain my history with not only my love of all animals, but my experience with my Pit Bulls. My strength from being in the Combat Arms in the military. But most importantly, my promise of being able to provide the perfect type of living situation for a dog of this caliber.

I sent that email during the morning hours while at work, and by six in the evening that same day, I had received a response. In my original email I had specified that a male puppy would have been my preference. In the response I received, I was told I could come see the puppies to see if the breed would be a good match. But more importantly, the breeders wanted to meet *me*. And basically, size me up.

The puppies were at a kennel in Shediac, New Brunswick. A short hour and a half drive from Hampton. So in the early morning on the following Saturday in January of 2015, I got in my car and drove up to Shediac. I was beyond excited to meet the puppies. I had the proper amount of cash and my GPS all set with the address.

Upon arriving, as I walked up to the front door of the building, the front door opened. This is where I met Shane. The breeder himself. What I was later to find out was that not only was he a passionate man about working dogs, but he was Canada's only black belt Jiu Jitsu World Champion. Trained and mentored by the one and only Jiu Jitsu Master himself, *Rickson Gracie.*

So this wasn't just your average dog breeder. As the door opened and I was greeted by this man, I was unknowingly going to develop a lifelong lasting friendship with a semi-retired World Champion fighter.

He first brought me into the training room. This was a simple room, concrete floors with various training aids in the room. Shane had been living in the apartment that was above the kennel.

Also soon to arrive was a very special woman. Vanessa. Daughter of the man who owned the actual kennel. A woman who not only is an amazing light all on her own, but she became a sister to me. And both these people, Shane and Vanessa, would be the two people by my side in years to come.

After sitting with Shane in the training room for about twenty minutes talking about the breed, he was ready for me to meet some of the dogs one by one. He was diligent in giving me a background on the actual *history* of these dogs. Explaining to me that this breed and their blood line was almost like holding a loaded fifty caliber machine gun in your hand, with the safety switch turned to *off.* And it was my duty to be capable in having total control of my animal at all times. Or else simply put, I wouldn't be fit to buy one.

When Shane returned to the training room from out back where the dogs were, I was expecting to see a room fill with some of the puppies. Many of them were still not spoken for. But Shane had his own plan. He knew he needed to see how I would not only react, but physically handle a full grown version of what my puppy had the potential to become.

In walks Shane with the stud on a leash. My eyes opened wide. This dog was huge. Tall. Pure muscle. Extremely intimidating. I have been around and seen a multitude of *bully breed* type dogs, but anything I had experienced in the past had nothing on what I was looking at. Shane gave me the leash and said *"Here. Take him for a walk around the room. I want to see how well he listens to you"* Basically an on the spot test to see if I could comfortably handle this breed. After a few small walks around the outskirts of the room, with Shane keeping his eyes locked on how his dog was responding to my lead, he was slightly impressed that all 115 pounds of me actually had a decent disposition with his dog.

He then took the stud back into the kennel out back and brought out three puppies that I was to ultimately choose from. As he came back into the room, three beautiful Presa puppies came tumbling out of his arms and excitedly onto the floor. Two of the three came right over to me. The other was more excited to wander around and do her sniffing. All three puppies were female. *"Oh, I'm interested in a male puppy. Are any male puppies unspoken for?"*

Ever so gently, Shane very clearly stated *"I'm not sending you home with a male Presa. A female is best suited for you"*.

And after really learning the breed, and with the months to come while raising the puppy I had taken home that day, Shane was right. A male would have been too powerful for me. Not just physically speaking, but *mind set*. Shane could see that I was strong, but not *male Presa* strong.

I was sitting cross legged on the floor while watching these puppies tumble and roll and one at a time come give me their sniffs and kisses. I had my eyes on one of the three who had markings like a tiger. But the colours were inverted. She looked like a baby African tiger cub. I couldn't get over how stunning she was. But ultimately, she wouldn't be the puppy who would win my heart. The smaller of the three who was mostly all black, or *black brindle*, she some-what nervously walked over to me, sniffed my knees, then ever so gently crawled into my lap. She did a few circles on my legs before she would plunk down and curl up in a little ball right between my legs. She took one look up at me, and with her deep brown eyes, she had just picked her new mummy. Once we locked eyes, I knew this shy, white toe'd, black brindle Presa puppy was the one I was going to bring home. Right away Vanessa says *"I think you found your baby. Or more so, your baby found you! That's Ritsa. Her name means human guardian."*

Everything about that moment lined up by the working of the stars. Ritsa was going to be my guardian. A heartbeat soft enough to be my sweet pokey girl, but with a bloodline running through her strong enough to keep me safe.

"Nala". I said out loud. *"I really love the name Nala. It's soft."* And at the very same moment Vanessa and I both said *"Nala Ritsa"*.

And there it was.

A done deal.

While driving back home with Nala in the passenger seat beside me, I remember how at ease I felt. How excited I was to fill my *soon to be* big home with a dog almost as big. During the entire drive she was nervous. She had her little blue fleece lined jacket on, with her front paws tucked under her chest, and with pure Nala Ritsa style, she sat quietly in the passenger seat.

Her behaviour was amazing. She had already had exposure to living with a friend of the breeders, so she had her *sit-stay* and *paw* pretty much down pat. It wasn't until we pulled into the McDonalds that she actually got up off her seat. I was stopping in quick to grab a coffee for the drive home, so obviously I bought a hash brown for us to share.

Right from the very first day I brought her home, she's had a gentle disposition. Now mind you, as she became larger, and has always kept her puppy-like excitement, her disposition is still gentle, but when she's excited about something, everything about her becomes huge and requires muscle to handle.

Getting home that day wasn't as calm as the actual car ride. Once back to the rental house in Hampton, Nala was going to meet my rescue kittens, plus one rescue bunny.

Tink
Tom (who had only three legs)
Rocky
And the bunny, SummerBean

This was the first accident Nala had on the floor.

Right as we entered, all three cats hissed and began growling at her. Even though Nala stood much taller and definitely a few pounds heavier, she peed right there on the floor, tail between her legs. She was terrified.

It took a few weeks of "meeting everyone" for all the animals to finally become one family unit.

And eventually, even the bunny would be eating out of the morning breakfast bowl that I would fill with veggies and place down on the centre of my kitchen floor.

We were all happy campers.

By the end of February, we were all settled in the new house. The cats were adjusting to the huge increase of space we had. And Nala was soon to learn how to manage a 100 year old farmhouse staircase. Farmhouse staircases aren't like the ones that are built today. There's not a whole lot of *"building codes"* that go into them. So in a nut shell, they're fucking steep.

That winter in Titusville consisted of becoming settled. Adapting to my new routine of maintaining a huge home. And my most favourite part, having my morning coffee in bed on those Saturday mornings when Nala and I were able to sleep in. As each work week passed, and the spring got closer, not only was Nala continuing to get bigger, but I was beginning to wonder if getting her a friend would be a good idea.

My contract with my current position in Saint John was a mere few weeks from being over, and at that point, I still hadn't had any new contract lined up. So between job searching and slightly renovating the staircase, my hands were pretty well tied up.

About two weeks before I was to be officially jobless, I received an email on my work computer from a woman who was the Manager of a different department just a few streets away from my current office. It was a slight promotion in position level, but more so, from how she explained the job, it sounded as if I'd have a few years of promised job security. And after being a contract worker, scoring a position that had the potential to last more than one year was a very big deal.

After a formal interview and quick tour of my new-to-me working location, I was offered the position. This was *very good news*. With a new contract secured, now I could focus on enjoying the summer months that were a mere few weeks away. Focusing on my plans for all the gardens I was going to create. The huge 8x16 vegetable garden I had mapped out for a section in the back field. And best of all, my plan to bring home a brother for Nala was a definitely a green light.

At this point Nala was around six months old. So she was definitely much bigger, but this breed tends to grow very slowly. So I knew she still had a ways' to go. Therefore, her future brother would need to be comparable in size and strength. I really believe in *putting it out there* versus obsessively tracking something down just to fulfill that feeling of want or need. Forcing anything – never pans out. So put your intention out there, let it go, then what comes back to you is more than usually *for you*.

One sunny afternoon as I was sitting on my big red porch with a glass of wine, I was watching Nala roll and play on the front lawn. She was playing with the shrubs in the gardens. Tossing about small sticks that were laying around. She was pretty good at keeping herself busy, but I knew her days while I was at work would be ten times more fun if she had the company of another heart beat with her. So I called Shane.

"Hey, what do you think about getting Nala a brother? You think that would be a good idea?"

Shane's response…

"Yes, but she's a female Presa Canario, and although she's one of the more gentle of the litter, she's an alpha female Vicki, so whatever type of dog we find her, it will have to be male, no questions asked, and he will have to submit to her, immediately"

Agreed.

Shane said he would seek out a retired male German Sheppard from the Police Force. At first we both had in mind a dog maybe a bit older than Nala, but basically a dog that came with a very balanced disposition. And trained.

Regardless of where my mind drifts off to with the fantasy of having *lots of animals on my farm* Shane always kept in mind that he would never set me up with one or more dogs that would be too powerful for me. With any animal you own, you have the responsibility of ensuring you remain in control, to be *the Alpha of your pack*, to say. But it's not rocket science, when you have dog breeds that are large and strong, you *absolutely without question* are required to know what you're doing. Because if not, then your dog makes the front page news, and not for a good reason.

A few weeks went by since I had made that call to Shane. He had met a few Sheppard's from various shelters, or through people, but none that had him thinking would be a good match. It wasn't until he himself was contacted by his Uncle. And the reason for the phone call was because his Uncle had a six month old purebred Rottweiler, and due to his health issue of a recent stroke, ultimately having the Rottweiler was just too much for the family during his time of recovery.

It's early in the evening on a Sunday and I was lying in bed with Nala. I remember everything from that day. I was in bed because I had a really intense work out early that morning at the small gym in town. Mowed the lawn, and sanded down the death ridden staircase. So Nala and I were pretty wiped.

My phone rings.

It's Shane.

"Hey Vic, so… what are your thoughts on a Rottweiler?"

"Well, I mean, I never considered a Rottweiler. I don't know much about them. But I guess so?"

Shane then began to explain the situation. That his Uncle had owned a few purebred Rotties over the years. But unfortunately with his health, having this particular Rottie pupp just wasn't going to be in the cards. His Uncle had asked Shane if he could find him a good home. Shane has a huge amount of pull in the dog world, so being able to re-home any large breed high-drive dog is something Shane would more times than not be able to do.

I asked *"Well, what's he like? How big and how old is he?"*

"He's about one month older than Nala, and he's a big dude Vic, his name is Titan. And well he's… he's special, let's just say that. He eats his food like a Hoover Vacuum. I've really never seen anything like it"

Shane then sent a few photos of Titan.

I was in love.
It took less than one second for me to see his beautiful face, and I was in love. I knew ultimately Nala and him would need to meet before any decisions could be made. But the decision to have them meet in order to give the green light in bringing him back home with me, that decision was made during that phone call.

There was one thing though, *"Titan.. I don't know if I'm really feeling that name? It's sort of... to be expected, you know?"*

Shane:

"Well we can change his name Vic, what were you thinking?"

"Big Poppa"

Shane laughs.

"Ok, Big Poppa it is! I don't know how comfortable I feel calling him that... Hey Big Poppa! But if that's what you think suits him best, Big Poppa it is".

One short week later on an early Sunday morning Nala, myself and my dearest girlfriend Shana *(Southern New Brunswick's most talented and experienced hair dresser)* all pile into my Honda Accord and head up the highway to Shediac back to the Kennel. To meet the one and only...

Big Poppa.

When we pulled into the kennel, Vanessa had drove up as well to be there for the official meet and greet of Nala and Big Poppa. Before Shane brought him out, we sat in the training room and Shane went over everything about him. He explained that Big Poppa's drive was pretty intense. He did a little bit of work with him prior to me coming up and he said that with basic working training techniques, Big Poppa lit right up. The drive in Poppa was huge. And if trained properly, he would easily be an unreal protection dog.

Bravery was the emotion that put the beats into Big Poppa's heart.

This truth would be demonstrated to me every waking day that Big Poppa was with me.

Shane then went out back to the cages where Poppa was. Within a few short minutes he returned back with this very tall, very excited, stunningly beautiful Rottweiler. Big Poppa didn't even look at anyone else in the room. He locked eyes with Nala. And Nala locked eyes with him. There was no nervous sniffing or uncomfortable first few seconds of two dogs meeting one another. Within seconds Nala and Poppa were intertwined on the floor rolling, kissing and playing. We all just sort of stood there with our eyes wide open. It was pretty magical. It was pretty clear that they were destined to be together.

There wasn't an ounce of energy that pointed to the indication of possible alpha issues. Even though Poppa was as energetic and powerful as he was, something about their energy had Nala knowing that she was still secretly the alpha, and thus, they got along like peas and carrots.

That's what I would continue to say anytime someone would ask me *"What's it like having a Presa Canario and purebred Rottweiler? Do they ever fight?"*

My answer would always be the same.

"They get along like peas and carrots. My home is my most favourite place to be, because they are there".

As I type out and really, re-live this memory, tears are running down my face. And that is because some of Big Poppa is now in a small gold and diamond heart locket that sits on my chest, just above my heart.

But before he found his place forever locked into my heart, he made my world the most beautiful place it had ever been.

When Big Poppa came into my life, he ultimately saved my life. Little did I know then, that later in that year I was going to be going under the knife for the third time. My two previous corrective hip surgeries had done all that they could do, but the reality was finally settling in.

Due to *where and how* my hip broke, I had developed AVN. This condition is Avascular Necrosis. This is when there is not enough blood supply getting to the joint, therefore, the joint ultimately will begin to rot away until it dies.

And for a hip, this means nothing more than a total hip replacement. Once AVN begins to become unbearable is when the top of the hip ball is flattening (caving in) to a point where your hip is actually sitting loose in the socket. This feeling of my hip failing began to set in during the early winter months, just before I moved into my Titusville home. And although the pain was getting pretty bad, for the most part, it was only a few hours during the end hours of my days when I would be limping and in need of finally just lying in bed. I tried to keep holding out, in hopes that maybe one more winter was in the cards for me. But ultimately, I knew deep down, that it was time.

My replacement surgery was scheduled for December 14th of 2015. This date had my nerves tied up in a pretty heavy knot during the months leading up to it, but with having Nala and Big Poppa at home with me, there was no time to feel sorry for myself. I had two very big, very demanding dogs, plus a boat load of animals to care for.

In addition to bringing Big Poppa home, that summer my neighbour had brought a truck load of cows onto his property. At first, the cows where fenced in just on his land, but because my neighbour and I got along so well, I told him he was more than welcome to use my land.

Coming home to cows and bulls wandering your property?

Yes. Without question, *yes.*

His cows became our cows. And my land became our land.

Within no time, Nala and Big Poppa would be in the fields with me and the cows during the evenings when I was home from work. I had names for almost every one of them.

There was Wanda.
Sally May
Mama Tilley
Dill Pickle Donna
Trish (she was named after my fellow stripper friend, Trisha)
Goldie Hawn
Dallas Deluxe

And when the baby calves were born…

Twinkie
Tulip
Hershey
Cream Pie
Pound Cake (he was a chubby calf)

And the bulls...

Big Daddy Ron
And,
Kevin Costner

It was one very big, very happy, very funny farm-type family.

Running out the back door to go see the cows when I would get home from work was Big Poppa and Nala's favourite part of their day. My back field was big. Tall grass. Apple trees, a weeping willow, poplar tress and of course, my rhubarb patch, for all those pies I baked that summer.

Like clockwork, every evening that summer we'd be sitting out there, just the three of us with our cows. I'd have a bourbon in one hand, and my camera in the other. Nala and Big Poppa would get more and more comfortable with actually *kissing* the cows. Wanda was the easiest to steal kisses from. She was probably the sweetest of the group.

Between my long hours at my new job, keeping my house in good order and managing the animals, I had enough distractions in the fore-front of my mind to keep my nerves at bay with my surgery date slowly getting closer.

With everything Big Poppa did, he did it bravely. He acted first, thought second. And for humans, that's usually not a good thing, but for a protection dog, it's a perfect thing.

I was always safe with Big Poppa with me. He also helped bring out Nala's courage, as she's always been a little more timid. If the three of us were lying in bed and there was a sudden noise downstairs, before I would even be able to process the noise, Poppa would be half way down the staircase ready to evacuate whatever the source of that noise was.

It didn't matter if he was tired from his busy day out in the woods, or in a deep sleep, Big Poppa would fly up out of bed and take down anything and anyone who wasn't supposed to be there.

His demeanor wasn't naturally aggressive, because he knew the difference between good people and bad. Anytime anyone I invited over would show up, he would always greet them with a huge *Big Poppa welcome*. He would overwhelm you with being right at your feet from the moment you'd walk in the house, to the moment you'd finally get to a chair in the living room. And even then he'd still find a way to get up onto your lap and be right close pressed up against you.

He loved his people.

In seeing how brave Big Poppa was no matter what he was doing or facing, it showed me just how to be brave. I always considered myself a stronger than most type of woman, but to this very day I have yet to meet any person or animal who possess the strength Big Poppa did.

Big Poppa's name would eventually evolve into *Big Poppa John*.

And that easily came to be all because of one night after driving home in a snowstorm, I had stopped in town to pick up a veggie pizza from Big Poppa John's Pizza.

It took about an hour to drive my usual 25 minute drive home. The roads were bad, very bad.

After getting in, I walked into the kitchen covered in snow just from the walk from my car to the house, put my purse, water bottle, cell phone and pizza onto the counter top.

I then walked back into the mudroom to take my boots off.

When I came back into the kitchen a mere three minutes later, all I could see was a cardboard *Big Poppa John's Pizza* box sitting on the floor.

No pizza.

Just the box.

I peeked my head into the living room, and all I saw was Nala sitting in her usual over-sized chair with that look on her face as if to say *"it totally wasn't me, mum"*. I then looked over to Big Poppa.

He wouldn't make eye contact with me.

He had this blank stare and was looking straight at a bare wall.

Not even at the TV, which I had left on for them while at work. He was just starring at the wall.

He was *so guilty.*

As I stood in front of him and asked him if he ate the pizza, he very slowly licked his nose and began to look up at me. I leaned in, kissed his face, and could smell nothing but the amazing seasonings from my veggie pizza that I clearly wouldn't be eating.

It was that night that Big Poppa became *Big Poppa John.*

And not that I was surprised, but I also learned it was clearly his favourite pizza, as well.

In the months to come where my surgery was getting closer, being *Big Poppa John Strong* would be the unspoken mantra that would be ingrained in the back of my mind anytime I felt scared or weak.

Because if you are *Big Poppa John Strong*, you're doing big things.

You're doing *all things.*

My surgery date was fast approaching. Come the second week of December I would need to come to terms with finally saying good bye to my little left hip that truly did withstand much more time for me than what any of the Doctors ever predicted. For my two previous surgeries, I wasn't very scared going into them. The first surgery happened so fast due to the breaks needing pretty much immediate repair. And the second, due to certain bolts and plates being taken out, that surgery didn't play with my mind too much either. But this surgery, when I look back I can see the heightened state of pure anxiety I was operating in the months leading up to it.

Physically I had pushed for as long as I could with the necrosis pretty much flattening the top of my hip bone. The pain was becoming so bad that during most mornings those first few steps walking out of bed were so painful my eyes would fill with tears.

Going into any big surgery, being mentally and physically ready really do need to go hand in hand.
Physically, I was ready. I was *over-due* ready. But mentally, I was so scared.

Since I was alone for both my first surgeries, it never crossed my mind that I would want or need anyone by my side for the full replacement surgery. I had one of my closest girlfriends Shana already lined up to be my driver that morning. I knew I was scheduled to stay in the hospital for three days post-surgery, however apparently if I was able to walk around with a walker or crutch, I'd be free to go home if the surgeon gave me the 'A Ok.

I really, *really* don't enjoy anything about being at a hospital. I'm not huge on IV's, or the every four hour wake up calls to swallow a paper cup full of pain killers. If I'm in recovery mode post-surgery, the only place I want to be is at my home with my dogs. No people with me. No hired nurse floating about. I just want my quiet and privacy.

Being somewhat of an athlete for most of my life, if I'm physically not doing well, I don't like anyone around me to see it happening. Call it an ego or pride, but either way, I'm too stubborn to accept help.

It might take me twenty or more minutes to slide out of my bed after a surgery, but twenty minutes or five minutes, I'm slinking out of that bed on my own.

Come late November I was working away in my office in Saint John. The entire night before and for that entire morning I remember being on the edge of tears. With the operation a mere couple weeks out, I was becoming scared.

In my head I kept thinking about the things I would no longer be able to do. Or at least, *do well.*

Even though an entire new hip and half-femur is pretty much like a "whole new you", you don't come back with the movement abilities that you have with your natural hip joint. There will be limitations on how and where I can move my body. Certain angles with my knee would be a no-go. Jumping off a ledge maybe four or three feet or higher would be super risky. Horseback riding would leave me sore for days afterwards. And running outside on pavement, or even a trail through the woods would no longer be a possibility for me.

This was what broke my heart the most because running was a true source of therapy for me. I was almost scared as to how I would handle that one. On my worst days, putting on my running shoes and heading down a country road at dusk or dawn would be the only way I knew how to work my way through whatever was bothering me. Running gave me relief and joy at the same time. The physical impact on the hard pavement would be what would hinder my ability to run longer than maybe fifty yards before I would become extremely sore.

Part way through that morning in my office, I got up and went into a separate part of the building where there was a private room and I could close the door. I picked up the phone and called my dad. I wasn't sure if he was in Toronto at work or somewhere else in the world travelling for work. But the fear of the surgery was taking me to my breaking point.

Once he picked up the phone, I tried with everything I had to not start crying, but I couldn't help it. The tears just ran down my face. I asked him if he would be able to fly into Saint John to be with me for the surgery. I had never asked my dad or anyone in my family to be with me during a surgery. For one, I never wanted to inconvenience people. But more so, I was just never very scared until now. He began to tell me that he had a conference in Japan scheduled on that day where he would be giving a talk to a few hundred Doctors.

My heart sank.

My dad is pretty much world famous in the medical world. So I knew that if there was a conference scheduled and he was set to speak, asking him to pull out with only a few weeks' notice wouldn't look very good on him.

I could hear in his voice how awful he felt. I asked him a second time, *"Please dad, I'm scared, and I'm not ready to have my bones taken away"'*

During our short phone call it didn't feel like there was much he could do in terms of making the trip in. And of course I understood. But I was still so paralyzed in fear about the whole thing.

I told him I loved him and hung up the call.

I sat in the chair in that empty office for a few minutes and just stared at the bare wood surface of the desk. My tears slowly kept dripping onto the keyboard that was in front of me.

I knew I had to clean up my face and walk back into my Department and continue on with my work day. But I'll never forget how hopeless I was in that moment. It was a mixed bucket of being angry at the reality of needing this surgery, with being angry that I was scared and couldn't tough this one out.

My emotions were winning over my logic. And it was killing me.

Later that day as I was pulling in my driveway about to get some groceries out the back seat, I heard my phone make a text message sound.

I've never been huge with texting people, so my phone might go off once or twice per day. And if it's not my mom pocket texting me, it's one of my girlfriends.

I picked up the phone to see on the screen a message from my dad.

"We will be flying in the day before your surgery. We have booked a room at a hotel by the hospital. Everything is going to be ok. Love you! –Dad"

Immediately I sent a message back *"What about Japan? The conference?"*

His response, *"I told them my daughter needs me."*

Dad Moment of the Year

I took the biggest sigh of relief.

I was still nervous as shit about the whole thing, but knowing my dad would be with me up until I was wheeled into that operating room, that simple knowingness took about one hundred pounds of fear off my shoulders.

It was a cold snowy December morning and I was just finishing putting on my mascara. I had driven Nala and Big Poppa John to Shane's place in Shediac the day before. He would be taking care of them for a few days until I was strong enough to have them back home with me.

Shana texts me *"On my way! See you soon, surgery girl!"*

Even though I was about an hour away from getting into a hospital gown, I still wanted to get my make up right.

I had my nails did right. A fresh gel fill just a few days prior. A few dabs of my nicest perfume. I even shaved my legs the night before and made sure I was all done up in my self-tanning body lotion. The next time I would be able to shower or bath wouldn't be for another three weeks or so. So I got ready that morning as if I was getting ready for a hot date with the world's richest man.

A quick half hour drive into the city and we were there. Parked right out front of the Saint John Regional Hospital.

I was never a cheerleader in high school, but that morning between Shana's car to the main entrance of the hospital, I was all high kicks and no fucks. It was my last stretch of terrain with my little hip so I was going to get my last flexible movements with my left side before the bones were to be drilled out and sawed off and thrown into a medical waste bin.

Right as we walked into the main lobby, my dad and Maureen were right there with big smiles waiting for me. It was so good having them there. It brought a whole different level of comfort to me that day.

After I checked in at the front desk, my dad led the way to where I was to register and get changed. It was comical walking behind my dad and Maureen. I didn't have a fucking clue where I was supposed to be going other than getting myself to the actual hospital. But due to their Doctor and Nurse instincts, they knew exactly where we had to go without even reading the signs.

I need a sign to instruct me on how to get out of my car some days.

But not my dad. He has a road map in the back of his head for just about everything it seems.

Including East Coast Hospitals.

Everything that morning went really fast. I was changed into a green hospital gown, told to lay in a bed with a warm white hospital blanket over me, handed two paper cups of various pills, and then told to basically just wait. Maureen said the nurses were just prepping me before I would be wheeled in to where I would meet with the anesthesiologist.

I only waited there for maybe ten minutes before two nurses came and said *"Ok, are you ready?"*

The two of them grabbed both ends of the bed and started wheeling me down a long hallway.

My dad, Maureen and Shana were right behind me the entire way down that hall.

As soon as we got to the set of double doors, the one nurse told me to say good bye to my family and that they'd be seeing me soon.

I looked behind me and as they stood alongside the beige hospital wall reminding me not to be nervous and that everything is going to go well, my dad's face was the last thing I saw before the doors closed.

A few years prior, my dad had confessed to me over dinner one night that he has always blamed himself for my hip injury. He told me that the very first night I called him while I was in military training and told him it was hard for me to walk, he explained to me that he regretted not taking that phone call as serious as he should have. Because ultimately, my bones were fractured during that first call I made to him, but nobody, not even myself could have ever known. He, just like everyone else, assumed it was a torn muscle and I was just having a hard time while going through training. My dad more than anyone wanted me to succeed in my military career, so seeing me push through the training was important to him.

But what he ended up doing was blaming himself for my hip ultimately breaking.
He wishes he had instead urged me to get an x-ray versus letting the base hospital staff dismiss me as pitifully as they did.

I could see the weight of my fear written all over his face that morning.

In my head I remember saying to myself *"I love you dad, I'm going to be ok"* right as the doors were closing behind me.

I have never once for a second blamed anyone for this injury, other than publicly shame the two fucking idiots who miss-diagnosed me, and twice at that. And one of them is still gainfully employed at the base hospital on base Gagetown to this very day.

She must shove horse shoes up her ass each morning. Because my mind is sure fucking blown that she still has the ability to even practice medicine. And on our troops at that.

But my dad blamed himself for not stepping in and making sure my injuries were properly aided to.

The injury happened because idiots were on staff that day in October of 2008. It never had anything to do with anything other than that. But being someone who understands the pains of not protecting something or someone you love, I understand why my dad holds himself responsible.

Ultimately, I'm his daughter. So I'm sure for any of you out there who are parents, if your baby girl gets hurt, you're going to kick yourself for not being able to prevent it from happening.

But what I hope my dad does remind himself of is that without his support or without the efforts he has made over the past ten years, everything about all three of my surgeries would have been a nightmare to navigate.

For everything with my hip - the good and the bad, my dad has been my *complete superhero.*

My saving grace through it all.

Before, during, or after any part of the recoveries, I've had a world class medical expert guiding me through any issues or worries I had. He was always a text message or phone call away.

It doesn't matter what you're going through. When you have the best of the best surrounding you, you know things are going to pan out in your favour. Because the best of the best don't let you *not be ok.*

My mum, being a Registered Nurse her entire life, my step dad, who is a self-made successful business man, and a double stroke survivor who thrived to a 90% recovery, I had the most incredible voices reminding me to recover well and *recover strong.*

The Man in Red and White

Waking up in recovery was a pretty bizarre moment. Between my former hip surgeries, waking up in recovery was always a bit dramatic. I would never react that well to the various medications, so I was usually very confused or crying until I would clue in as to where the hell I was.

When I woke up that evening, I opened my eyes but I wasn't able to hear anything just yet. My dad was sitting in a chair down by the foot of my bed. I think Moe was out grabbing some food. And Shana, my beautiful friend Shana, she was standing against the wall having small talk with my dad. As my eyes looked throughout the room they both noticed I was waking up. My dad immediately let me know that the surgery went well and all was expected to heal well.

Shana on the other hand, with her brutal honesty that I love so much, *"How ya feeling!? You look great for being all cut open and put back together again! Your eye brows didn't even rub off!"*

I remember feeling as if I had been hit by a truck. The more minutes that passed as I was awake, I was starting to feel my entire left side. My stomach, both hips, entire leg, rib cage, all of it – I was in *so much pain*. But I knew I didn't want any more pain killers floating through my system so I didn't say much when the nurse came back in to check on me.

She started adjusting the knob on one of the IV bags. I looked up and asked her what that was *"It's just your morphine drip"*.

The second she left the room I pulled the IV needle out of the top of my hand. Morphine makes me very light headed. So light headed to the point that if I try and stand up, I'll feel so dizzy and nauseous that I'll need to sit right back down. I knew if I stood any chance of being released from the hospital within the next twelve or so hours, I was going to need to show the surgeon that I was able to walk.

What a lot of people don't realize is that the recovery period of a *hip replacement* is much different than *hip corrective* surgery. With a full replacement, it is expected that you will be able to get up and walk twenty four hours post-surgery. Now, granted, *not walk well*, but definitely be able to somewhat weight bare and keep your balance while having the aid of a walker or crutches. Because it's not the bones that require healing, only the muscles. Your bones were just removed completely, therefore your new "bones" are basically perfect.

After about a half hour or so went by, the nurse came back in with a little white paper cup of pills. *"Where's your IV?"* she says.

I told her I was choosing to fore-go pain meds. And to be completely honest, recovering naturally hurts, sure, but it's a way better way to gauge your progress. All too often people get hopped up on pain killers to the point where they're actually doing more harm than good because they can't really feel if they're in pain or not. If I can feel every inch of the pain, I can gauge when I should rest and when I can actually push.

In saying that, regardless of the reasons why I choose to go med-free for the recovery, the pain I had that first week was almost unbearable. It was pure fucking hell, in a nut shell.

The nurse looks over at my dad, as if to hear some form of verbal support that his daughter should put the damn IV back in. My dad said nothing other than *"If she doesn't want that IV in, nobody in this room is going to be able to convince her otherwise"*.

My dad asked the nurse about discharge. The nurse explained they wanted me to remain under their care for at least one night, then in the morning if I was able to show the surgeon I was capable of walking up a set of stairs, they would have no choice but to discharge me as legally, they couldn't keep me there against my will. Most people remain at the hospital for three or four days after a surgery like this, but being in that place was making my skin crawl. I knew being at home where it was quiet and private was the only place I needed to be.

After one shitty night of sleep, around nine the next morning my dad arrived with McDonald's coffees and French fries. The surgeon was on his way to see if I was moving enough for him to give me the *A 'Ok* to leave the hospital. Because I was living in my farm house where my bedroom was on the second level, I had to climb a set of stairs for him.

The surgeon did his due diligence in explaining to my dad that it really was best if I stayed at the hospital for at least one more night, and as much as my dad probably agreed with him, he very respectfully explained to the surgeon that I wasn't one who said *"Ok, yes sir, good idea"* very easily. My dad also reassured the surgeon that I was a lot stronger than most people ever expect and that he personally wasn't concerned about my abilities to be at home post-surgery alone. My dad knew that if *I knew* I was ready, then I was probably ready.

Moe helped me sit up from the bed and as she pulled the hospital walker out in front of me, I placed both my hands on either side of my hips on the mattress. With I think my wrist muscles alone, I pushed myself up into a standing position. Once my hands were locked onto that walker, I looked up at the surgeon and said *"where are these stairs. Let's go climbing"*.

The physio room was about fifty meters down the hall. Using that walker to make my way down to the room felt like an eight hundred meter track challenge. The thing about your muscles needing to re-fuse themselves after being cut open, is by mid-morning, you are fucking exhausted. After three hours of slightly moving around, your entire body is ready to sleep for twelve hours. By the time we got to the door way of the physio room I was out of breath and dizzy, but I didn't let anyone know because I just wanted to get home. On the other side of the physio room there was a mock staircase of about eight or nine steps with a railing going up along one side of it. The surgeon wanted me to crutch my way over to the base of the staircase and show him how I would move my legs and in *what order* to be able to climb up and come back down a set of stairs. Luckily, I've tackled staircases twice before because of my other hip surgeries. So the actual technique was just muscle memory for me.

As I got to the top of the staircase I had to turn myself around and come back down. It was here when I saw the staples that were running up my thigh and up onto my lower back. There were thirty four of them. Thirty four extra-large surgical staples. (I counted them later that day) For whatever reason, the tape that was holding the gauze started to peel back exposing the staples that looked like a CN Railway journey going up my entire leg and butt cheek.

It was horror story material. Right as I was about to take my first step down to the stair below me, I caught sight of my leg. It took everything I had plus the blessings of God and any of his angels who gave a shit that morning not to throw up on myself. I remember my eyes were slowly filling with tears because the simplicity of seeing what my body had become was hard for me to look at.

Like my first two scars, this scar was going to be another permanent reminder.

Despite wanting to vomit on myself, I got to the bottom of the stairs without a hitch, looked up at the surgeon and asked him *"Good to go?"*

He gave me the thumbs up and said he'd have his dis-charge nurse make her way to my room to go over my recovery movements. There was a lot of new/altered ways of moving my leg that I was going to forever need to follow in order to prevent any form of re-injury or dislocation. And the nurse ensured I fully understood this before letting me pack up my belongings and head home.

The first few weeks of being at home were hard. I was alone, by choice, however looking back I don't know why I didn't opt out for hired help. Some mornings it would take me around twenty minutes or so just to slink myself in a parallel type way out of my bed, crutch down the hall to my washroom, bath at my bathroom sink and then approach the top of my staircase.

There were even some mornings where I would take breaks between my attempts of trying to get out of bed. Engaging my core muscles was a really hard thing to do because it put pressure on my hip. There were a few mornings where my day would begin with nothing but tears in my eyes because I'd be lying in my bed being completely stuck. Then after a few stubborn shifts from my body and a few seconds of pain, I'd get myself into a position that would allow me to let my right leg (the good leg) hang down over the bed so I'd be able to get my footing on the hardwood to let the rest of my body follow suit.

It was always during these moments where I knew I had to get strong enough so I could get in my car and drive the two hours to pick up my dogs from Shane's place. I didn't like being at the house alone. I was completely vulnerable to anything or anyone. A very easy *non-moving* target.

After the first week I decided to get fully dressed in my gym clothes and drive the ten minutes into town so I could start rehabbing myself at the town gym. This was really big for me. I could only manage to put on gym shorts versus actual spandex pants, but I dressed with what I could and started spending about two hours in the gym each day. I wouldn't do much other than slowly walk around and do various balancing activities. Re-learning how to go up onto my tippy toes with both feet. Laying on my back and starting with small leg lifts. At first, I could only raise my left leg off the ground by about two inches or so. But I kept at. And with each day, my progress started to speak for itself. There were always minor hiccups along the way during this time in January, like when I realized I had to put gas in my car as I was on empty.

I was in yoga gym shorts, so basically underwear, knee high socks, and a winter jacket.
I pulled into the Shell station on Hampton Main Street one afternoon after my gym session to only receive looks as if I was some kind of hussy showing off whatever the hell people thought I was trying to show off. I was embarrassed enough as it was simply due to needing a good two minutes or so to lift myself up out of my driver's seat so I could grab the gas pump. It wasn't until a lady with the look of pure disgust on her face looked me up and down as if I was trying to dress skimpy on purpose that I lifted up the side of my jacket to expose to her my thirty four staples. I just held a blank stare towards her with my hand holding up the side of my jacket.

I've never seen someone look away as fast as that woman did.

Silently I was saying in my head *"What's the matter old gal, never seen a cute leg before. Take a good hard look then"*.

By the end of week three I decided to go back to work. Being at home was starting to give me that cabin-fever type feeling. Doing anything I could that would make me feel as if things were *back to normal* was the best plan of action for my mental well-being.

Those first few months back at work were tough. I had a bedroom pillow on my chair in my office, but my energy levels were still low. But as each week went by, my progress remained on a slow but steady rate of improvement. However, the reality of healing through that surgery, and how tough some days were living alone in my big farm house had me re-thinking what was realistic for me, lifestyle wise.

I think deep down a lot of us always picture owning that big beautiful family home. The one that will pretty much foot the bill to meet all the needs of a growing family. But my life wasn't going in that direction. I was very insecure about my scars. And also just the way I moved in general. I had physical limitations that would no doubt spill over into the bedroom. Dating wasn't on the table for me in any way during the spring of 2016.

Despite people always saying *scars are beautiful* or *they make you look tough.* I've heard it all. But I have yet to hear that from a person with actual *big scars* being the one delivering those words. And what I mean by that is it's easy for people to say what they think you want or need to hear. But I see no beauty in my scars.

I only see reminders.

And they bring me a lot of anger.

I was thinking heavily about selling the farm and downsizing to something more manageable to maintain. The entire idea of selling had me un-easy, but I kept thinking about my future and what it would look like after another surgery.

I was tired. My hands were tired. And my mind was tired.

Recovering alone had taken its toll on me more so mentally than anything else.

I remember feeling like I was 75 years old and ready to retire to a bungalow in Florida where people came to mow your small patch of grass once a week.

Heating the farm during the winter was expensive as well. Initially, I was planning on having a wood stove put in before the fall of 2015, but when the decision of my surgery was realized, I knew that splitting wood that winter wouldn't be a very realistic option.

After going back and forth in my mind about the pros and cons of selling, I decided that ultimately selling would be the wise choice for me at that time. It almost felt like a heartbreak watching the For Sale sign go onto the front lawn of my farm. Even though I knew I would own a home like Titusville again someday, the magic and the love that place brought me would ultimately be irreplaceable.

During those early days of spring, between house hunting online and working my days away at the office, I was becoming stronger with my hip. I was also unknowingly going to meet a very distinguished, pretty powerful man.

This man wasn't like anyone I've ever been with in just about every way possible. He was older, about *17 years older*, and unlike the handful of men from my past, he had nothing to do with any type of uniform. Initially, I was somewhat attracted to his much older, handsome ways. He had jet black hair. (More salt and pepper nowadays), but when I first met him, it was jet black. And depending on how he was shaving that week, very clean side burns or a beard of some kind. There isn't anyone I can think of off the top of my head who looks anything like him. What started off as something not so serious eventually turned into the best kind of love that has ever come into my life.

That very fact is what has made the past year so hard.

We began to get to know one another the same way anyone nowadays gets to know a person.

Texting.

Sending pictures back and forth.

And little by little we began to learn a thing or two about one another.

When he came into my life I was still incredibly insecure about my newly installed hip. I hadn't been with anyone in quite a long time by this point. I was still learning how to accept my new self after the surgery. So I really didn't expect this man to come in and do that for me, or do it *himself* for that matter.

The best way I can describe how he loves me would be simply, *he gives me the kind of love that has taught me how to love myself.*

In my previous relationships it was always about doing everything I could to make sure the person I was with felt loved or important. And I did it to the point where eventually there was nothing left around me that made *me* feel loved. When I look back, my relationships, although different, had the same one thing in common, they were more of a *one-way* love story. I never really felt as if I got in return the equivalent to what I was giving. Which made those relationships incredibly unbalanced. And anything unbalanced will eventually fail. Which as we know, they all did.

Nothing about getting to know this man felt anything like the experiences from my past.
He is a motorcycle man who spent the majority of his time on the road. Between the East Coast, Toronto, and the West Coast, he was always on the go. Initially, spending time with him was few and far between. But it was sort of nice this way. Just the simplicity of getting to know him as a friend, a *person,* was all I could really handle during that time. I didn't have many expectations when it came to having him in my life. But the more days that passed during the spring of 2016, the more I was beginning to find a piece of happiness with having this man around me.

By trade, he is a certified Red Seal Chef. What a lot of people don't know is how incredibly smart he is. With literally, *everything* it seems. He is a gifted self-teacher. Self-learner. He is a natural entrepreneur. He can run numbers the way I used to run long distance races. He's just good at it. *Fast at it.*

He had built two retail stores from the ground up. One in Toronto, and one here in New Brunswick. These stores sold all kinds of gear. From sweaters to t-shirts, hats, handmade leather belts (which he designed and hand-made himself)

He was a good old fashioned working man.

And thanks to him, I had a pastry and baked goods expert on speed dial anytime I would run into a problem in the kitchen with a blueberry cheesecake or any kind of fancy cookie I was attempting to make. More than half the pictures I would send to his phone anytime he was on the road wouldn't be sexy selfies or anything of that kind. They would be wedding cakes. Or birthday cakes. And I would ask him *"What type of icing is that? Fondant?"* To which he'd reply *"That's Royal Icing baby girl, it's different than fondant. Just icing sugar and egg whites".*

I didn't get to know this man with the idea of falling in love and being his dream girl. It was the complete opposite. I began to let him into my life because he brought this kind of love around me that had me feeling that no matter what, everything was simply going to be ok from now on.

It was the most comforting feeling I have ever felt from a person.

He didn't care about my scars, or the metal in my hip. He didn't give a damn about anything from my past. He saw me for exactly who I was. He was able to see my weaknesses, and *better than I had thought at that.* But standing in front of him, my weak places didn't feel weak. My emotional moments weren't crucified or looked down upon. And anytime I would express the things that upset me, he would patiently listen, *always patiently listen,* and then offer his feedback and advice on the matter.

There was one hiccup about the kind of relationship we would ever have, or lifestyle for that matter. He is a very senior member of the most powerful motorcycle club in the world. So time away on the road came first. And being able to adapt to that reality was crucial if I was going to stand any chance at remaining in his life. At first I found it hard. Like any woman, having the person you care about away most of the time, it can wear you down. You have your moments where you get frustrated with it.

There were times I wished he was with me. But I knew his club came first. And I also knew that if I wasn't happy, I could have chosen to walk away and no longer have him in my life.
But after a few months of having his love around me, kicking him out of my life wasn't something I saw as a possibility. In a time where I was weak, and really starting to learn how to love myself as a whole, he brought with him the kind of love I should have had around me my whole life.

Without many words, he showed me time after time how beautiful I was. How special I was. How I deserved to be spoken to. And I laugh when I think back, because there were times I had *crazy Vicki moments* and any other man from my past would have handled those super-emotional moments of mine in a much different manner. Ways that would only have left me feeling more alone, and even *more* unstable or ashamed of myself.

But not Robin.

With him, I felt strong. In front of him, I felt beautiful. And loved.

So loved.

Anything I was doing, *or wanted to do*, he always encouraged me to pursue. When I began my online Spanish courses, he would send me text messages *only in Spanish.* When I would run by him certain foods I was adding in or removing from my diet and fitness regime, he would always be sure to add in certain foods that held important nutrients he knew I was missing.

By the summer of 2016, I had moved into a new home. A small bungalow about thirty minutes East of Fredericton. I was still working in Saint John, so my commute was about an hour each way. But my plan was to eventually transfer to a new job in the Fredericton area. And I was so sure about making this happen that I bought my third house in the area I would need to be in for that to happen.

Commuting wasn't anything new to me, and I knew it was only a temporary situation until I was able to land a new contract in Fredericton.

That summer brought with it a lot of changes. My early mornings of needing to wake up at 4:30 a.m kept my evenings pretty mellow. As well, earlier that year I had taken a huge financial loss on one of my cars. I purchased a beautiful Audi A4. And when I bought this car, I was *so proud* as it marked a certain level of accomplishment for me. Almost that same feeling of when a person or family buys their first home. You feel proud and as if *"I've made it"*.

After that car had me feeling all accomplished and strong in my solo independence, it only took a few coil packs in the engine and the timing belt to completely let go, and *voila*, I blew the turbo engine.

Twenty nine years old, a German Sports car that no longer runs, and a certain lump sum of cash still owing to the bank on it.

That lesson of thinking material gains fulfill or represent personal growth ended very quickly that year for me.
I had forty two thousand dollars to pay the bank and a car in the drive way that now held a whopping five grand value.

With the monthly interest rate alone on that debt, I knew if I didn't do something aggressive, paying down that forty two grand wouldn't ever happen.

So what does the girl with the nine hour work days and two hour commute do to earn extra cash outside of day time working hours?

Become a phone sex operator, obviously.

Putting on an act, or taking on a certain persona has never been a problem for me. Some days it feels like I can act like a totally different identity more easily than I can actually be myself. So I knew getting on the hot lines every night and pretty much becoming whatever the customer needed me to be – for 0.50 cents per minute plus tips, the decision was easy.

I gave myself a flat rate goal of needing to earn minimum $2,500.00 per month working the phones. At first I knew it would be trial and error. Also, landing certain clients who will become your regulars via calling back and requesting you (we all have numbers, sort of like service numbers when you're in the military, but these are Character ID numbers) would take time.

The first week adjusting to my new schedule of being on the phones at night was a bit of a tough one. It took me a few weeks to really learn how to conserve my energy when performing a call. It's very easy to give a client a forty five minute phone call where you are legitimately emotionally fulfilling a part of them. If you're not careful, the calls will leave you drained. That first week of working from eight at night until one or so in the mornings – then up at 4:30 for my day job -- I was a zombie. But I knew I didn't have any other choice. I had forty two grand that I needed to fall from the sky. The mortgage would keep coming, the dogs would always need to eat, and my *new-to-me* simplified F150 that I purchased would always require gas and some level of insurance. I could survive on crackers and ice cubes, but my dogs, I always made sure they ate. And well at that. Fresh veggies with all their meals. Homemade sweet potato treats. A proper amount of second hand blankets from Value Village for their bedding – *always.*

I can't really explain how it felt during this time with the overwhelming amount of financial debt sitting over my head. But I can tell you that I broke down, and a few times at that.

I was usually pretty good at keeping my social media "positive – strong – look at me I'm so independent" but what most people never realized was how many moments throughout the past few years where I've been the exact opposite.

One Saturday afternoon in August after mowing my lawn, I sat down on the small wooden porch that was attached to the front of my shed. I took my boots off and sat there with the sun beaming down on my back. It was hot that day. I was covered in sweat, head to toe. And just overall exhausted. I was starring across the yard watching Nala and Big Poppa John run and play. Like kids, usually unaware of the very adult things taking place unless you expose to them that you're actually scared, or sad, or scared *and sad.*

It was in that moment where I started thinking about my mum. With Robin on the road for most of the summer, and of course, I hadn't opened up to him quite yet about what I was doing at night to earn extra money, I had successfully put myself in a very lonely place. I remember saying to myself *"Thank you God... I don't have kids. How in the hell would I be dealing right now if I had two little mouths and minds to take care of?"*.

The memories of my mum began to flood my mind. I remember as a little girl watching her struggle because of the finances. There were many times I saw her break down. I didn't understand necessarily her tears back then, but as I grew older I was always aware of how hard she worked to do the absolute best that she could.

She would have her good days, and her not so good days. But on every day, she was a warrior.
All of a sudden my level of understanding, but more so, *compassion* for my mum completely overwhelmed me. I began to cry, sitting there on that shitty broke down porch that was basically falling off the front of my shed.

You see, the year my mum and dad decided to separate, my mum had lost her parents that same year.

Who I call my Nana and Bumpa, were my grandparents. The spring of 1994 my Bumpa passed away from lung cancer. A few months later, my parent's separation went through. And to wrap up the year, come November, my Nana had passed away from cancer as well.

In one year, and within months apart, my mum lost her dad, her husband, and then her mum.

The timeline was so close I don't think my mum could have even completed one grieving cycle before the next one would hit her.

So in the years to follow, when my mum would work extra-long shifts at the hospital in order to keep the roof over our heads, behind the various women from my home town that took it upon themselves to gossip about the end of my parent's marriage, or what my mum was doing or where she was working to keep her daughters fed, -- while you ladies were being stay at home *comfortably kept* wives, merely starring out your rose coloured glasses flipping through Chatelaine magazines in the comfort of your *mortgage will always be paid* secure life, my mum was being a warrior.

And shame on all of you for being such shitty women during that time.

I'd list your names, just in case you by chance bought this book.

But typing your names on one of my pages isn't worth the cost of ink.

There were a handful, and I mean – handful -- of beautiful women – beautiful mothers – that stuck by my mum's side during those years. Three women on my home town street who were working women and didn't care to have anything to do with the Starbucks sitting, gossiping women. Those three women had sons who to this very day I proudly call brothers.

Byron, Aran, Bill, Luke, Daniel and David.

Your mothers stepped in and gave my sister and I love and a second table to eat at any time my mum was working late nights at the hospital. And between all of you, I had brothers. Brothers who would always be there for me.

After sitting there on that porch and remembering everything my mum continued to face during the hard years, I felt a huge sense of responsibility to create the solution for myself. Never mind the problem, but be orientated towards the solution. I at least had privacy on my side. My personal failures and financial issues at that time weren't widely known among the people around me.

If there was one thing I took away from the whole situation, it was simply – *where's there's a will, there's a way.* As simple and as commonly overused as that phrase is, when you remove the bullshit mental obstacles that aren't even relevant to the actual root of the problem, and when you start to focus day by day doing a little bit more of whatever it is that needs to be done in order to reach your end goal – now you're head is in the right place.

Now you are in a place where you can start making your gains.

That night as I logged onto the phones, I decided I was going to be the best of whatever it was the caller wanted me to be. Getting those additional tips from the callers was going to be the fastest way I would start really bringing the money home.

If a caller wanted me to be a dirty cheerio, I was the dirtiest cheerio in the box. If a caller wanted me to talk dirty to my ceiling fan, I was talking dirty to that damn ceiling fan for as long as it took. If a caller wanted me to be *Perverted Penny home alone at the farm,* I was going to be the most perverted Penny any farm has ever seen.

Before I knew it, I had banked around ten regular callers who would call in on their usual day, at their usual time. And for each special request, the company would add ten cents more per minute to my calls. It doesn't sound like much, but it adds up fast. And the more callers you can retain, the more time your character profile will get featured on the front page of the website. And you need this type of free advertising to help gain more callers.

After a short emotional breakdown on the porch of my poorly built shed that afternoon, I had put hours on the phones almost every night that month and ended up surpassing my monthly goal for *Total Earnings'*.

I knew I still had thousands to go, but slowing down anytime soon wasn't in the cards. When you've got momentum, keep rolling with it.

Between the long days of working in Saint John and most of my evenings being spent on the phone lines, any room for a personal life wasn't all that possible. But that didn't stop Robin from always having me know that he was there. Whether a phone call or highway drive away, we spoke almost every day just to touch base and check in. He became the biggest source of love for me in a time where there was very little around me. My dogs are what really kept me going during the fall of that year.

There's times in your life when a person can come in and be that one heart beat you need to help take the edge off during the *not so sunny* days.

Robin was that.

He was my love, my comfort, and my encouragement.

Our relationship wasn't based on wild sex, date nights, or trips to the movies. Those types of normality's became irrelevant to the purpose of him being in my life. I didn't need dinner at Boston Pizza to feel loved. I needed a kind, unconditionally loving, *forgiving,* and calm but strong love around me.

And he gave me that, and he *continues to give me that.*

Before I knew it our situation was beginning to clearly demonstrate a foundation that was being built on trust, truthfulness, friendship, support, and unconditional love. I was very *un-knowingly* building the type of relationship I had tried to build with my past relationships. However this time I wasn't trying. It was just happening.

I have a certain spectrum let's call it… of emotional instability within myself. Mental weaknesses, let's call them. And it has been these weaknesses within me that have usually left me hurt when I would experience any form of rejection. After the years that have gone by, and with many moments of reflecting, if you were to ask me to write down on a piece of paper all the times I had a fight with Robin to which I was left feeling bad about myself, or bad about the situation as a whole, I wouldn't be able to.

It's as simple as that.

Almost three years, and I have had only one fight with that man.

Just one.

And I of course started it due to being emotional about God knows what that day.

But I can't even tell you what he sounds like when he raises his voice, and that's because I've never heard him raise it.

In moments when my behaviour or emotional reactions to a circumstance may be more on the irrational side of things, the way he reacts to me is what puts him in a much different, *much higher* place then the men who have loved me before could ever be.

When I've been in pain over something and decided he was going to be the lucky candidate who received my feelings on the issue, he wouldn't react with anger or yelling.

Zero violence.

Zero name calling.

He instead could always see the very simple truth to the matter.

Which was that I was more than likely struggling with some form of inner battle or hard memory that really, never had anything to do with him at all.

And with that, he would carefully and lovingly hold me until I was calm again.
He would listen to everything I would be venting about, hold me still just enough so I wouldn't hurt myself, *or him*, and before I knew it, my face would be pressed into his chest, his arms around me, and his voice quietly saying over and over again *"It's ok baby girl, I'm here, I'm home. It's ok sweetness, just breath"*

And this is why this man holds my heart. For the very simple realization that I learned I could *give him my heart,* and he would be gentle with it.

If your man isn't aware that he needs to be gentle with your heart, then you should consider finding a new man.

There is nobody on this planet who has held my hurting places as gently as he has.

He has taught me what love is supposed to look like.
He's showed me that I am in fact able to be loved.
And he will roll his eyes and jokingly say that loving me isn't always easy, but he still does it.
Even when he doesn't have to, he still does it.

On the days when I'm not very loveable, he still loves me.
He still loves me until I am *in my eyes*, loveable again.

Crazy Victoria moments and all.

Unconditional acceptance. For everything that I am, and everything that I am not.

And with that, we didn't need to wake up beside each other in the same bed every day to re-inforce the "I love you's". Nor did we need a title to what we were, or official date nights and anniversary flowers. Once I realized how this man was loving me, I realized how unimportant 99% of things couples fight about were.

Partnership isn't social media status updates. Partnership isn't to be funded or proved by fancy gifts or paid vacations. Partnerships shouldn't be made believable due to how many times you can flaunt the fact that you're *engaged* or a *bride to be*. It's the expectations of what people unknowingly place on each other that usually ends up burning the union to the ground.

Don't love the man you *want him to be*, love the man he *already is*.
And if you can recognize that he loves you exactly the way you *currently are*, then that's a very simple, very special thing that you shouldn't be quick to dismiss, or feel as if it's "not enough".

Once you remove the material junk that funds your expectations of what you think it will take for you to be happy, you're left with facing the person standing in front of you. You're better half has every possibility to go out and earn a great living. He also has every possibility to get fired from a great paying job and need you to cover the bills until he can sort his life out. So with those very real life possibilities, what are the things about your partner that has you telling people *"I'm with him"*.

I know deep into my core the kind of man Robin is, with or without luxuries or sunny days.
On the good days, or the not so good days.
The days where everyone is winning financially, or the days when we're hustling 90+ hours a week to keep the houses paid for. Or for him in some cases, 24/7 it would seem.

It doesn't matter what's taking place.

I'm with him.

I'm *always* with him.

So before you put too much focus on the little things, just be sure you're secure with the big things. Because if you need a diamond ring or both names on a hydro bill to feel secure in a partnership, you probably have a much bigger hole to fill, and it's not a hole you should be burdening your partner with.

There is very little out there that anyone can see or hold onto when it comes to my relationship with him.

But the relationship I have built with him is one hundred times stronger than some relationships out there living inside four brick walls with a document stating by law that they are "together".

Our relationship has always been far from traditional, but at that time my life wasn't all that traditional either, so when things between us started building, it just worked. He had his total freedom for everything and anything he wanted or needed to do. He fulfilled his various obligations that required tending to, and I fulfilled mine. And somewhere in-between that we found time to love one another.

I have never been more independent than I am now.
And a large part of that is due to everything I have learned about myself with him being the heart beat by my side.

It's almost as if he put me back up onto the balance beam that I fell so hard off of, and quietly let go of my hands because he knew I could re-balance myself all *by myself.*

A big part of my *going it solo* power I have today as a woman is attributed to the man who helped me re-build it.

That's partnership.

A person who makes you *a better you.*

That Christmas I decided to stay in New Brunswick. Flying home to Toronto can be expensive in December. And with the money I was making to get the Audi debt paid down, I really didn't want to take time off in my evenings that would put those extra earnings to a halt.

With the snow on the ground, the quietness of having no holiday plans, and Robin's motorcycle being parked for the season, we made plans to spend Christmas Eve together. At the time, he had a condo on the North side of the river. He was only ever at the condo when he would be in town between travel trips. For him, Christmas Eve was a working night. But working at home. Going over various clothing designs, orders in, shipments out, invoices; the whole shebang. Christmas Eve was also down time for him to be able to go through the never ending Christmas cards that came his way. Cards from people all over. He's a very well-known man within his organization. Well known and very much respected due to having more than a decade behind him of being devoted to his club.

When I arrived to the condo that evening, he had an industrial sized cooking pot on the stove with a *from scratch-home-made* turkey soup broth cooking. I don't eat meat, but the smell of the soup base was amazing. He had just the right amount of this, a pinch of that, stirring a little, then stirring a little more. Watching him with food is literally an experience in itself. He's a master with his hands and more so his mind when he's in a kitchen preparing food.

With nothing more than some classical music playing in the background, (he loves classical music) his soup creation on the stove top, and the city lights reflecting off the river, it was one of the most relaxing nights I've had in a long time.

We spent the rest of the night in the California King he had in the bedroom. I had a busy week prior, so I was pretty drained. It wasn't before long that I was drifting in and out of sleep while being curled up under one of his arms. He'd be occasionally checking his phones for business emails, or replying to various text messages. With a movie playing on the big screen TV that stood at the foot of the bed, I spent the rest of the night being in the only place I needed to be.

He knows I have a busy mind, so every few minutes when I'd wake up he'd rub my shoulder or gently rub my cheek until my eyes would close again. Having my head on his chest and being able to completely relax and drift off to sleep is the most simple but loved luxury I have with him.

These were the quiet and most needed times with him. I appreciated his busy life, because *my life* was busy. But being with him taught me how to be less demanding of a person's time or attention, and be more demanding of myself. Demanding more from yourself versus your partner will force you to almost level up. And before you know it, you're accomplishing a lot of your goals at a much faster rate than you probably initially saw as possible.

I was beginning to really like the woman I was becoming with him by my side.
This was making the reality of having him as my "person" for the long term a very easy decision to make.

In fact, when I sit and think about it, I don't think it was ever really a decision to begin with. And that was probably because there was nothing to decide on.

With him in my life, my world was becoming better.

And that's all there really was to it.

An unspoken commitment, really.

He didn't need to have me tell him I was his, he already knew.

And I never needed to ask him if he was planning on sticking around, because time and time again, even on the days when I'd shut down and attempt to push him away, he'd never leave.

He continued to show me that he wasn't going to ever bail on me.

And I knew all of this without needing a conversation or words of promise from him.

Our actions towards one another said everything we both needed to know.

In the months to follow after our quiet Christmas Eve, spring was soon approaching.
I never necessarily loved the small bungalow I was living in, as I always viewed it as a transition house. A small and quiet place to live while I paid down my debt from the Audi.

So when the idea of renting the bungalow out came to the table, I thought it was a pretty decent idea considering it would prevent me from breaking another mortgage term early. Robin and I both loved the idea of having a farm house with lots of land. I always knew I would eventually have another Titusville at one point or another, I just wasn't expecting to start looking for it so soon.

The reality of having more than one home is always something him and I agreed on. He knows how much I love my private space. And with him, he's on the road so much, he really only ever needed *stop-over-houses*. But the idea of having a family-type farm again was ultimately the dream. I would live there full time and take care of the actual home, the bungalow would be rented out, and he would stay at the farm any time he wanted or needed those quiet nights between travelling.

The reality of living in a lifestyle of having the man you care about being at the home once or twice a week never bothered me when I became involved with him. The way him and I view that type of living was never really concretely discussed, but with the way our relationship was becoming, anything different would have probably felt odd for us. A lot of people had a hard time understanding how or why I decided to start this kind of life, but it didn't matter if I explained myself or not, I knew ultimately I didn't need anyone to understand. As long as I was happy, I really didn't care what anyone thought.

The other aspect of the relationship that seems to still blow people's mind is that I'm not the only woman in the relationship. There is in fact another girlfriend who although may be different from me in terms of how we live our lives, but the one huge thing we both have in common is that we found similar reasons as to why Robin is the man we're choosing to be with.

The other girlfriend is a stunning model. She's tall, very unique looking. Think classic 40's pin up, but with an alternative and sensual twist to it. She's from Toronto as well originally. Between the East Coast and Toronto, she would be on the road just as much if not more than Robin would be. Her and I have never lived together, nor will we probably ever. But anytime we touch base about anything, it's always easy conversations with a dash of team work.

This is probably the biggest factor in what makes my way of living viewed as non-traditional. But how many traditional ways of living have ended up in divorce, secrets, or cheating?

Lots.

Now, *lots haven't*, as well.

But if there's one true fact about my previous relationships, it's that all of them were supposed to be traditional, or at least *appeared* that way to other people. But behind closed doors they were all flooded with a lot of unhappiness.

So when my life with him began on this very non-traditional path, I really didn't have anything to lose. Who was I to say it wouldn't work out unless he was "all mine".

I'm not a jealous person, for one. And for two, once you can get over yourself and stop expecting a person to have eyes for you and *only you* until the end of time, you can actually just enjoy living.

And being.

And living and being *happy* with a person who is good to you.

If you focus on that, then the fact that there is another woman in the picture doesn't disrupt anything I've built with him.

She has something very special and important with him, as do I.

That as a whole *is far* from a terrible thing.

Cancer is a terrible thing.

Genocide is a terrible thing.

Losing your loved one in a car accident – that is a terrible thing.

I know people who have shared the same partner with another person, except one of the partners had no idea it was happening.

That's a sad, kinda shitty, *kinda terrible thing.*

So you can hold onto your judgements before you throw shade our way.

Baby Angel

In the early days of Spring I found a 125 year old homestead that sat high up on a hill overlooking the Saint John River. It was three stories, six bedrooms, two wood stoves, and sat on just about 100 acres. The house itself needed updating, but Robin wasn't concerned with any of that because he knew I enjoyed those non-major, mostly cosmetic, room by room renovations. There was a large deck that wrapped around three quarters of the home. A few sheds for storage and hobby farm type ideas, and then land. Lots of land.

When I first went through the home Robin was away for business. I walked through the entire thing with the overall idea of *"yes, this will most likely foot the bill I think".* The amount of updating was a bit overwhelming, but a lot of the rooms had some vintage shag rugs that honestly only needed a steam cleaning, and with some Pinterest worthy bedroom themes, would end up giving the rooms a really cool feel to them.

The upstairs bathroom did require about a Costco sized crate of Comet Cleanser in order to remove the yellow stains from the sink and bath tub, but again – not a deal breaker. This was to be a farm house. And unless we were rolling in hundreds of thousands per year, our farm house wasn't going to be featured in any Country Living magazine. It was going to be a home where dogs, kids, us – could all walk in with mud on our boots and nobody would have a panic attack over the floors getting dirty.

There were a few aspects to this home that I wasn't sold on, so I knew no decision would be made until Robin was back in town and be able to come see it for himself.

I continued to look at other places, but as of yet, nothing was really comparing to the location, size, and *land size* of the home on the hill.

As soon as Robin was back in town he took a drive down to the property to see the house for himself. He knew the area very well as he had grown up right down the road from the place. He was even wondering if he would have known the family or the son who was selling the place. In small towns out here on the East Coast, there's always someone who knows you, or knows *of you*. The entire Maritimes has that *"news travels fast"* vibe.

After about twenty minutes of him being at the property, my phone rang. *"Hi baby girl, so I'm here at the house, overall the house is kinda cool, I know you'll do your thing with the décor, but the land lay out isn't really useable land. It's a lot of steep hills with thick bush"*

I never really considered that. In my eyes, land was land. And owning land, was simply that, *owning land*. But he made a few really valid points. If the land wasn't usable, what type of value would it add to our property other than being listed under our names on the land title.

He had more of an idea of actual *rolling hills*. Land where you could set out for an afternoon on a couple four wheelers and actually enjoy the land. Versus just stare at it.

We went back and forth with the pros and cons for about a week or so. I thought a lot about simply wanting to leave the bungalow and get into something bigger. We eventually decided that although that particular farm house wasn't the "big winner" but it would do no harm for us to take it, live in it, enjoy it, do some upgrades, and then when we'd come across something more ideal, sell it – and purchase the more ideal long-term property.

But I guess the universe had something different in store for us after all. Usually when presenting an offer on a property, the sellers have a twenty four hour window to send back their counter offer, or, acceptance of your proposal. After submitting our offer, it took just over three days until the other realtor contacted my realtor with their counter offer. Robin was firm with the fact that we weren't going to over-pay for any part of this property. He and I both knew that ultimately if they didn't come down to our number, then we'd walk.

After almost twelve days had passed, the sellers stood firm on their number. I was at work in Saint John when my realtor called me with their final selling price. I called Robin from my office and gave him the latest update. He suggested we walk. He knew the area very well simply from growing up nearby. He also knew the return value that property would give us, so with those two variables, we decided it wasn't worth it to buy. If the return on investment is only a small-time gain, then it's not worth your time.

I was a little bummed out, however he reminded me that old homesteads like this pop up all the time in this province. And that if this deal didn't pan out, it was simply not meant to be.

It was nice having someone with me while potentially buying another home. All my homes I've had to go through the buyer and seller woes alone. Remaining firm with or against a realtor can be tough at times. Especially if you're not sure that the final purchase price is legitimately a fair one. But Robin is a business man at heart. So standing firm on a number he saw as reasonable was easy for him. He wasn't sweating the counter-offer from the sellers, or the fact that we may not get the house. He just let the facts run the show.

If the selling price was fair, we'd purchase. But if he had any inkling that our future return on investment wouldn't be all that great, our money would be better used elsewhere.

And with that, we sat tight remaining with the little bungalow I didn't love living in, but was comfortable in.

During this time, I started to really become comfortable in the life we had created together. Our way of living was something I had become very happy with. My hopes for a baby of my own started to become an option again for me. I didn't know how he would feel with the topic, after all, he was in his late forties nearing fifty. But I was incredibly happy with how our life was at this time. And with the way he showed his love and constant support with me, I could already see how ideal it would be to have him as the father of the baby.

We never argued about money.
There were basically zero angry phone calls or even disagreements about big time ideas or current things we were handling.
Our flow just worked.
And on the days we would see things differently, those moments never lasted very long because we resolved things pretty easily with a few short, but effective back and forth sentences.

He communicated calm with me even during times when I wasn't very calm. The way Robin treated me had me very early on realize that if I ever had a son, I would want my son to treat a woman and conduct himself in the same manner he did.

I went back and forth for almost a month in my head with the idea before I brought it to the table for discussion with him. At this point we had our foundation already built with the simple fact that we understood one another; how we lived, how we *liked to live*, and what the other needed to feel secure or cared about. There was very little Robin ever needed from me. Which has always been one of the most refreshing things about his love. It's so incredibly *non-demanding*. It's more so based on what I've always needed *from him*.

That unconditional type love. The calm he brings into my world. The friendship. He's a brilliant man, so I learn from him. And if I can't learn from a man, then I don't remain very interested in a man.

And when I'm in front of him, or speaking to him over the phone, he always gives me his undivided attention. The amount of respect that man has given to me in a matter of a handful of years outweighs the respect I've ever received from my previous relationships combined.

I knew the discussion of *"let's have a baby, baby!"* would be discussed in the same manner all of our decisions are discussed. With logic, ensuring the decision made sense, is it economically wise, and of course, would it be beneficial to our future as being partners.

As black and white and as slightly emotionless as that may sound, this is what I love most about him. Making horrendously, regretful decisions that were fueled by emotionally charged thinking patterns were directly to blame for some of my biggest personal downfalls in life.

With Robin, I learned how to quiet my heart, and enlighten my logic. And when you do that, your life begins to involve less hurricanes.

Sunny days, almost every day.

I will always remember the day I proposed the idea to him. He was in Toronto for business. I was visiting one of my closest girlfriends who owned the tanning salon in town. She had been a single mum for basically her entire daughter's upbringing. Knowing the living dynamic Robin and I had and would continue to have, I wanted her insight on how it really felt being alone during nights when your baby won't stop crying, and nobody is there to be with you through it.

She gave me her full honesty on the issue that *nothing about it was easy*, but that no matter what, every single day with her baby girl was a miracle. And seeing how her little girl was growing up into the most amazing little lady, she was so easily able to tell me how worth it all those alone-moments were. And if she could go back in time, she wouldn't change a thing.

She also reminded me of something very important, *"You know Vicki, you've accomplished a lot completely on your own. Regardless if he is your better half for the long haul, you have to know that if you decide to become a mum with knowing most of your days will be spent doing it alone, you out of anyone I know could do it. You might regret not doing it. But you'll never regret doing it"*.

I took everything she said to heart that day. Her honesty and *more so* support meant a lot to me. And with that, I sent one of my *chapter book length* text messages to Robin.

I don't remember the meat and potatoes of the text message, and that's probably because it was mostly composed of a lot of emotional jibber jabber, but I do very much so remember his response. And how little time it took for him to provide it.

"Sugar bear, you knew my thoughts on the topic months ago. Nothing has changed."

His response was what it was because we had openly and *very lightly* talked about the idea of having a baby, but there was never any serious conversation about it. I definitely never proposed the idea with the intention of actually making it happen. So when I read his response, I knew that giving me the gift of a baby was something he felt very comfortable doing.

I almost began to cry while reading his response over to myself. Of course I just *had to be sure* he understood what I was *really asking*, so with my emotions now running the show, I immediately called him to just ensure he was *totally sure*.

Years ago, in one of my relationships I was told something that broke me down right to my core. And they are words I have yet to erase from my memory. But during a fight with an ex, he very clearly stated to me, *"Victoria, I don't think you're emotionally capable of raising a child"*. And when this man spoke those words to me, it shattered me.

So much to the point where even after a couple years of building this beautiful, *healthy as ever* foundation with this beautiful man, that insecurity that was planted by a *not so nice* person actually hindered my ability to completely rejoice in the happiness of the moment.

A simple reminder to anyone out there before you decide to throw words at a person when you know you're going to hit them where it hurts.

Don't fucking do it?!

How about that option.

Don't be a dick.

Low people throw low blows.

So for anyone who has been hit hard with a low blow, don't dwell on the pain they caused you, instead, pity the broken person who *attempted* to break you.

Ring ring -

"Hi baby girl"

"Hi! So – are you sure? Like, you're really sure you want to make this happen? I just need to know why. Justify to me why you're on board – I need to hear it."

"Well baby it's not really a difficult decision for me. You're smart. You have so much love to give. You're beautiful inside and out, so our baby will be beautiful inside and out. I trust you. You take care of just about anything and everything on your plate. The answer for me is easy sweetness. You just say when and well start working at it".

And just like that. My whole world began to open up with this entirely new shade of sunshine for my future.

I was going to be a mummy.

This was going to be a planned, and *happily received* pregnancy. And I would be doing it with the one man who made everything about my life better.

He was expected to be back home from Toronto in about two weeks' time. And with that, I stocked up with the best pre-natal money can buy. I began making fertility-friendly weird hippie tasting smoothies every morning. I was doing holistic remedies to detoxify my Jack Daniels ridden liver, meditation sessions for inner-calmness and stress management – everything.

With everything I was doing on my end to prepare *body for baby* – it was no surprise that it only took us a handful of moments together to actually conceive.

I was driving home from Saint John one weekday afternoon when I was thinking about how and when I would tell Robin we had made our little baby. During that week he was away for work, but was expected to be back in town soon. I wanted to tell him in person, but at the same time I was so excited I wasn't sure if I could wait or not.

The spring of 2017 was shaping up to being an incredibly busy time for him. The clothing line for his club was thriving here in the Maritimes. Orders were being shipped out worldwide. The other girlfriend was hugely involved with that. Her modeling schedule had a lot more flexibility in it. So being on the road with him was a lot more do able for her. Between being vendors at various Motorcycle and Tattoo Expo's across the country, they were busy. I was strapped down to my Monday to Friday day job. And with still working most nights on the phone lines, my time was pretty limited. But he also knew I liked my life for the most part the way it was. He always knew I was a homebody at heart. Being on the road was his thing.

As much as I wanted that *"special in person moment"* who was I kidding, we didn't care about normality's like those. A phone call was no less special or important as a face to face conversation for us. I never know when he's in meetings and when he's free, so I usually send a text message first just to see if he's free for a call.

I send a text *"Hey babe, can you call when you have a free minute? It's important."*

Not even five minutes pass, and my phone rings.

"Hey sugar pie what's up"

"Ohh nothing... I'm just driving home from work..."

Immediately he says *"What's with the big sigh baby girl, do you have something to tell me".*

Like the back of his hand that man knows when I've got a confession coming.

"I'm pregnant"

"Aww sugar bear that's great news! How do you feel, do you feel ok?"

And just like that, within a whole whopping seven second time frame, our *"Yay! We made a baby!"* conversation was accomplished.

"Ok baby girl drive safe and shoot me a text so I know you've made it home. I'm home in a few days. We'll talk more then. Love you".

In the coming weeks, baby Moulton was a tiny growing baby that made me insanely exhausted and pretty grumpy at that. I can easily say, and Robin will agree, I was not a happy pregnant girl. He was on the road for most of the first trimester, but I'm sort of glad he was. I was temperamental on a good day to say the least.

He knew when to give me my space, and could read between the lines on those days I wasn't being overly kind or loving. But he continued to be his strong and sturdy self. Which really, was all I ever needed anyways. Of course there were nights where I would be in bed by 7:00 pm wishing he was there to cuddle me while I ate salted crackers and sipped pineapple juice, but for the five or six minutes those moments would last, before I knew it, I'd be falling asleep with the pupps on either side of me.

Many women may see this as lonely, or "un-fair", and I won't lie, *of course* it was lonely. But this is what I had signed up for. I went into this entire relationship understanding the type of life that would become my reality. I also would remind myself that my hormones were elevating every emotion in me *ten-fold.* So on the nights he'd receive my bitchy text messages, he knew I had probably withheld many more in the days prior.

But he had been through this before. He has children already. Beautiful children. So understanding the emotional upheavals some of us women go through during pregnancy wasn't anything that ever got him riled up. As long as I was home, safe, eating well, and getting enough sleep, he'd let me yell, cry or be as bitchy as I needed to be. He'd never react to my various *"I'm so alone, can't you just be here"* phone calls, but instead he'd tell me he loved me and he would gently remind me he was on the road working because money isn't going to fall from the sky and give us a secure life.

With his continued logic at work, I would usually calm myself down and tell him I was sorry for being emotional, to which he would always respond *"don't be sorry baby girl, you're just a bit crazy from the hormones. You can yell all you want sweetness. We have lots more of these phone calls to get through until your hormones level out".*

I would end up laughing with him before ending our call. Because he was just so good. He was always just so – good with me.

But our next phone call about our baby wasn't going to be a good one.

He had been home for a short time frame until he was headed off to Halifax for a weekend with other support clubs. I was a day or two away from hitting the ten week mark. So close to being through first trimester.

But our baby wouldn't see another day.

That weekend I lost the baby. The physical pains of miss-carrying wasn't new to me.

Robin was never aware of my previous pregnancies. Mostly due to the complete shame I held with the failures of them. I knew regardless he wouldn't have cared if I was ever pregnant before or not, but it never occurred to me how much guilt and sadness I still held in me with those unsuccessful pregnancies until having a baby became a possibility again.

A miss-carriage and an abortion had put me in a place in my mind where I basically convinced myself I couldn't have a successful pregnancy. The abortion itself was so terribly morbid for me. I held that moment of my life secretive from almost everyone.

I was laying in my bed that night knowing the cramping was so deep that the outcome couldn't possibly be good. Not only that, but I was so nauseous as well. The pain had me in tears. I decided to call an ambulance to be taken to the local hospital down the road. I wasn't sure if I would need a D & C or not, but I knew I needed help, that was for sure.

It took a few hours until I decided how I would get in touch with Robin. I knew he would most likely be out having a really good night with various friends and brothers from his club. The conversation would take place no matter what, but choosing the time to tell him, that was something I didn't take lightly.

I ended up sending a text to one of the guys who had been working closely with him the past few months. He had become a dear friend of mine during that time. I sent him a message asking him to let Robin know I needed him to call me in the morning. I assured him everything was fine, just that it was important Robin called me.

Of course everything *wasn't* fine, but when you keep the big picture in mind, yes – it was heart breaking; *my heart* was breaking. But, this wasn't an emergency, it was simply something sad.

The next morning after arriving home early from the hospital, I ran a hot bath.
It wasn't long after getting in the tub when my phone rang.

It was Robin.

After sniffling through a running nose and tears telling him the news, in the loving way he always handles things with me, he very warmly said *"When you're ready my love, we can try again"*. And with that, as sad as I was, I was somewhat able to come to peace during that moment with losing our baby.

The remainder of the day was very somber for me. Of course the drop in pregnancy hormones over the next few days didn't help. But I knew enough that most of my thoughts and emotions were caused solely to that. So I just rode the wave of it all.

I went back to work the very next day. I was still exhausted from everything that happens to your body when you miss-carry, but I needed something else to put my mind to. *"Nothing a few mood stabilizers and extra-large Maxi Pads can't take care of"*, I said to myself. Robin wasn't expected back for a few days yet. So until then, I kept myself busy with work.

Losing our baby wouldn't be the only heartbreak that would hit home that year. I didn't know it then, but our time together was going to become limited, and within a few short months at that.

As summer rolled in, I wasn't overly focused on trying again to conceive. I knew when I felt ready, we would give it another try. But I think my body was still feeling the loss. I had a certain numbness around me. And it wasn't from any mood stabilizer pills. I think I just became very sad during this time. With how Robin and I lead our relationship, business and practical things almost always came first. Even though I knew he was always there *when or if* I needed him, but this wasn't something I wanted to burden him with. His clothing stores were up and running, with deliveries and new designs to keep getting out into the market. He was extremely busy during this time.

The world wasn't going to stop just because I had a miss-carriage.

Although when I look back, I wish I didn't *solo-navigate* my feelings as much as I did. I really do wish I would have chosen to be with him more that summer. And have more of our nights spent together versus apart. Business for him continued on as per, so if I wasn't giving him grief over the phone or telling him to come home early, as far as he was concerned, I was probably ok, and just throwing myself into work like I always do. But little did I know, *he did in fact know* something was up. But it's not like him to push. He knows when I'm ready, I'll come to him with whatever it is I need to get off my chest.

By June of 2017 we were barely seeing one another. It was a lot of good morning text messages, but rarely having visits to actually catch up and spend time together.

I decided to throw myself back into an industry that I seem to fall back into anytime I isolate myself from just about everyone due to something breaking my heart. With my Audi debt paid off, I didn't have any real need to work multiple jobs. However, giving up the phones was something I never ended up doing, even after I paid back the 42 grand to the bank. The routine of basically becoming a workaholic had become my new normal. And actually *re-building* my savings was something I couldn't justify slowing down. With my two decently lucrative income sources, I was doing more than ok. But still, I found *God knows what type of reason* to justify taking part in more work.

The Adult Companion industry has been forever thriving. Most refer to it as *Escorting*. And by general definition, we can all come to a pretty quick conclusion on what an escort is, or what an escort does. But I don't necessarily see it that way. Because being an Adult Companion has so much more to it. I've had a client who was in his late 80's. He was years away from needing any form of nursing home. And financially, appeared to be from a family with old money. With no family living close, he just wanted someone to play chess with for two hours every Sunday afternoon. And lucky for him, I can play a mean game of chess. I've had a client who wanted merely one hour of my time per week to literally meet him at a restaurant in town and share a meal with him.

Loneliness is a quiet killer. And people will pay a large amount in order to avoid dealing with it.

I think I threw myself back into this world in order to avoid dealing with how I was really feeling.
I mean, being an outsider looking in, it probably doesn't take a whole lot to connect the dots.

I was avoiding my loneliness by serving those who were lonelier than I was. And with that, I was no longer lonely.

I was now needed. And more so, was feeling appreciated.

Going to work and doing whatever it is your boss needs you to do to earn a paycheque, that's all fine and dandy. But actually taking part in human connection and giving a person something they have been missing, such as a kind conversation, or someone to listen to their story of their white poodle who's going blind in one eye -- As mediocre as these things may sound, being that source of light in a person's day is something I really do believe in.

I've always cherished most of my clients because they all had one defining trait in common, they were all very kind, but more so, extremely lonely. Whatever took place in their life, or whatever they had done in their life to end up so alone, those details were none of my business. But what was my business? Was sharing with them a piece of whatever sunshine in me I had to give.

Life is so short, you know. And we too often get caught up in all the things that really aren't that important at the end of the day.

Human connection. Feeling loved. And having something to truly smile about in your day, what more do we need?

I believe through these various client meetings, I was unknowingly slowly healing from losing our baby. When other people share their stories with you, whether stories of joy, pain or loss, somewhere along the journey of it all you heal. Because your pains aren't alone anymore.

Strength in numbers they call it.

Come late July, it had been almost two months since Robin and I had seen each other. I was missing him, I was missing him *a lot.* But I think I put distance between us mostly because I was simply hurting. And I've never really mastered the *"art of healing without pushing people away"*, so when it all came full circle on how I was coping, I hadn't really surprised myself. And little to my knowing, my behaviour wasn't shocking to him either.

He was home for a few days before heading out of town again. We made plans for a sushi dinner date in Fredericton. I was really happy to finally be seeing him.

After getting freshened up with a cute little summer's night outfit on, I made my way into the city to meet him at the restaurant. I was still a bit emotional deep down about our loss. But I was going to try and hold it together, at least until we were done at the restaurant. I also knew I had to tell him what I had been up to the past two months. There isn't anything I really keep from him, so a simple explanation of why I had been so closed off – he was more than entitled to that. He was after all, my guy.

I hadn't even managed to eat two sushi rolls until my eyes teared up. He sat at the table across from me, and like usual, *calm as ever.* I told him I had been working. He didn't need me to expand on the details, because he knew what I meant by the way I looked at him while saying it.

"It's ok baby girl, I just wish you would have told me, so at least I'd always know where you were, or that you were safe".

And he was right. There was never any need or decent reason for me to have kept that from him. But I did. For whatever reason during that time I felt closed off from everyone and everything, including the person I loved the most. He didn't want or need to dwell on the topic for any length of time. So we had our dinner. And once we were done, hand in hand, we left the restaurant.

My truck was parked a few minutes away. I knew he was on the road within the next day or two, so a simple kiss goodnight to end our dinner date was good enough for me.

As we got to my truck, he opened the driver side door and with one hand under the butt cheek of my wobbly side, he lifted me up into the driver's seat. We had a few more kisses before he told me to text him when I was home, and to drive safe.

Those kisses would be the last kisses I would have with him, and for years to come at that.
And I still remember those last moments with him like they were yesterday.

Waking Up without Getting the Goodbye

It was nearing the end of August. I had been busy with my day job, and for the first time in over a year, I started cutting back my hours with the phone lines at night. I was starting to get back into the groove of "prepping body for baby". With Robin back and forth with his travelling, I was looking forward to getting the house ready to be put back on the market. I had decided that we'd off load the bungalow completely, and either build something, or buy something bigger for the New Year that was to come.

But my plans for a bright family-filled future would unknowingly come to a full stop. It was around 4:00 in the morning on a Friday when I got the phone call. I picked up the phone, still almost fully asleep, to hear on the other end *"Robin has been arrested"*.

"What?" I say in confusion.

"They pulled him over two days ago, along the Trans Canada. Apparently they seized guns and some other stuff from different locations. All the news channels are flipping out about this".

My heart stopped.

A big part of what Robin and I respect about one another is that we've never meddled in each other's business. Anything he did when he was away from me wasn't any of my business, nor concern. What he brought to my life when we were together is the only thing I focused on. And whatever the news was talking about wasn't ever anything he brought around me or into my life.

What felt like a knife in my heart wasn't necessarily because he had been arrested, but more so because he had been in prison years prior while in Ontario. This meant that being possibly convicted as a second time felony offender, the consequences would most likely be much more severe.

I hung up the phone and sat up in my bed. The dogs were still sleeping. I hadn't spoken to Robin for the past couple of days. Nothing about not hearing from him while he was on the road was out of the ordinary for us. But as I sat there, I began to panic, and in my *non-sense making* type thinking, I called his iPhone – it was off. So I called his blackberry – it was also off.

His phones are *never* off.

A hurricane could come through town, and he'd still ensure his phones would have some type of cell service.

With both his phones being off, the fact that he was behind bars became real. But as nutty as it sounds, even though that phone call was all I needed to hear to drive the point home, a part of me was still in disbelief. I'm pretty sure I was in shock.

"I'll just text him later. I'm sure he'll explain everything. Ya, I'll text him tonight when I'm home from work. Everything is fine".

Apparently the story had been "breaking news" the night prior, but I never had cable TV, so catching up on the evening news wasn't something I ever did.

During that morning as I put the coffee on and got the dogs fed, my entire body was on auto-pilot. By 6:00 am my phone was getting flooded with messages that included links to the story online. Websites upon news websites were publishing his arrest like hot cakes. And all the stories had various versions it seemed. Some said the RCMP and local police authorities had been building a case against him for over a year. Where other sites stated he had been followed by undercover police very closely the last three months leading up to his arrest.

The news was all over the place. I knew nothing was going to be concrete until I heard from him directly. But hearing from him, in terms of *when that would happen*, that was a huge question mark.

While driving to work I was getting to the half way point on the highway. I had about thirty minutes left of my drive. Then it hit me – like a ton of bricks – *everything* hit me. I had to pull over because my tears were flooding my vision. There wouldn't be any text messages or phone call later that night. I wasn't going to hear from him and have everything sorted after a few lawyer visits.

This wasn't a small thing.

He was gone. Hand cuffed and God knows where at the moment.

And just like that, my whole world fell apart right in front of me, on the side of that highway.

I had finally gotten to a place where I had this man, this partner in my life who made *absolutely everything* in my world better. So much better. I loved who I was as a woman with him in my life. I loved our unique but beautiful partnership. Our phone calls. Our moments together. My ability to have a family of my own because I had found a man who I'd proudly do that with – all of that shattered. The realization of all those things falling apart so fast took the breaths out of my chest.

When I started to breathe again, I let out the biggest cry.

I was sobbing.

On the side of that highway at 6:30 in the morning as the sun was rising, with my forehead laying on my steering wheel.

I was devastated.

I arrived to work and sat in my office starring at a black computer screen. It took me almost forty minutes that morning to actually turn the damn thing on. I grabbed my stack of files that needed completing, and began to work.

As numb and as scared as I was, I just plugged away at my work while soaking in the chaos that was taking place on the news.

Radio stations, websites, nothing would let up.
His face was plastered everywhere.

It wasn't until I read online a few days later did I learn of his next court appearance.

This would be the first of many court appearances where I would begin to adjust to my new way of life.

An entire month went by before I would hear from him. Apparently they had him on 23 hour lockdown the first few weeks he was arrested.

It was Thanksgiving Monday in early October. I was at home on my computer running some numbers for my phone earnings for the month of September. My cell phone rings. I look at the screen, and it's this odd 1-866 number. Immediately I figured it was a telemarketer, but something in me told me to pick up the call.

"Hello?"

It was fuzzy, a pretty shitty connection.

"Hi baby girl"

My whole body went limp in my chair. *"Baby!?"*

I say into the phone.

"Hi baby girl, I'm here. How are you. Holding up strong?"

Hearing his voice that evening was the only thing I had needed since the moment he had been arrested one month prior. I knew I would hear from him eventually, but I had never been through this sort of ordeal with someone. So in terms of the logistics to it all, I had no idea how the whole thing worked.

I wanted our call to be filled with love and solution-oriented steps we needed to be taking, but I couldn't hold myself together. I was a wreck. He could barely make out what I was saying, my tears were over taking the call. But he continued to remind me we were going to get through this. It was merely the beginning of a long, painful and frustrating road navigating the legal system, but come hell or high water, we were getting through this.

When the man you love becomes incarcerated, everything changes, and fast at that. First and foremost, you have a decision to make. You can stay, or walk away. A lot of women choose not to stay, to which I can understand merely because it's incredibly difficult even on the good days to push through life alone. Knowing you need to remain strong for your loved one who is on the inside. There is no shame in that either, walking away. I personally believe, at least.

I was so angry. I was angry at him, but wouldn't tell him. I was angry that life had thrown this wrench at me. But again, I didn't tell him any of this. When you're in a dark place, the last thing you want to do is make it any darker than we both knew it already was. There was no going back in time. What was done, had been done. The additional sources of income he had in his life came from criminal activity. It was never anything I ever had my nose, eyes or ears in. Even though I knew he had been to prison before. But I truly never believed he would ever land back in prison.

We had only a minute or two left on our call, so before we would get disconnected I sat up in my chair and wiped the tears off my cheeks.

"I'm here. I'm planted right here. Ok? Do you understand? I'm not going anywhere. You're right, we will get through this".

The decision of walking or staying wasn't much of a decision for me. After a month of not hearing from him, the continuous nights alone gave me more than enough time to process my feelings with all of it.

He fucked up, sure. But guess what, *we all fuck up*. I know criminals who wear a suit and tie and never see the inside of a jail cell their entire lives. It's the select few who live their life honestly, and not hiding from anyone or anything who end up paying the highest prices at times.

The man had done nothing to deserve my desertion. The man had shown me time and time again what it means to stand strong by my side, even during some of my *not so nice* moments. He had never asked anything *of me*, or *from me* since the first day I ever met him. Now it was time for me to show him my money would always be found where my mouth was. I told him I was with him, sunny days or not so sunny days.

So now here we were, with a lot of *not so sunny* days ahead of us. And I wasn't going anywhere.

The time frame from being arrested to getting to the actual sentencing day, that's where the most work takes place. That's where everything is still completely up in the air. Things that were left unfinished required finishing. He had a complete clothing line that needed to continue running. After all, when he hires the best criminal defense lawyer in the entire Atlantic Region, the fee for that doesn't pay itself. With everything taking place, he needed the people he could trust, and the people who truly loved him to remain by his side.

There has been hundreds, and I mean *hundreds* of girls who blow up his Facebook account, or send boat loads of messages to his various social media platforms.
Messages that the other girlfriend had to sort through and eventually just start to ignore. When you see your man through those *not so easy times*, then have random women from different parts of Canada professing their love to him, you sort of just want to swat those cling on's and random women away.

At the multiple court appearances that took place leading up to his sentencing date, the people who were there? It wasn't the fan club of random women, nor was it other dudes he barely knew who would boast about being his "friend". It's awfully cute when things get real how many people disappear.

Myself, his mum, his Aunty, the other girlfriend, and one of his guys from a support club.

That was it.

Every time.

Just us five.

If there was one court date I wasn't able to make due to my workload, the other girlfriend would be there. If she couldn't be there, I would make sure I was there. Either way, the both of us weren't going anywhere.

The other girlfriend single handedly took over the clothing line. She basically became a business women over night. Not only that, but with Robin sending her sketches from his jail cell, she was able to add new designs to the line, and even got the women's line up and running. She was amazing. I took care of various house stuff. With the other girlfriend travelling for work at times, anytime the house we had just North of Fredericton would be left for weeks at a time, I would ensure to make trips up to run the water or check on the property for security reasons.

Whether new insulation needed to be put in, or a contractor was coming up to look at the furnace or electrical system, I'd make time in my week to tee-up with whoever Robin needed me to in order to give him a full update on what we may or may not need for the home, pricing out various small upgrades, the list goes on.

The biggest pull that winter was keeping the clothes selling. With the orders being placed and paid for online, the other girlfriend would receive all the customer orders, then forward them to me via email. Once or twice a week I'd make my way to the property North of the city where all his things were moved to, and in the living room, the official "shipping and handling" of his company would continue. I'd be leaving the house with boxes of customer orders. Trips to the post office became a common occurrence that winter.

Before we knew it, *Team Robin* was established. None of us gave a shit about any outsider's opinions. We were simply doing what needed to be done in order to keep things flowing as smoothly as possible until all this was behind us.

We were still months away from knowing which of the 12 or so charges were going to actually stick. Every other day the news would state some "new charge" placed upon him. It was almost comical to see how many ways the authorities could split two or three actual charges into 12 or more. They were scraping the bottom of the barrel it seemed. The entire system wanted to throw the book at him. Make an example out of him as if to "ward off" motorcycle clubs from re-entering the Maritimes.

But I didn't give a shit about any of it.

I was standing by my man.

I knew the road ahead wasn't going to be easy, but my mind was made up.

And that was that.

The Fight for His Life

Come early January of 2018, once things with Robin were beginning to get ironed out, with a possible idea of future court appearances and what charges will actually go through, the heaviest of the storm was slightly behind us. *So I thought.*

It was the early morning of January 24th when I woke up to a horror that will forever haunt me.
My three year old baby, my Rottweiler Big Poppa John, was waking up as well. But nothing about the way he was waking up was good.

As I got out of bed, Nala still asleep under the blankets, I made my way to the end of the bed where Big Poppa John was asleep on his circle bed. Surrounding his head was a pool of blood. There was blood dripping out of his mouth, his ears, and even through the sides of his eyes. I gasped in pure fear, to which he awoke suddenly. As he stood up he immediately fell back over. With that much blood loss I could only imagine how light headed and weak he was.

I gently but frantically examined his head, trying to understand where all the blood was coming from. But to my worst fear, there was no cut, or something stupid and sharp that he had gotten into. It was his body. His body wasn't able to stop his blood from seeping out of him it seemed.

There was a huge book-sized patch on his back that was filled with blood. It was this jelly like consistency of dried yet wet blood covering the surface of his skin.

And all of this came on within a matter of hours it seemed overnight.

I grabbed my cell phone, called my vet – she told me to bring him in immediately.

I threw on a pair of pants and one of Robin's old sweaters. Slid my winter boots on, put Nala out for a quick pee and filled her bowl with her breakfast. While I was doing all of this Big Poppa was trying to walk down the hallway to come join us in the kitchen, but he was struggling. Bumping into the walls, pausing with his eyes rolling back in his head. It was a nightmare. I'll never get out of my memory the amount of blood that was on my bedroom floor that morning. I knew he would be too weak to jump up in to the truck the way he always did.

Big Poppa was well over 100 lbs, but like any mother out there who's had a sick baby, it doesn't matter how much your baby weighs, within seconds you possess this *sumo-mommy* type strength. I slid my arms under his body, got myself into a full squat position and forced my body up high enough so that I could slide him into the back seat of the truck. I flew into the front seat, started up the engine and flew out of the driveway.

The vet was only about fifteen minutes down the highway, but it was the longest fifteen minutes I've ever driven.

At that point I didn't know what was wrong with him. I didn't know if we had two hours or two minutes. Big Poppa was the strongest Rottweiler, physically and in spirit, so seeing him like this was scary.

It was beyond scary.

Throughout the drive I kept reaching one of my hands back to try and catch the blood he was throwing up. Hearing him choke on his own fluids was crushing my heart. I couldn't pull over and tend to him because we just needed to get to the vet.

Once we arrived, I opened the back door of the truck. Big Poppa knew exactly where we were. He loved all the girls at the vet. So as weak as he was, as soon as that door opened, he still had it in him to jump out in hopes of seeing the vet tech girls he loved so much. We slowly walked up to the front door of the clinic. Once inside one of the girls got us into an exam room. Within minutes the doctor came in. We went over all the basics to try and narrow down what could have happened. I've been to this vet clinic many times over the years. The team knew how much I loved my animals, but more so how well I took care of them.

With Big Poppa's age being still so young, cancer was a possibility, however it was listed as possibility number five on our list out of 1-5 possible causes. After a few minutes on the ground with Big Poppa, and carefully examining his skin, the vet had a pretty good idea what was most likely going on. He began to explain to me what an auto-immune disease in dogs can look like. Although rare, and difficult to treat, he's seen it a few times in his career.

It is most known as AIHA. This is a disease where the body basically attacks itself from the inside. The white blood cells attack the production of red blood cells. Without red blood cells, our bodies won't breath. He explained the continuous bleeding from his mouth and skin due to Big Poppa most likely having little to no platelets left. Platelets are what stop us from bleeding to death when we get a cut or go in for surgery. Platelets are one thousand percent necessary for us. As well, the red blood cells. Without his body responding to treatment (and some dogs don't) Big Poppa would die.

As the vet was explaining to me the disease, I began to understand very quickly that this wasn't something small, *at all*. This wasn't something a few medications was going to fix. This was big time. This was *so deadly* that most families who receive this diagnosis with their pets, they choose to euthanize because it can take anywhere from five to ten grand just to get through this first week of treatment, and that's with absolutely no guarantee of the dog surviving.

People with families can't gamble that money when they have their own kids to think about.

With no babies of my own, and the man I love behind bars, I knew immediately we were going to start treatment.

No questions asked.

I had lots to sell to keep the money flowing.

Whatever my baby needed, he was getting.

The first order of business was to get Big Poppa new blood. He was so faint, so weak, his gums were almost white. He needed a blood transfusion, and fast.

The closest clinic that was equipped to perform a transfusion was in Moncton.

Two hours away.

I said to my vet *"will he make it that long? Do we have two hours? Will I need to pull over on the highway and watch my dog die?"*

My vet assured me that although Big Poppa was in very bad shape, he had no concern with him holding up well enough to make the trip to Moncton. Once we were back on the road, my vet had called ahead to Moncton with Big Poppa's blood type so they could prep the transfusion equipment and get the right blood match ready to go.

I think I got to Moncton in just under an hour and a half. I'm pretty sure I hit that highway going about 150 kms per hour the entire way. It was cold, and icy. But with my new tires I had recently put on, I put the truck in four wheel drive and white knuckled it to the clinic.

Once arriving, we got Big Poppa into a private exam room. The vet went over the entire procedure. How long it would take, how they matched his blood, everything. Due to the transfusion being a pretty big process, he would need to remain there overnight so the staff could monitor how his body received the new blood.

Just before they were about to take him out back to start the transfusion, I laid on the floor with him in the exam room. He could barely lift his head. His eyes were so tired. I was scared. I knew if anyone could beat this, it would be Poppa. But another part of me had this very real, very morbid realization that this disease is in fact a deadly one.

I had just lost my man to the system. I needed both my pupps by my side. Losing Poppa too, I couldn't even fathom the idea.

That afternoon Vanessa, my pupps official Aunty had met us at the clinic in Moncton. She has one of the Presa pupps, a sister of Nala's. She was also there the day Nala and Big Poppa first met. She's basically family to me.

Her and my breeder live very close to the clinic, so having them there with me was a big relief. They are the guardian angels to my dogs. Shane, my breeder, he loves Nala and Big Poppa as if they're his own. He has Nala's mum and some of her brothers at his place.

With Vanessa and Shane by my side for this battle, none of us were going anywhere until Big Poppa was healthy again. That night as I drove home, I couldn't help but feel completely helpless.

In a matter of a few short months my world was becoming extremely tough, and extremely sad.

With the onset of Big Poppa's sickness, it was times like this where I became angry that Robin was away.

These are the moments when you need your partner physically there *with you*. You need and *want* their support. Their reassuring words. Even to just have their body standing beside you while you take in the never ending devastating information the vet is telling you.

But that is the down fall to deciding to stay with your loved one while they serve time. You need to learn how to cope and handle things like this *alone*.

What doesn't kill you makes you stronger

They say.

I like to think of it more as:

What doesn't kill you makes you cynical, quick to anger, and slightly ruthless.

But to each their own.

Later that night as I got home, once getting in the house, I turned the kitchen lights on and just slinked down the wall by the door and sat on the cold floor. With being gone all day, the heat was still sitting at a pretty modest temperature. I was too tired to really move. Nala soon came over and sat down right beside me. She kept starring at Big Poppa's circle bed. She was confused as to why he wasn't home.

I kept thinking to myself *"this can't be happening. This can't be real. He's only three years old"*.

As I was preparing supper for Nala, I got a call from the Moncton clinic with an update on Big Poppa.

He had taken the transfusion very well. His red blood cell count was up. His energy much better. All in all, things were stable. This was a huge relief for me. I felt confident in the possibility of beating this.

The next day as I headed back to the clinic, with Nala in the back seat, we made our way back down the highway into Moncton.

Shane and Vanessa were meeting me there.

When I arrived, the latest update on Poppa wasn't good. His red blood cell count had again, dropped, and he was now back down to dangerously low levels.

They brought him out into the private family area where we were waiting. Shane, Vanessa, Nala and I surrounded Poppa as he lay weak on the floor. Shane began to discuss with the vet other solutions or courses of action to conquer this disease. But the vet didn't have very much to tell us. She was basically guiding us to the decision of euthanization. I was way too emotional to deal with any of that sort of talk.

Vanessa nor Shane were satisfied with their quick ability to simply *give up on Poppa.*

Nor was I.

Vanessa had asked if any of the vets had reached out to any of the doctors at the Veterinary College on the island, *Prince Edward Island.* For anyone who is familiar with veterinary care, the college on the island in terms of expertise is equivalent to Guelph University in Ontario. Guelph and P.E.I are the gold standard of veterinary hospitals in the country. The vet kindly stated they *had not* reached out, and that she wasn't sure that they could do anything more than what had already been done at the Moncton clinic.

As I lay on the ground with Poppa, Shane had Nala by her leash, Vanessa sitting in a chair right beside me, Vanessa looked to Shane and simply said *"We're going to PEI".* She thanked the vet for their attempt to provide care, advised them we'd call in a few hours with my Visa card to settle the bill. And with that, Shane opened the back door that was apparently only for emergency exits, he loaded Nala up in his SUV to take her back to his place for the day, Vanessa and I got Big John in the back of my truck, and we were off. We had about an hour and half before we'd arrive to the College on the island. Vanessa made the call to let them know we were on our way.

This was a family undertaking. We were going to save Big John, and that's all there was to it.

During the drive I called my dad. I had called him the night prior explaining everything to him that was taking place. Like the reliable, super smart dad that he is, he had some very uplifting and supportive news for us to hear while on the drive.

"Hi sweetie, so I've been researching this auto-immune disease. A lot of cases have been reported particularly in the Boxer breed. From everything I'm reading, it appears that if we can keep Big Poppa alive for the first 7-9 days of treatment via blood transfusions, that will give his body a chance to respond to the drugs. But in order for this to happen, he needs to survive the first week or so, as it can take up to nine or ten days for the drugs to actually kick in and start working. If we can do that, he has an excellent chance at recovering".

Boxers usually weight anywhere from 60 to 80 pounds, so with Big John surpassing 100 lbs, it only made sense that his body would take longer to process the drugs through his system, as simply put, he's a bigger dog. More body to treat.

Once arriving to the hospital on the island, we were lead back to a room where we met the vet student who would be the lead vet of his care team. This young woman was brilliant. A truly brilliant – thriving veterinary student who has already treated and saved loads of animals. While listening to her explain the treatment process, as scared as I was, I began to feel calm simply due to her level of expertise as she spoke about the various variables that can add unfavourable hiccups during treatment. She explained that some days we may take one two step forward only to take two steps back. That recovery with this disease was literally an hour by hour process.

We had an understanding that we would need to leave Big Poppa with them for a minimum of seven days. They knew we had many more blood transfusions to continue with. These transfusions would take place every 24 hours until his body would reach a point where his red blood cells would begin to survive on their own. But most importantly, his bone marrow would re-produce them naturally, and his white cells would seize from attacking them. It was the medications he would require for many months to come that would inhibit his white cells from attacking his very much needed red blood cells.

During the drive home from the island, as exhausted as I was, I knew he was in the right place. Vanessa was by my side that entire trip reassuring me he was the in the best possible care on this side of the country. We had one quick stop to make at Shane's to pick up Nala, then I would drop Vanessa off and make my way home with Nala fast asleep in the back seat of the truck.

Only in the Maritimes can you cross three provinces in one day.

The following week involved trips to the island to visit Poppa while he was in recovery. Everything in my world came to a halt the day I awoke to find Poppa helpless on my bedroom floor in a pool of his own blood. I was barely remembering to eat during this time let alone respond to some text message or even take a shower. Every day that week consisted of sitting by the phone awaiting the every two hour phone calls from the college with updates on how he was doing. *Did the transfusion take? How many hours does the fresh blood last until his body kills it off? Has his immune system let up any?*

It was the longest, and by far most painful sequence of days.

As each day went on, there was always good news about the transfusion being a success, followed by a dinner time phone call letting me know his levels had once again dropped, and another transfusion would be needed to keep him alive another night.

On night eight, I kneeled in front of my small white Christmas tree that I had ordered off Amazon that fall for me and the pupps to enjoy over the holidays. In front of me was a half chewed Christmas ornament that Poppa had chewed the year before. I put my hands by my chin, closed my eyes, and with everything I had, I begged God to give my boy the strength he needed to overcome this. I prayed for his lungs – for them to remain strong. I prayed for his heart – for it to continue beating with the strength of mine. I prayed for his brain – to remain protected and to not be flooded by seeping blood that his body couldn't stop from running through him. And lastly, I'd pray for his bone marrow. For his bone marrow to produce the strongest, bravest red blood cells any dog as ever seen.

I said these prayers over and over again until my knees became numb from sitting on the hardwood floor for so long.

On day nine, Vanessa and I had planned to drive back up to the college for another visit. Upon arriving, Poppa's progression was speaking for itself. His body was slowly – but surely beginning to respond to the treatments. On day nine it appeared the drugs were *in fact* kicking in. His body was holding his red blood cell count on its own for much longer periods of time.

This in itself was a miracle.

During that afternoon visit, as Vanessa and I lay on the ground with a much healthier looking Big Poppa. The vet advised us she had yet to draw his levels for that day. The latest results we had still showed his red blood cell count at around 19. The normal/healthy levels for dogs was in the 30s. But anything above 15 – and we were out of the danger zone. His platelets were still at zero, unfortunately. But any progress was still to be celebrated. So during that afternoon, we were celebrating his red blood cells.

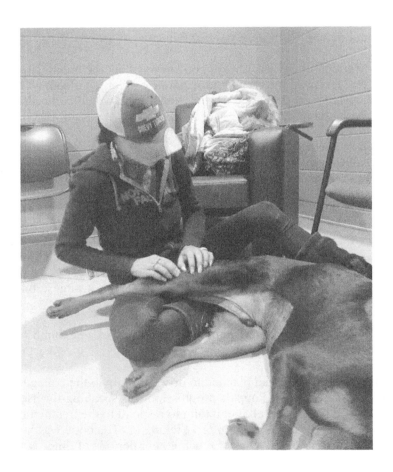

It was about thirty or so minutes after we left the hospital when we got a call from Meredith, the lead student who was working with Poppa. She had news for us. And this news was the latest results from his most recent blood work.

As Vanessa and I had the call on speaker phone through the truck, we held our breath just as we began crossing the confederation bridge. *"His red blood cell count had – on its own – increased to twenty seven. And his platelets, they have gone from zero, to 70 thousand"*.

Hearing Meredith say those numbers over the phone felt like I had just won the fucking lottery.

Vanessa and I both yelled in sheer excitement and relief. I kept saying *"Yes Big Poppa!! Yes!! Yes!! That's my boy!!"*

I remember taking a big, deep breath. I think I had shrunk down to 100 lbs just from the stress of the past eleven days. And that moment after hearing Meredith give us the numbers was probably the first time I took a full chested breath of oxygen since the morning Big John awoke sick on my bedroom floor.

Tears of joy streamed down my face. Meredith explained that they wanted to keep him at least another night just to ensure his body continued to stabilize. But if things remained solid until the next day, I could come back and go over discharge instructions and most importantly, my new *long-term Big Poppa John treatment plan* for his recovery.

Recovery for this diseases isn't a five or six day thing.

Recovery from this disease – due to how fragile a place his body got to – six months, minimum, until we were *really* out of the danger zone. But I didn't care. I didn't need time with friends or Saturday nights out on the town. I needed my boy to be healthy again. And to be home with *both my babies* so I could keep the money coming in and support my loved one who was sitting behind bars.

After spending a total of just under twenty two thousand dollars, my boy was coming home.

Twenty two thousand of the best dollars I've ever spent.

We regret spending money on "things", cars (an Audi that fails you), poor stock choices, a housing investment gone badly, or hell, even two 200 bucks on an ex-girlfriend or boyfriend who ended up doing you dirty.

But we never *ever* regret spending money on our babies.

I sold diamonds, my gold jewelry, precious stones, fucking furniture – I pawned and sold almost half my god damn house to keep the cash flow going to ensure Big Poppa got what he needed.

I remember saying to Vanessa after the phone call with Meredith *"Van, thank sweet God – we went through with treatment. Could you imagine? Had I "opted out" due to finances with the very real fact that Big John would survive this?!"*

Money is replaceable.

They make it all the time.

Family isn't.

Big Poppa John showed me time and time again he was going to fight for me, therefore I was without question going to fight for him.

If he needed time and resources to end up coming out on the other side of this, then giving him the time and getting him the resources - that's what I was going to do.

And I am forever glad that I did.

After two days had passed and Big Poppa was still holding steady with all his levels, Vanessa and I made our way back to the island. This was a celebratory day. I had Nala with us in the back seat, we stopped and got some Tim Hortons, this was the end of a long eleven days of pure hell. But we did it. Poppa made it through treatment.

Once arriving to the hospital and making our way inside we only had to wait a few minutes until Meredith brought Big Poppa out to us. And in pure Big Poppa fashion, he was basically pulling Meredith by the leash.

His energy was back.

My boy was back.

Meredith and one other vet went over a very detailed long-term care recovery plan. We were coming home with a pharmacy it seemed. His pill schedule was more complicated than a pill schedule from the nut house.

There was only one big *"shit"* moment during the discharge instructions. One of his prescriptions, his main prescription that he would most likely be needing for at least the next six months, this pill was almost $600.00 a box. One box will last about a month.

In my head I thought to myself *"fuck me!"*. But then I looked down at his big brown fighting eyes and before I knew it, the $600.00 price tag didn't mean anything compared to having him back home with us. The cheque book will balance itself out. It always does. The only thing that mattered was that he was surviving this. I'll eat napkins and tap water for the next six months. I'd do whatever it would take to have enough cash to ensure his recovery process goes as smooth as possible.

Once getting home, the simplicity of watching him run into the house and hop up onto his oversized chair that he'd sleep in during the day, seeing that – my entire body was all of a sudden at ease.

I still had to be cautious. Limit his play time with Nala. Ensure he didn't get any type of scratch or cut. With the heavy dose of steroids he was on, any cut or scratch where blood would seep out would be risky for his newly returned platelets.

The very next day after spending the night in bed with both Nala and Poppa sleeping soundly by my side, I went to the grocery store to stock up on everything Big John would need in his diet going forward.

He was now considered anemic, and would probably always be a bit anemic for the rest of his life. So ensuring his meals were high in iron was an absolute daily necessity.

My 32nd birthday was just around the corner, but that was the furthest thing from my mind. I actually didn't even remember until Facebook reminded me. My birthday was spent at home prepping John's meals for the following day. I didn't need or want any kind of celebration. My gift was already here. Having both my babies together again.

The next two months my life was on a very tight *very strict* schedule. Due to John's meds needing to be taken at various times in the day, having any type of social life was off the books.

The minute I was done at work, I'd be on the highway headed straight home to be with my pupps. Even though the recovery was slow and steady – just how it should be, I was still completely pre-occupied with being by Big John's side as much as I could. Routine check-ups at my vet here in town about twice a week simply to draw his blood to ensure his levels were all remaining steady.

The girls at the vet were so impressed with his recovery. And slowly, our maintenance-check-ups would become once a week, once every ten days, so on and so forth.

It's pretty incredible the perspective you get when tragedy hits home. Before Big Poppa got sick, I was slowly becoming more comfortable with Robin being behind bars. My new-solo everyday routines with our evening phone calls from the jail was becoming my new normal, so I had started setting more goals to achieve with various one or two year time lines. And like a lot of people, some of these goals were pretty superficial.

But after going through everything with Big Poppa, none of those things I once saw as important held much weight. The fruits of your labour are only ever really enjoyed when you have the ones you love most enjoying them with you. Ever since bringing Poppa home, seeing how much spice he added to mine and Nala's life, I never have – nor could I picture a life without him.

As I sat in my living room one evening with my semi-decent Canadian Tire Fireplace burning, a double Jacks on ice in my hand, Big Poppa sleeping on his circle bed by my feet, and Nala curled up beside me, in that moment – despite wishing my better half wasn't on the inside, but in that moment I felt for the first time in a *long time* how lucky of a woman I was. I had a roof over my head. Running water. Food in the fridge. A day job that covered most of the bills. And most importantly, the two heart beats that warmed that house – they were both beating strong.

If you have your health, you have your wealth.

But this moment in time – this peace and happiness – the bliss -- wouldn't last long. The road was about to take a much darker turn. It was a turn I never thought I'd see.

During the first week of April, after almost a month of steady progress, I awoke to find Big Poppa not looking too well. I put him and Nala outside to see if his energy would perk up. Anytime they go outside he becomes *Big Poppa John Strong.*

I let them out – but nothing. Nala ran onto the lawn and found her favorite sticks to chew and run with. But not Poppa. He slowly sat down at the edge of the porch staircase, licked his lips and looked over his shoulder at me. I stood quietly in the door way just watching him. Looking for any sign of weakness, or maybe pain.

Anything.

He eventually took a few steps down the stairs and onto the lawn. I could tell he was about to throw up.

This wasn't a good sign at all. Throwing up a little bit here and there was sort of expected while in recovery, but this wasn't him throwing up because he ate his food too fast. It was stomach bile. He had a very somber look in his eyes. I called him back in the house.

As he walked into the kitchen, right as I was wrapping my arms around him to give him a hug and a cuddle, he threw up almost a bucket's worth of clear fluid right onto me.

He then went and made his way down the hallway and laid down behind my bed.

This was hugely out of character for him. He never lays down anywhere anyone can't see him. He's an attention loving dog. He'll sit right on your lap if you let him. When I went into my bedroom and tried to tempt him out from behind my bed with a cookie, he wouldn't move.

That was all I needed to see. I grabbed my phone and called the vet. They told me to bring him in right away.

At first while examining him, they couldn't see why all of a sudden his progress went from hero to zero practically overnight. I went over everything he ate, his activities the day before - everything. Nothing that took place at home was out of the ordinary.

After a few hours of having him on an IV for fluid replacement, with *little to no* improvement with his energy they decided to do an X ray.

Just to rule out anything serious.

What my vet found was devastating news.

It appeared he had some type of long string in his lower intestine. When the body attempts to digest a string with no success, the string will eventually remain in a part of the intestine and slowly begin to get stuck in a manner where it almost becomes a saw. Each time the digestive tract would move food through the intestines, the rope would slowly cut through the skin as it would be moved back and forth by the motion of the intestine.

With scenarios likes this, it's a day surgery. The vet will open up the dog and remove whatever is lodged in their stomach. It's a common surgery for a lot of vets due to how many time animals get their paws on either poorly made chew toys that they end up swallowing parts of, or various sharp or dangerous objects in a yard.

It is expected that a dog will awake from this type of surgery and pretty much walk out of the operating room.

When we realized what was causing him to feel so ill, at first I said to the vet *"ok! Well this is good news, Right? I mean, we can fix it with surgery. And everything should be ok, right?"*

The vet then began to explain to me that due to Big Poppa being on such a high dose of steroids for the last few months, cutting open his skin to perform the actual surgery is a risk all its own.

Removing the string wouldn't be the hard part. It would be sewing him back up afterwards so he can heal.

You see, due to the medications he was on, his skin would lack the ability to hold tight with the stitches. So even if the removal of the string was successful, there was a very high probability that his skin would fall away from the stitches. Ultimately, his bowels would fall apart from the inside.

I knew if we didn't do the surgery, he would be dead within a day or two. So although the surgery was high risk, with the fact that there was still a chance his body may in fact hold after being stitched up, I knew we had to try. We had gotten this far and I couldn't grasp the idea that a poorly made chew toy would be what ultimately took Big Poppa down for good.

What killed me the most about this was that I had stopped buying rope toys for the pupps months prior. I began to see how Nala would shred them, and having the pupps swallow the strings was dangerous. But with the snow melting, Big Poppa must have found an old one that had become exposed in the yard from the snow melting.

The decision was made to go through with the surgery.

And it was the longest five hours I've ever sat through.

I drove down to a local restaurant a few minutes after Poppa was taken back and prepped for surgery. I took a seat at the bar and asked the bartender for a short glass with a double Jacks. I sat there and just sipped the drink while starring at the screen of my phone. I kept going over in my head all the variables about this surgery. Whether or not his body would heal and hold the interior stitches long enough for the incisions to scar over. The rest of his life was riding on the outcome of the surgery. I held onto the hope of him once again, overcoming the odds that were so unfairly stacked against him, but at the same time, it felt as if death himself was sitting in the chair next to me. I had the most unsettling gut feeling that this might not pan out.

My phone rings.

It's the vet.

I pick up immediately.

The vet explained to me that they have successfully removed all the string. And that they were now beginning to sew him up. He had a certain tone to his voice. I could almost feel through the phone the lack of hope he had for Poppa to pull through this. I told him I was on my way back and would see them shortly.

While waiting in the front room of the clinic, I could see some of the staff coming out of the operating room. I could tell who had been in the room with him just by the look on their faces. Everyone at that clinic was so proud of Poppa and how brave he was in battling the auto-immune disease. The entire building had a very somber vibe. It was if everyone knew this would be Poppa's last night with us.

It wasn't very long until one of the Vet's came out and brought me into an exam room. Poppa was still out back in recovery, but he wanted to discuss with me how the surgery went. He didn't need to say very much. It was written all over his face. As he kneeled down beside me, while holding my hand, he ever so gently said to me *"Victoria, Big Poppa has fought a long, hard battle. You have done 100 times more for him than we've ever seen any animal owner do"*.

Tears began to fill my eyes because I knew where this conversation was going.

"We could tell by how fragile his skin was… the stitches most likely won't hold longer than 12 hours."

"Do you think he has a 50 or 60 percent chance at healing?" I asked. In complete desperation the vet would agree.

"Unfortunately no, I am so sorry Victoria"

"Ok, so maybe a 20 percent chance at healing? Because Big Poppa can do a whole lot with even just 20 percent".

The vet then very gently said to me *"Victoria, I can honestly tell you, Big Poppa has about a 1% chance, maybe less, of surviving this. I'm so sorry"*.

I nodded my head as I held a blank stare down at my feet.

I understood.

This was the end of the road for us. This was the end of the road for Big Poppa.

The vet then explained to me that since they did the surgery, we owed it to Poppa to see how he handles sleeping through the night. But if by morning he wasn't walking or showing signs of energy, that would indicate to us that his bowels were in fact slowly letting go of the stitches.

And we would need to put him down.

I drove home from the vet that night blaming myself.

Everyone has told me that I have zero reason to carry his death on my hands, but what people say doesn't matter. Big Poppa didn't eat the rope toy because the trees in the backyard bought it. He didn't ingest the toy because the garden shed put the rope toy in the yard.

He ate the rope toy because *I had bought it*, and left it out in the yard.

And with that, his death was not his fault, but mine.

After pulling in my driveway, I could hear Nala barking from the living room. This would be another night I'd be coming home without Poppa. I sat in my truck and asked God with every last bit of energy I had in me to wrap his healing hands around my boy. I was no longer praying for Poppa to beat this, or survive. With the amount of trauma and sickness his body had gone through, even if he did recover from the surgery, he'd need to be on puppy bed rest for weeks just to ensure a stitch didn't open up. His quality of life would be completely compromised.

So I asked God if he could wrap his hands around my boy and keep him warm until the morning when I would be back at the clinic.

I walked into the house and sat down on the kitchen floor with Nala. I had never felt as helpless as I did that night. We literally had done everything possible, but we weren't going to win this time.

By six a.m. Nala and I were up and out of bed. I threw on some gym pants and a hoodie, wrapped Nala up in one of John's blankets and made my way back to the vet.

During the drive in, the vet called me to give an update on how John was doing.
The call lasted about forty seconds.

It was time to say good bye to Big Poppa.

I remember how his face, his bark, his crazy and hilarious Big Poppa John antics started flooding my vision as I drove down that highway. A part of me wanted to believe this wasn't real. But it was. And I was moments away from losing him forever.

When I got to the clinic I came in through the side door. Out back, laying in his recovery bed, Poppa was half asleep. They had him on some mild pain medication to keep him comfortable.

I crawled into the bed with him and was his big spoon that morning for the very last time. I had my face pressed right up into the back of his neck. I never wanted to forget his smell. I never wanted to forget what he felt like while sleeping in my arms. I laid with him in that small bed for about a half hour or so before the vet came back in. I told Big Poppa that Nala and I were so proud of him. That he was our Big Brave Boy.

As I rubbed his ears and told him everything was going to be ok, I looked up
at the vet and gave him the go ahead to go through with the injection. With
Poppa's back pressed up to my chest and his body wrapped in my arms, I felt
his heart make that Big Poppa John beat for the very last time.

After three months of fighting for his life, the road had now ended.

He was three years old.

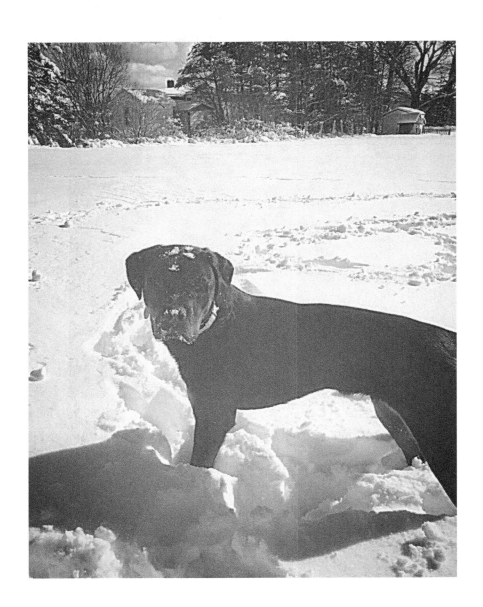

Don't Let the Pain from your Past
Dictate how you
Re-Introduce yourself to your Future

After losing Big Poppa, my entire world changed. What I thought I had wanted out of life for myself, those images were now very different. The weight of his loss completely shifted my entire state of being into another world.

For anyone who has lost someone or an animal they loved, your life is never the same after that. There has been scientific research done that has linked losing an animal or family pet as being equivalent to losing an actual person. And I believe it. The pain of both my dog's deaths has stayed with me much longer than the pain of losing any relationship.

I was set to move into my fourth home. The moving day was May 18th of 2018. I had finally sold my small bungalow to a young guy who nickle'd and dime'd me on the listing price until I was ready to throw the keys at him and tell him just to have the damn thing. Being a part of any back and forth negotiating with the selling price wasn't something I gave any shit about. And of course, he wanted all my appliances. Including the washer and dryer my dad had bought for me as a gift for my Titusville farm house. But with Big Poppa gone, and in no way even close to coming to terms with his loss, just about everything at that time held zero relevance. If the young buck was a cheap fuck, then that was his life journey, not mine, so I gave him what he wanted and moved on.

That washer and dryer set may be the only set the poor guy will have for years to come. So I let the bugger have them. And after fighting for three months to save Big Poppa's life, I simply didn't have much fight left in me anymore.

Moving into the new house was very bittersweet. Mostly because Big Poppa was supposed to be a part of that new beginning. There was more land. The home was bigger. Sky lights in the kitchen. Peaked roof in the main living area. Much more privacy with only having one neighbour who I could barely even see due to all the trees surrounding my lot. Not having his *bull in a China shop* energy in the house was very heavily felt during the first few months of moving in.

But Nala and I made the home *our home*, as best as we could while holding his memories with us. I knew she missed him. She fell into a puppy depression after we lost him. It killed me to see that sparkle in her eyes now gone. He was her light. He was the spice to her soul. He was the pillar of strength for us both. Driving home from the vet with his ashes now in a box, as I held the box close to my chest while making my way down the highway, I looked down at this six inch by four inch cardboard box that used to be my giant Rottweiler, and I asked him where he wanted to go for one last truck ride with mum.

So with thinking of where Big Poppa would most likely want to go, we made our way down the highway to our most favourite spot, just the box of ashes and I.

Robin was of course always there in the background. There wasn't anything he could do from a jail cell other than give me his words of support during our phone calls. He reminded me how good of a dog mum I was. He reminded me that I did all that could have been done, and that Big Poppa had a great life while he was with us.

That's the hardest part about your better half being behind bars. On the days when you're struggling, yet you've got loved ones surrounding you, various ways and resources to manage a problem or handle a bad day, you almost feel guilty to complain to them. It's a balancing act of knowing you can tell them about *any and all* of your bad days because they're your partner, but at the same time, you want to be strong for them. Because if you're falling apart while on the outside, there isn't anything from the inside they can do to help.

Even though he does listen to anything *not so wonderful* I might have on my mind that particular day, you don't want to be a big bag of tears anytime they call. You want to be that uplifting phone call for them. You want them to walk away from the call knowing things at home are ok, things are being taken care of, the bills are being handled, everyone is healthy, everyone is managing – all of it. They have very long and very lonely nights in those cells to think or worry about something shitty you may have told them during one of your calls.

Robin hardly ever gave me anything to ever worry about when he was out here, on the outside. So now that he was facing years of being behind bars, I didn't want to give him additional things to worry about. Yet despite being behind bars, he still remains my strong and steady. Most calls he's helping *keep me* together. His ability to master mind over matter is pretty impressive.

Mourning the loss of Big Poppa John would take place while continuing to handle everything that was still in front of me.

I have had a few people over the past year or so ask me about what I really want for myself. That family I wanted. Or simply just being able to be a mum all on my own. People who just overall look out for my best interests, or simply inquire because they are trying to be a good friend. And I appreciate any and all the loving advice that has come my way, I truly do. However, what I really want has changed drastically ever since losing Robin to the system and Big Poppa to the heavens.

Waking up each morning and putting the coffee on with the simplicity of peace in my heart, healthy loved ones, and having the love of a good man.

That's it.

Nothing else.

The list of "goals" prior to losing them both looked very different than what it is now.

It looked more like this:

Making six figures in 2019.
Having enough monthly revenue to comfortably lease a Range Rover.
By 2020 have a lifestyle that would allow me to spend two or so months in Florida during the winter.

List number two sort of makes me look like a self-absorbed woman focused on material gains.

Even though the financial loss I took on my Audi which almost bankrupt me absolutely served its lesson with making me fully understand that material gains do not represent growth. They may display a certain status, but they don't in any way represent true happiness. Despite that major lesson that had me talking dirty to a multitude of perverts for 0.50 cents per minute, before losing my loved ones I still had my mind focused on all the wrong things. All the things that only fill a hole inside you that you'd be better off filling with something a bit more concrete, like self-acceptance.

My dad is one of the world's leading Radiation Oncologists in the cancer world.
He's basically famous in the medical world. There's not enough room on this page for me to type out all the additional letters in his signature block that come after "MD".

He's incredible with what he does.

I believe today he is currently driving the fourth vehicle he's ever had as an adult.

It's his fourth Honda.

No Lexus. No Range Rover. Not even a fully loaded Jeep Cherokee.

It's a Honda SUV.

With *cloth interior.*

The home he lives in during the week while he's in the city for work is smaller than the home I live in now.

He makes *ten times* what I make in a year. And when I actually run the numbers in my calculator as I type this, I think even maybe a bit more.

But he knows all too well that having the best of the best means absolutely dick all unless you have the people you love the most with you to share it with. And even then, how expensive does your living room sofa need to be in order for everyone to sit on the cushions it provides to have a good time?

It's easy to get caught up in wanting to be the best of the best. And when we go without those various achievements or material possessions, we make ourselves believe that we are lacking, or not as successful as the people around us.

That fact couldn't be further from the truth.

It's all a bunch of bullshit.

And even though I always knew the logic of that fact, I never really understood what it meant until I woke up and felt the weight of that actual reality.

"Never wear your wealth" Robin would always say to me.

When Big John became sick, coming home that first day without him, all those fancy jewelry items I had, the expensive watches, or the custom designed sofa set, it was all irrelevant. When Big John was sick, the only purpose those items gave me was the dollar value they held so I could *get rid of them* in order to take care of the thing that *actually* mattered, which was Big John.

These days I wake up every day very clear with what's important, versus what's not.

You couldn't bother me with any mediocre level, non-serious worry that will dissipate from conversation before it even turns into anything to even really worry about.

If a person rubs me the wrong way, or adds no purpose or benefit to my life, they don't stay in my life. And I don't take more than one second to even think about it.

Before the pin hits the floor, I get rid of them.

The prison sentence that we knew was coming was eventually put in place for the man who gives me so much.

There was one thing and *only one thing* that has helped get me through the past year, and that has been my family. My family and a handful of friends that I basically consider family.

Not a day goes by where I don't feel moments of loneliness due to Robin being behind bars. That's something that doesn't ever get easier. Sure, I have my daily routines that help keep me focused on the good things in my life. But ultimately there is a lonely place in my day that I simply cannot change with a simple *mind over matter* switch in perspective.

But waking up every morning, while putting on the coffee, and getting ready for another day, I'm thankful for the pains I've had over the past ten years. I'm thankful because they have allowed me to relate, and more so *understand* a multitude of women who have experienced similar situations. It has allowed me to help someone realize that *I too*, have had days where I hated *everything about myself.* That I as well have fought through those never ending months of depression that can actually hurt so bad and feel so hopeless that you wallow in your self-pity.

I've had three unsuccessful pregnancies, a divorce, failed relationships, failed military career, crashed a few cars, was minutes from declaring bankruptcy by age 29, three major hip operations which eventually led to the complete removal of a couple *pretty big time* bones. I've done regretful things. I've said regretful things. I've hurt people who I love. I've put a price on myself as a person you could rent in order to pay my bills. And I've made big decisions for the wrong reasons.

I have a lot to shame myself about.

But holding onto those mistakes, "living in the past" we call it, serves you no purpose. It will only keep you stuck.

Some days I laugh because I think to myself, *"I honestly think the only thing that's left is to be set on fire"*.

What has made navigating through my twenties most difficult, wasn't the heart break from the Special Forces guy, nor was it losing my marriage. What has made things on a *day to day* basis a little difficult for me is the diagnosis I received a few years ago.

Now, when I finally received this diagnosis, I was a bit relieved because it gave me some clarity on why I would find it hard to simply sit and watch a half hour TV show without feeling uneasy or restless.

I was diagnosed with Borderline Personality Disorder and Identity Dissociation.

This is a mental illness that isn't very commonly known. It's usually miss-understood if anything. Many people are mistaken as bi-polar, when in fact they are Borderline. A bi-polar individual can have over one hundred highs and lows in the matter of a day. A Borderline individual will have highs and lows that can last days, sometimes weeks.

Now, it's not multiple personality disorder. That is quite different. That is legit having *multiple personalities*.

To put into perspective the general severity of Borderline Personality Disorder, I came across this statistic from an article I found on the internet about a year ago or so.

And the statistic read that on average around 80% of Federal Inmates in the USA who were sentenced for violent crimes who were diagnosed as sociopaths, when further psychiatric sessions took place, they were re-diagnosed as actually being *Borderline*.

The best way I can explain what it feels like to live as a Borderline is this:

"Borderline individuals are the psychological equivalent of third-degree burn patients. They simply have, so to speak, no emotional skin. Even the slightest touch or movement can create immense suffering for this person".
-- Marsha Linehan

With Identity Dissociation, it's a severe form of actual *dissociation from self.* It's mostly thought of as almost a coping mechanism. Where a person can literally dissociate from a place or situation.
We often *"check out"* in order to *"check in"* with another state of mind. When this happens, I usually can't remember what took place between the times I started to dissociate from my present state or current reality to when it stops.

Which is a bit scary, mostly due to my lapses in memory.

I've had people come up to me whether at a grocery store or the local gym, and they'll say something such as *"it was so good seeing you the other day!"*. I'll play along with them as if I feel the same, when in fact, I haven't a damn clue what they're talking about because I don't remember it happening.

Now, the causes of these two mental disorders?

Trauma.

Of any kind.

When I received the diagnosis, the only thing I was sure about was simple;

I wasn't born this way.

And with that fact clear in my mind, that is why you couldn't pay me all the money in the world to re-live my twenties.

In the past, when I have reacted a certain way to a situation, I couldn't understand why nobody could see why I would be feeling that way. To me, it was clear, but why couldn't anyone else understand? Was I seeing something they weren't?

Imagine walking outside and its pouring rain. Everyone outside has rain jackets and umbrellas, but not you, you're just out there in a t-shirt and jeans. All of a sudden you start to become drenched due to the water falling from the sky. You are wet and cold. But nobody around you feels that way because they have rain gear on. In this example, the rain gear isn't actually *rain gear,* it's the emotional disposition of a *non-mentally ill* individual.

So with this analogy, a Borderline lives in a life where they never have rain gear. So whatever is happening around them, they feel it much more intensely than the person standing next to them. Making the way we react appear to be extremely irrational due to the person standing three feet away not being able to see what the big deal is. If a hurtful word is used, a Borderline will digest that word as if it's a knife being thrown at them. Therefore, our reaction can be vicious. Much too vicious of a response in comparison to the mediocre level of severity of the actual word. A non-mentally ill individual may have an easier time brushing it off, or not letting the mean word cause them any upset in their day.

When living each day now being aware of my emotional triggers, it has been a difficult but needed education process. On my worst days, I push people away who actually love me. I become suspicious of why people are contacting me. I no longer see reality for what it actually is. My ability to understand the true workings of what is taking place outside my front door becomes difficult. Making it incredibly easy for me to stay at home as much as I possibly can.

My home is safe.

My home is quiet.

And I don't give out my address to *anyone* unless absolutely necessary.

Busy airports. Loud crowds with multiple strangers brushing by you on a sidewalk, all of these things are extremely uncomfortable for me.

Looking back to when I moved home to Toronto to live with my sister, it's no surprise that I struggled as much and I did. But more so, literally flee from the busy spot we were living in a mere three weeks after moving in. I was incredibly uncomfortable to the point where I just had to go. It didn't matter to me at the time who I was hurting or the rift that happened with my sister and I because of it, I just *had to go.*

Something as simple as the volume on my TV during a movie. If a scene in the movie displays a car crash or something loud taking place and the volume of that scene automatically gets louder simply due to the theater effects of the movie, if it lasts for too long I'll jump out of bed and scramble for the volume button as fast as I can. My whole body will begin to feel like a pin bag with tiny pins being pressed into my skin. The intensity of the *intense movie scene* can completely set me off.

As much as it hurt to receive this diagnosis, it has helped shed a lot of clarity on moments of my life where my reaction was not justified by the actual situation that took place. I've had moments where an individual has pulled up behind me at a stop sign, and for whatever reason, they honk at me as if I'm taking too long of a pause at the stop sign. The last man who did that has probably never done it to anyone since.

I jammed my car in park, flung open my driver's side door, flew out of my car with nothing but red in my eyes. They were probably as red as the stop sign itself. I remember as I stormed towards his car window, I think he thought he was about to die. I was losing my shit at this man in his mid 40's with his petrified wife in the passenger seat beside him. With the palm of my hand, I slammed my hand onto his window and asked him which stick that had been shoved up his ass would he like me to pull out first. Because only *"miserable fucking dick heads"* honk at a person who's actually stopping at a stop sign.

I saw this as completely rational. I *one hundred percent* saw this as a completely appropriate way to react.

And it was, if *going to jail every week* was how I saw as a normal way to live.

As I made my way back to my car, he rolled his window down a crack and *said "you're a very angry little girl"* to which I replied *"good observation, fuck face! Looks like you're not totally fucking brain dead after all!"*

Living with Borderline isn't always manageable.

As clearly demonstrated with the above example.

Now, thankfully it's been about two years since that incident took place. And nothing close to that level of rage has taken place since.

You can see how having a not so kind relationship with a man could be basically lethal for me, as with an un-kind partner, a Borderline will simply suffer due to the multitude of emotional triggers placed upon them by the unhappiness of the relationship they are in.

Psychologists have said during various documentaries that if you ever needed to hire bodyguards or personal security, forget going through an agency, just hire a couple Borderlines. You can guarantee that nobody will be successful in harming you.

Sociopaths put a multitude of calculated thinking between the *thought* and the actual *harming phase.*

But not Borderlines.

We have very little, *if any* space between the initial *thought* to the *taking action* part.

This is what makes us the highest *most likely to kill* on the scale of the mentally ill.

With the sheer anger I've possessed during my various Borderline moments, I can absolutely agree with that statistic.

Our emotions are just overall completely off the charts in terms of being rational.

When Robin came into my life, not only was his love healthy and kind to begin with, but how he handled me in my moments of emotional upheaval has been a very big part of my healing process. His partnership has been the biggest benefit in helping me manage the day to day woes of this illness.

So you can see how deserting this relationship simply due to him serving time in prison wasn't something I ever saw as a decision to make.

I don't remain by his side because I *need him*, but I remain by his side because like I stated earlier, my life is profoundly better *with him.*

What made my coming together with Robin vastly different from my previous relationships was that I told Robin very early on what my issues were. I almost did it in a way to probably push him away. But because how he entered my life was much different than the previous men, the journey as a whole has been one never having any form of expectations placed upon me by him.

He didn't come into my life expecting me to turn myself into a Betty Crocker homemaker and to always have dinner on the table by six. Nor did he ever give me grief or ask me questions about the way I live my life. He has not once, *not ever* pushed me into a different line of work that would earn more money for everyone. He's only encouraged me to gain weight and nourish my body in ways any parent would want their children to adequately take care of their health. He's encouraged me to pursue my passion projects. He reminds me to let the bullshit go and focus on the things that matter. He reminds me to be good to my mum. As so many of us young women can have good days and bad days with the mother-daughter relationship at times. He reminds me – all the time – that I am smart, hardworking, and that I take care of *any and all* things that need to be handled.

He reinforces my strengths to the point where they end up pushing any of my weakness completely off the table.

The only kind of words the man has ever said to me when I'd be erratic would be *"You're just having one of your moments sugar bear, take a deep breath, it will pass"*.

Not once has he kicked me while I've been down.
I can't say that about the previous men.

Not once has he ever for a second allowed me to dwell on my weaknesses.

With him, I have become a better woman.

I have become a wiser person with his advice and sound logic being with me through anything I've had to face that's been challenging.

His constant mindset that is more times than not set on *optimism only* has shown me just how powerful of a person you can be when you start making friends with the positive thinking process that your mind has been wanting to give you this whole time.

The heart break of losing Big Poppa remains strong in my heart beat.

I couldn't be more proud or more in love with my family.

I am beyond blessed that I wake up every day as a woman who is loved by these incredible people who I get to call my loved ones.

Every painful step I take when I get out of bed in the mornings because of my hip implant reminds me that I'm walking out of bed, not lowering myself down into a wheelchair.

But that I'm *walking* out of bed.

Every bad memory from a relationship that was more *un-kind* versus *kind* has given me huge downfalls where out of them came the biggest lessons I have learned, and they didn't even cost money. A little bit of my mental well-being, but shit, when is our mental well-being *not at stake* over something.

I have learned to let myself be loved by someone and not require them to fall asleep beside me in bed each night in order to know I have it.

I have forgiven myself for the things I really wish I had never done. I have apologized to myself for allowing bad things into my life that never really deserved the parts of me that I gave away. I look down at my boy-ish shaped bare feet, and although I hate my abnormally long toes, I thank them for holding me up on the days it felt hard to walk out my front door.

I can now look back at times in my life where I was so erratic in my thinking pattern or behaviour, and I can laugh at myself because at least it made for a really good story to tell my girlfriends over wine.

If there's one thing I want the person who's reading this to take away from this story of mine, it would be this:

Love those who love you.
And just because something isn't the status quo, don't shy away from it.
If it feels good for you, it might just be the best thing for you.

And,

Don't ever honk your horn if you pull up behind me at a stop sign.

Robin, for surrounding me with love no matter where I am.
Thank you for loving me.
I'm yours.
I love you.

To my family who has time and time again been my back bone, my continuous source of open, accepting and supportive arms, I'm so proud of who we are. It doesn't matter what life has thrown our way, we always conquer those big hills.

To the women out there facing something hard, *keep going.*
-   *Don't stop, don't sit, don't dwell*
You're strong enough to move through it.
Find safety in the knowing that we all question ourselves and having regrets is completely ok.
It's ok to derail sometimes. But ultimately, you are the only person who is going to put your train back on the tracks.
And when you do, be selective in the company you allow with you when driving your train.

And lastly,

Only give your heart to the person who's going to be gentle with it.

Made in the USA
Coppell, TX
31 May 2023

17558524R00164